VU
D.

CUSTOM WOODWORKING

Tables, Desks & Chairs

CUSTOM WOODWORKING

Tables, Desks & Chairs

By the editors of *Woodsmith* magazine

CONTENTS

CUSTOM WOODWORKING

Tables, Desks & Chairs

TABLES 6

Dining Table

Oak Desk

Rocking Chair

TABLES

Every home features an assortment of tables. They can be used simply for decoration, for display, or for eating or work surfaces. Whatever your needs, this section offers a variety of sizes and styles to choose from.

The first project is actually a set of three tables. These nestled tables with inlaid tops are built to stack together, but you can also choose to build one end table with a drawer.

The coffee table also offers two options. Whether you build the standard style or the small end table (or both), you'll be pleased with the diagonal grain that highlights their tops.

For some tables, one style is plenty. The Queen Anne end table is one such classic piece. With shop-made cabriole legs and a drawer that features half-blind dovetails, this walnut table is sure to become a family heirloom.

Style can also go hand-in-hand with function. While the dining table has the look of solid oak, it has convenient sliding leaves under the top. And if you'd like a less formal look, you can build the square version with a laminate top.

Nestled Tables

These matching tables feature inlaid banding on their tops and a special sliding system that allows them to "nestle" together. Or if you prefer, you can build a single end table with a drawer.

Deciding to make a set of nestled tables with inlaid tops was easy. The hardest part of this project was trying to name it. There was an ongoing debate around the shop as to which name was the most appropriate: "nestled" tables, "nested" tables, or "stacked" tables.

But the debate was settled as soon as I started to build "the tables." Normally, three progressively smaller end tables are just stacked on top of each other (stacked tables). But the set I built is different. Rather than just stacking the tables directly on top of each other, each of the tables is "nestled" into the next larger one by means of a drawer-like sliding system.

CONSTRUCTION. At first glance, the construction of these tables appears to be rather simple. However, they have their own unique set of problems.

First of all, the largest two tables don't have front aprons. Eliminating this front apron serves two purposes. Aesthetically, the difference between the sizes of the tables can be kept to a minimum. And functionally, the tables can then be "nestled" with a simple sliding system.

SLIDING SYSTEM. The idea behind the sliding system isn't very complicated, but accuracy is very important. Each smaller table has molded top edges that slide into grooves cut under the top of the next larger table.

So in order for this system to suspend the smaller tables off the floor, the grooves and molded edges must be located and cut accurately.

INLAY. To give these tables a bit of a different look, I decided to inlay banding strips around their top panels.

I got some rather formal-looking banding strips from a mail order catalog (see Sources on page 126 for information). However, you could use a different style, or even experiment with making your own banding.

SINGLE TABLE. If you don't want to build all three tables, you can build a single large table with a drawer at one end. See the Designer's Notebook on pages 14-15 for details.

EXPLODED VIEW

OVERALL DIMENSIONS:
22W x 15D x 21H

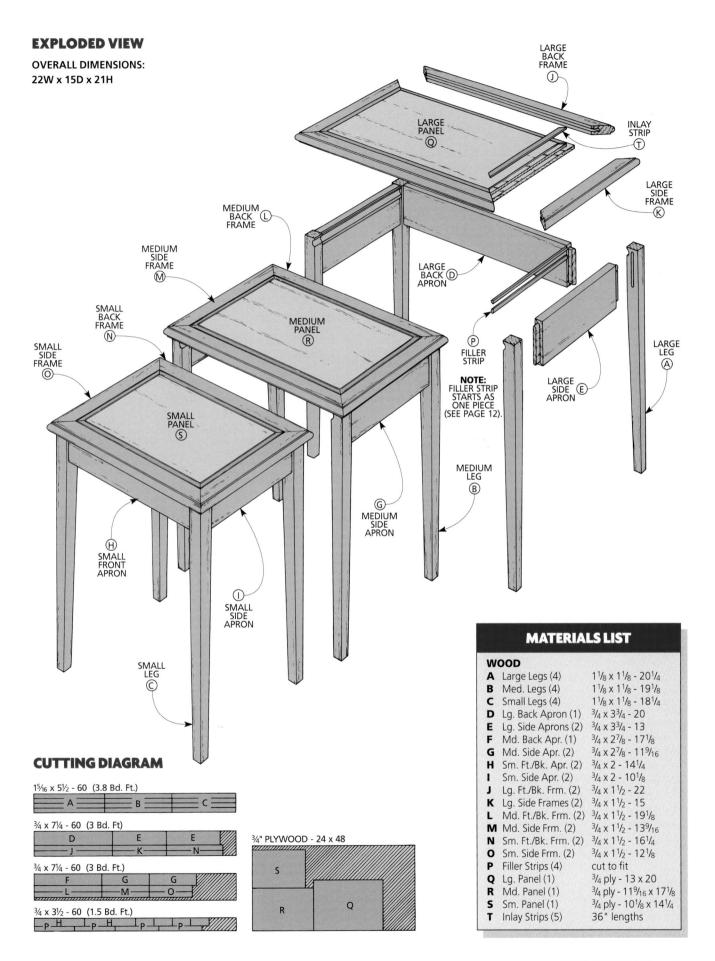

LARGE BACK FRAME (J)

INLAY STRIP (T)

LARGE PANEL (Q)

LARGE SIDE FRAME (K)

MEDIUM BACK FRAME (L)

MEDIUM SIDE FRAME (M)

LARGE BACK APRON (D)

SMALL BACK FRAME (N)

MEDIUM PANEL (R)

SMALL SIDE FRAME (O)

SMALL PANEL (S)

FILLER STRIP (P)

LARGE SIDE APRON (E)

LARGE LEG (A)

NOTE: FILLER STRIP STARTS AS ONE PIECE (SEE PAGE 12).

MEDIUM SIDE APRON (G)

MEDIUM LEG (B)

SMALL FRONT APRON (H)

SMALL SIDE APRON (I)

SMALL LEG (C)

CUTTING DIAGRAM

1⁵⁄₁₆ x 5½ - 60 (3.8 Bd. Ft.)

| A | B | C |

¾ x 7¼ - 60 (3 Bd. Ft)

| D | E | E |
| J | K | N |

¾ x 7¼ - 60 (3 Bd. Ft.)

| F | G | G |
| L | M | O |

¾ x 3½ - 60 (1.5 Bd. Ft.)

| P H | P H | P | P |

¾" PLYWOOD - 24 x 48

S
R
Q

MATERIALS LIST

WOOD

A	Large Legs (4)	1⅛ x 1⅛ - 20¼
B	Med. Legs (4)	1⅛ x 1⅛ - 19⅛
C	Small Legs (4)	1⅛ x 1⅛ - 18¼
D	Lg. Back Apron (1)	¾ x 3¾ - 20
E	Lg. Side Aprons (2)	¾ x 3¾ - 13
F	Md. Back Apr. (1)	¾ x 2⅞ - 17⅛
G	Md. Side Apr. (2)	¾ x 2⅞ - 11⁹⁄₁₆
H	Sm. Ft./Bk. Apr. (2)	¾ x 2 - 14¼
I	Sm. Side Apr. (2)	¾ x 2 - 10⅛
J	Lg. Ft./Bk. Frm. (2)	¾ x 1½ - 22
K	Lg. Side Frames (2)	¾ x 1½ - 15
L	Md. Ft./Bk. Frm. (2)	¾ x 1½ - 19⅛
M	Md. Side Frm. (2)	¾ x 1½ - 13⁹⁄₁₆
N	Sm. Ft./Bk. Frm. (2)	¾ x 1½ - 16¼
O	Sm. Side Frm. (2)	¾ x 1½ - 12⅛
P	Filler Strips (4)	cut to fit
Q	Lg. Panel (1)	¾ ply - 13 x 20
R	Md. Panel (1)	¾ ply - 11⁹⁄₁₆ x 17⅛
S	Sm. Panel (1)	¾ ply - 10⅛ x 14¼
T	Inlay Strips (5)	36" lengths

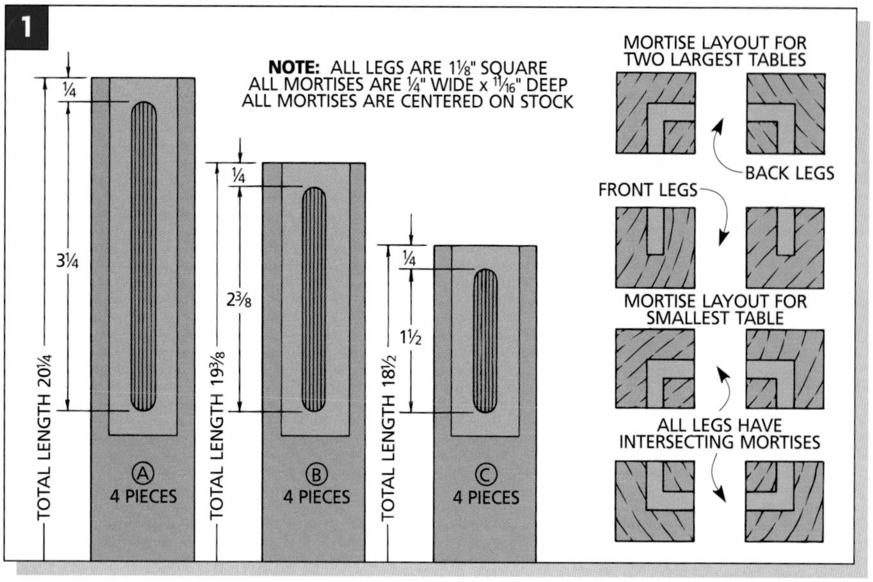
1
NOTE: ALL LEGS ARE 1⅛" SQUARE
ALL MORTISES ARE ¼" WIDE x 11⁄16" DEEP
ALL MORTISES ARE CENTERED ON STOCK
¼
3¼
TOTAL LENGTH 20¼
Ⓐ
4 PIECES
¼
2⅜
TOTAL LENGTH 19⅜
Ⓑ
4 PIECES
¼
1½
TOTAL LENGTH 18½
Ⓒ
4 PIECES
MORTISE LAYOUT FOR TWO LARGEST TABLES
FRONT LEGS
BACK LEGS
MORTISE LAYOUT FOR SMALLEST TABLE
ALL LEGS HAVE INTERSECTING MORTISES

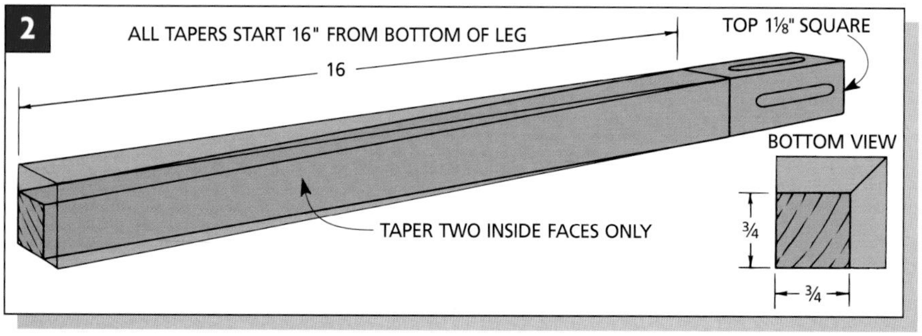
2
ALL TAPERS START 16" FROM BOTTOM OF LEG
16
TOP 1⅛" SQUARE
BOTTOM VIEW
TAPER TWO INSIDE FACES ONLY
¾
¾

LEGS

The legs for all three tables are the same except for their length. They're all $1^{1}/_{8}$"-square pieces of stock (I used walnut) with gentle tapers cut on the two inside faces *(Fig. 2)*. These tapers create a delicate appearance, while allowing the heavier, full-thickness stock to be used where it's actually needed most — for additional strength around the mortises at the top of each leg.

CUT TO SIZE. The first step is to rip enough 6/4 ($1^{5}/_{16}$"-thick) stock to produce all twelve $1^{1}/_{8}$" x $1^{1}/_{8}$" square legs. Then the four legs on the largest table (A) are cut $20^{1}/_{4}$" long.

However, because of the drawer-like sliding system used to "nestle" the tables, the legs on both of the two smaller tables (B and C) clear the floor by $^{1}/_{4}$". But rather than cut them to their exact length at this stage, they're cut $^{1}/_{4}$" longer than their final length, as if they extend to the floor. This way their tapers can be cut to duplicate the tapers on the legs of the largest table exactly.

With the additional $^{1}/_{4}$", the length of the legs on the smallest table is $18^{1}/_{2}$" long, and for the middle sized table, $19^{3}/_{8}$" long.

MORTISES. After the leg blanks are cut to length, they need to be both mortised and tapered. I decided to cut all of the mortises before tapering the legs to prevent accidentally drilling angled mortises because of a tilting leg.

Before the mortises are cut, lay out all four legs for each table and label their positions (for instance, left front leg), and their orientations (front face). Then mark the locations of the mortises on each leg *(Fig. 1)*. Be sure that only the smallest table is marked for mortises between the front legs for a front apron.

I used the drill press to drill $^{1}/_{4}$"-wide

SHOP JIG .... Router Mortising Jig

Even if you don't have a drill press, you can still make mortises that are centered precisely on your workpieces (like the ones needed at the tops of the legs on the Nestled Tables). To do this, I use a simple jig and a router (see drawing at right).

MAKE THE JIG. To make the jig, I trimmed two 2x4s to exactly the same thickness. Then I cut a spacer to exactly the same thickness as the piece being mortised. This spacer is screwed to the side of one of the 2x4s.

Now the piece being mortised is placed between the 2x4s (butted against the spacer, and flush with the top edges). The whole arrangement is then clamped together sandwich-style. (I normally clamp the end with the spacer block in a vise, and the opposite end with a C-clamp.)

To cut the mortise, I use a hand-held router equipped with an edge guide that rides on the outside of the 2x4s, and a router bit that's slightly smaller than the mortise.

After the length of the mortise is marked out, I make the first cut using one side of the fixture as a guide.

Then, without changing the setting on the edge guide, I make another cut, this time using the *opposite* side of the fixture for the guide. This assures that the mortise will be centered exactly on the stock.

If more than one identical mortise is to be cut, a set of stops can be tacked to the top of the fixture.

Note: This type of setup isn't only good for cutting a slot mortise on a narrow workpiece as shown. The same basic principles can also be used for cutting a clean groove along a piece to accept a panel.

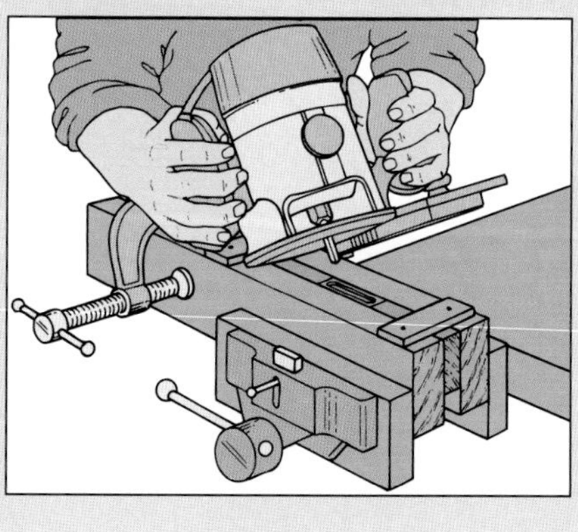

slot mortises $^{11}/_{16}$" deep, centered on the width of the $1^{1}/_{8}$"-thick legs. (The mortises could also be cut using a router and a simple jig. See the Shop Jig box on the opposite page.)

Note: On the legs which are mortised on two sides, the mortises intersect to form an L-shape (see mortise details in *Fig. 1*).

TAPER. After the mortises are drilled, it's time to taper the two inside faces of all twelve legs.

The taper jig is set up so that it starts cutting the taper 16" from the bottom of the leg, and leaves a $^{3}/_{4}$"-wide foot at the bottom of the leg *(Fig. 2)*.

Once the jig is set up, it can be left in the same position and used to cut the tapers on the legs for all three tables. (Although the overall lengths of the legs are not the same, the tapered area below the mortise is exactly the same on all twelve legs.)

TRIM TO LENGTH. After the tapers are cut, the last step on the legs is to trim $^{1}/_{4}$" off the tapered ends of the legs on the smallest two tables.

Note: To produce a square end, be sure to keep the two straight edges of the legs on the table and against the miter gauge while removing the $^{1}/_{4}$" excess length.

APRONS

When the legs are complete, the next step is to cut the aprons for all three tables. Only the smallest of the three tables has the typical arrangement of four aprons; the largest two tables have only three aprons each *(Fig. 4)*.

1 started by ripping enough material for all 10 aprons to width, and slightly longer than needed *(Fig. 3)*.

The next step is to cut the aprons exactly to the lengths shown in *Fig. 3* (these measurements include the lengths of the tenons on both ends of the aprons).

TENONS. Once the aprons are cut to length, set up the table saw to cut $^{5}/_{8}$"-long tenons to fit the mortises in the legs. The final shoulder-to-shoulder measurement of the aprons, shown in *Fig. 3*, is critical — it must be correct in order to have equal spacing between the legs on the three tables. Accuracy (or the lack of it) in these measurements will also determine if, and how much, custom-fitting is needed for the table's sliding system to work properly.

After the tenons are cut, round over the corners of the tenons to fit the mortises in the legs. The ends of the tenons that meet in the eight L-shaped mortises have to be mitered before they can be driven home *(Fig. 5)*. Then I assembled the tables and checked them for square.

LEG/APRON ASSEMBLY

The legs and aprons are assembled in two steps: first the side aprons are joined to two legs.

Then these two side assemblies are joined with the back apron (and the front apron on the smallest table) to form the table's base units.

The only problem with this assembly procedure is that if the bases aren't glued up perfectly square, the error will show up as unequal spacing between the legs of the three tables when they're nestled together (and the sliding system will never work as smoothly as it should). And if the assemblies have any twist, the effect is the same as if they were out of square.

To check the side assemblies for twist, dry-clamp the side apron and the legs on a flat surface. If there is any twisting, it can be detected by looking for the ends of the legs lifting off the flat surface *(Fig. 6)*. Any twist that's found should be removed by trimming the sides of the tenons accordingly.

Once the side assemblies are twist-free, finish-sand the aprons. Also, lightly sand (or scrape with a cabinet scraper) the faces of the legs around the mortises.

At this point, glue the side aprons and legs of each table together as a sub-assembly. (Don't glue these sub-assemblies to the back aprons yet.) Check these side assemblies for square by measuring the distance between the outside edges of the tops of the legs (near the aprons). This distance should equal the distance between the outside edges of the legs, measured at their feet. If they don't match exactly, try slightly loosening or tightening the clamps at the top of the legs. Sometimes the clamps can actually pull a leg in or out of alignment.

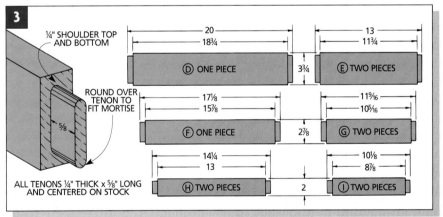

3

¼" SHOULDER TOP AND BOTTOM

ROUND OVER TENON TO FIT MORTISE

⅝

ALL TENONS ¼" THICK x ⅝" LONG AND CENTERED ON STOCK

20 / 18¾	3¾	13 / 11¾	
(D) ONE PIECE		(E) TWO PIECES	
17⅛ / 15⅞	2⅞	11⁹⁄₁₆ / 10⁵⁄₁₆	
(F) ONE PIECE		(G) TWO PIECES	
14¼ / 13	2	10⅛ / 8⅞	
(H) TWO PIECES		(I) TWO PIECES	

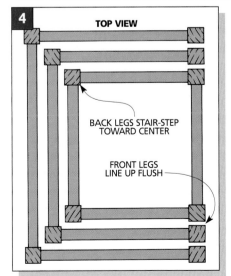

4

TOP VIEW

BACK LEGS STAIR-STEP TOWARD CENTER

FRONT LEGS LINE UP FLUSH

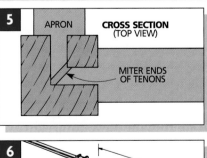

5

APRON

CROSS SECTION (TOP VIEW)

MITER ENDS OF TENONS

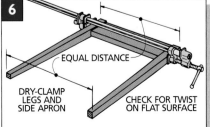

6

EQUAL DISTANCE

DRY-CLAMP LEGS AND SIDE APRON

CHECK FOR TWIST ON FLAT SURFACE

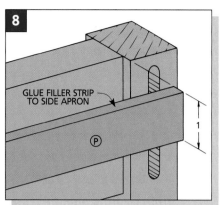

7

FRONT VIEW

LARGE TABLE

MIDDLE TABLE

SMALL TABLE

TABLE TOP SLIDES IN GROOVE

8

GLUE FILLER STRIP TO SIDE APRON

P

1

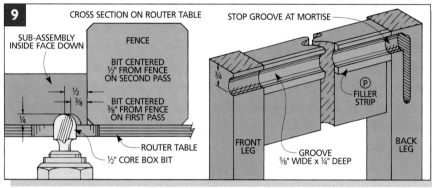

9

SUB-ASSEMBLY INSIDE FACE DOWN

CROSS SECTION ON ROUTER TABLE

FENCE

BIT CENTERED ½ FROM FENCE ON SECOND PASS

BIT CENTERED ⅜ FROM FENCE ON FIRST PASS

½
⅜
¼

ROUTER TABLE

½ CORE BOX BIT

STOP GROOVE AT MORTISE

¾

FILLER STRIP

P

FRONT LEG

BACK LEG

GROOVE ⅝" WIDE x ¼" DEEP

10

FRONT LEG

FENCE

STOP GROOVE AT MORTISE IN MIDDLE OF BACK LEG

ROUT RIGHT TO LEFT

BACK LEG

½" CORE BOX BIT   ROUTER TABLE   FILLER STRIP

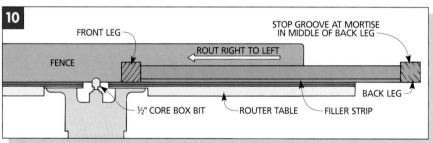

11

PLUNGE DOWN INTO MORTISE OF BACK LEG

BACK LEG

FILLER STRIP

ROUT THROUGH FRONT LEG

CLAMP SCRAP TO FRONT LEG TO PREVENT CHIPOUT

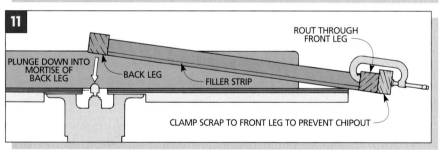

12

CHECK FOR SQUARE

BACK APRON

TEMPORARY SPACER USED WHEN CLAMPING TWO LARGEST TABLES

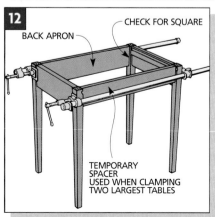

13

NEXT SMALLER SIDE FRAME EQUALS DISTANCE + ½"

NEXT SMALLER FRONT/BACK FRAME EQUALS DISTANCE - ⅛"

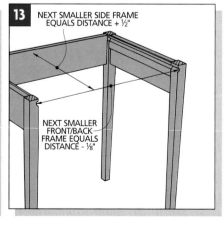

SLIDING SYSTEM

The heart of this drawer-type sliding system is a stopped groove cut in the side aprons of the two larger tables *(Fig. 7)*. When the tables are "nestled," the molded edges on the table tops slide in the stopped grooves, suspending the smaller two tables ¼" off the floor.

FILLER STRIP. Before the grooves are cut, a filler strip (P) must be added to fill the space between the side apron and the inside faces of the legs *(Fig. 8)*. Cut this strip slightly thicker than needed, and trim it to length. Then after it's glued in place, plane the strip flush with the inside faces of the legs.

CUT GROOVE. I used a ½" core box bit on the router table to cut a ⅝"-wide, ¼"-deep stopped groove (in two passes) so that its bottom edge is exactly ¾" from the top of the side apron *(Fig. 9)*. To rout the groove, center the bit ⅜" from the fence on the first pass, and ½" on the second pass.

The groove stops in the center of the mortise on the rear legs *(Fig. 9)*. On the right side, the routing starts at the front edge of the front leg, and stops at the rear mortise *(Fig. 10)*.

The left side requires starting the groove with a plunge cut in the middle of the mortise in the rear leg and continuing out through the front leg. Use a piece of scrap clamped to the front face of the leg to prevent any chipout *(Fig. 11)*.

ASSEMBLY. After the grooves are routed, the side assemblies are glued together with the back apron (and the front apron on the smallest table), again checking for twist and squareness. On the two larger tables, I also added a temporary spacer between the front two legs that was exactly as long as the shoulder-to-shoulder distance of the back apron *(Fig. 12)*.

TOP

Now the fun begins. All three table tops consist of a solid wood frame, a plywood insert, and an inlay banding.

FRAME. I started on the tops by making the frames first. Rip enough 4/4 stock to 1½" widths for all the frame members on the three tables. Then cut a ¼" groove, ½" deep in the edge of each piece *(Fig. 14a)*.

DETERMINE SIZE. Once the groove is cut, the frame members are ready to be mitered. To determine the length of all

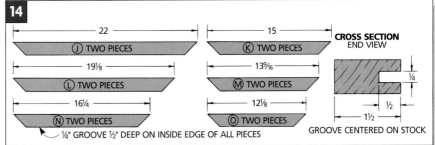

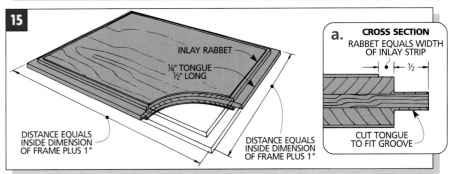

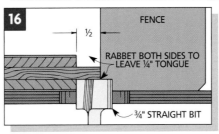

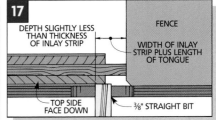

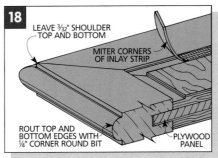

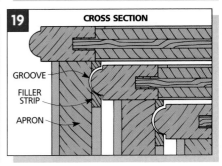

four frame members (J and K) for the largest table, simply add 1" (for a $^1/_2$" overhang on each of the four edges) to the distance between the outside edges of the table legs.

To determine the length of the front/back frame members (L and N) on the two smallest tables, measure the distance between the deepest point of the grooves in the side frames on the next larger table, and subtract $^1/_8$" *(Fig. 13)*.

To determine the length of the side frame members on the two smaller tables (M and O), measure the distance on the next larger table from the inside face of the back apron to the front face of the front leg, and add an additional $^1/_2$" for the front overhang.

PLYWOOD PANEL. After the miters on all three table tops are cut, measure the inside dimensions on all three frames. To find the size for the $^3/_4$"-thick plywood panel, add 1" to both dimensions for the $^1/_2$"-long tongues *(Fig. 15)*.

Note: This is one place where accuracy is a must. Any error in the size of the plywood insert will make it impossible to rout a rabbet accurately for the inlay banding later on.

PLYWOOD TONGUE. Next, cut the tongues on the edges of the plywood panels to fit the grooves in the frame members *(Figs. 15a and 16)*. Be sure the shoulder-to-shoulder measurement on the plywood matches the inside dimensions of the mitered frame.

Note: When cutting the tongue, make several duplicates to use when setting up for the inlay banding.

INLAY BANDING. When the tongues are cut on the plywood panels, the next step is to rabbet the face veneer on the plywood for the inlay banding *(Fig. 17)*.

The depth of the router bit for the rabbets is set so that it's slightly less

than the thickness of the inlay banding. Then the fence is set to cut the groove in the face veneer exactly the same width as the inlay *(Fig. 17)*.

Before cutting this rabbet, I routed a test rabbet on a duplicate piece cut earlier. Then this piece is slipped into a frame member, and the actual fit of the inlay banding is checked. Then the frame members and the plywood panels are glued together.

To inlay the banding strips, I simply mitered the corners, and glued them in place *(Fig. 18)*. Then finally, all three tops can be finish sanded.

MOLDING THE EDGE. The last step before the tops are attached to the base assembly is to rout the table top edges

using a $^1/_4$" roundover bit on the router table. Starting with the smallest table, rout the edge profile until it fits into the groove in the next larger table base *(Fig. 19)*. (If the top is too wide to fit the groove, use the table saw to reduce the width in $^1/_{32}$" increments.) Repeat this process on the middle table, and the largest table.

When the outside edges are molded, glue the tops to the base assemblies so they're centered on the width and overhang the front edge of the base by $^1/_2$". (This ensures that the fronts of the legs all line up when the tables are nestled.)

Finally, I finished the tables with three coats of $1^1/_2$ lb.-cut shellac, and two coats of furniture paste wax. ■

DESIGNER'S NOTEBOOK

Instead of "nestling" three different-sized tables together, you can make one end table with the same inlay banding on the top. This one features a deep drawer that is relatively simple to build.

CONSTRUCTION NOTES:

■ To make this table, start with the legs (A). Since it may be used as an end table or night stand, it should be a little taller than the Nestled Tables. I just added 2" to the length of the large legs *(Fig. 1)*.

Note: You don't need any parts from the smaller tables. Some of the part names are different here because of the orientation (the *side* of the table is now the *front*). See the Materials List on the opposite page for specific parts.

■ Start the leg tapers 18" from the bottom, instead of 16" *(Fig. 1)*.

■ The mortises are the same width ($1/4$")

and depth ($^{11}/_{16}$"), but are now 4" long to accommodate the wider aprons added later *(Fig. 1)*. Note that mortises are not needed on the inside faces of the legs on the *front* (small end) of this table.

■ Cut two long aprons (D) and a short apron (E) to a width of $4^{1}/_{2}$". They are 20" and 13" long, respectively.

■ Cut $^{5}/_{8}$"-long tenons on the ends of all the aprons to fit the mortises in the legs.

■ Then cut two $^{1}/_{4}$" grooves on the inside face of each long apron, $^{3}/_{4}$" from the top and bottom for rails and runners.

■ Assemble two side frames (a long

apron and two legs) by gluing the tenons on the aprons into the leg mortises. Put the short apron aside for now.

■ To hold a drawer (see opposite page), you'll need to add a series of rails, runners, and guides *(Fig. 2)*. Start by cutting two drawer rails (W) to width.

■ Rabbet the rail ends to leave $1/4$" tongues that fit the grooves in the long aprons *(Fig. 2a)*. The length of the rails exceeds that of the short apron because they extend to the long aprons.

■ To assemble the table frame, glue the drawer rails (W) and the short apron

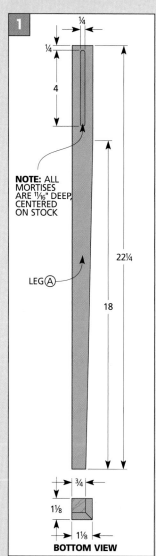

NOTE: ALL MORTISES ARE $^{11}/_{16}$" DEEP, CENTERED ON STOCK

LEG (A)

BOTTOM VIEW

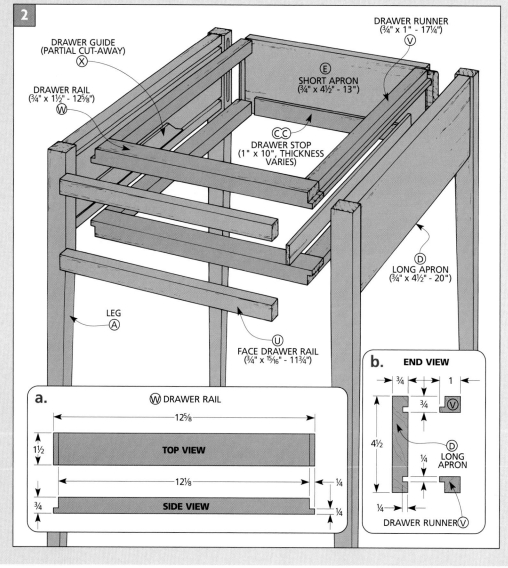

DRAWER GUIDE (PARTIAL CUT-AWAY) (X)

DRAWER RAIL ($^{3}/_{4}$" x $1^{1}/_{2}$" - $12^{5}/_{8}$") (W)

DRAWER RUNNER ($^{3}/_{4}$" x 1" - $17^{1}/_{4}$") (V)

SHORT APRON ($^{3}/_{4}$" x $4^{1}/_{2}$" - 13") (E)

DRAWER STOP (1" x 10", THICKNESS VARIES) (CC)

LEG (A)

LONG APRON ($^{3}/_{4}$" x $4^{1}/_{2}$" - 20") (D)

FACE DRAWER RAIL ($^{3}/_{4}$" x $^{15}/_{16}$" - $11^{3}/_{4}$") (U)

a. (W) DRAWER RAIL

TOP VIEW

SIDE VIEW

b. END VIEW

(V)

LONG APRON (D)

DRAWER RUNNER (V)

(E) between the two side assemblies you glued up earlier *(Fig. 2)*.

■ Now cut two face drawer rails (U) to length to fit between the front legs, and glue them to the drawer rails (W).

■ Cut four drawer runners (V) to width. These are rabbeted on the *edges* to fit the apron grooves *(Fig. 2)*. Cut them to length to fit between the drawer rails and the back legs, and glue them in place.

■ Add two drawer guides (X) that are cut to length to fit between the legs and to thickness ($^3/_{16}$") to fit flush with the inside edges of the legs *(Figs. 2 and 4)*.

■ Now it's just a matter of building the drawer to fit the table assembly.

Note: The measurements here are guides, but make sure you build the drawer to fit in the table, with $^1/_{16}$" of clearance on the ends and top *(Fig. 4)*.

■ Start by cutting two $^1/_2$"-thick sides (Z) to width and length. Cut $^1/_8$" dadoes $^1/_2$" from each end *(Figs. 3, 3a and 3b)*.

■ Cut a $^1/_2$" drawer back (AA) to width and length, with $^1/_8$" tongues on its ends to fit the side dadoes *(Figs. 3 and 3b)*.

■ Now cut a $^3/_4$"-thick drawer front (Y) to width and length, and cut simple locking rabbet joints on its ends to fit the dadoes in the sides *(Fig. 3a)*.

■ Cut grooves $^1/_2$" up from the bottom of each drawer piece to fit a $^1/_4$" plywood bottom. Then cut the bottom (BB) to fit, and glue the drawer together *(Fig. 3)*.

■ Finally, to keep the drawer front flush with the face rails, measure the gap between the back of the drawer and the back apron and cut a drawer stop (CC) to thickness to fill the gap *(Fig. 2)*. Glue the stop to the apron between the runners.

■ Now just attach a drawer knob, and add the table top (refer to page 13).

END TABLE
WITH DRAWER

MATERIALS LIST

CHANGED PARTS

A	Legs (4)	$1^1/_8$ x $1^1/_8$ - $22^1/_4$
D	Long Aprons (2)	$^3/_4$ x $4^1/_2$ - 20
E	Short Apron (1)	$^3/_4$ x $4^1/_2$ - 13

NEW PARTS

U	Face Drawer Rails (2)	$^3/_4$ x $^{15}/_{16}$ - $11^3/_4$
V	Drawer Runners (4)	$^3/_4$ x 1 - $17^1/_4$
W	Drawer Rails (2)	$^3/_4$ x $1^1/_2$ - $12^5/_8$
X	Drawer Guides (2)	$^3/_{16}$ x 1 - $18^3/_4$

Y	Drawer Front (1)	$^3/_4$ x $2^{15}/_{16}$ - $11^5/_8$
Z	Drawer Sides (2)	$^1/_2$ x $2^{15}/_{16}$ - $19^1/_4$
AA	Drawer Back (1)	$^1/_2$ x $2^{15}/_{16}$ - $11^1/_8$
BB	Drawer Bottom (1)	$^1/_4$ ply - $11^1/_8$ - $18^3/_4$
CC	Drawer Stop (1)	var.* x 1 - 10

* Cut so drawer is flush with front.

Note: Do not need parts B, C, F, G, H, I, L, M, N, O, P, R, S. Only need (2) inlay strips (part T). Need (1) drawer knob w/ screw.

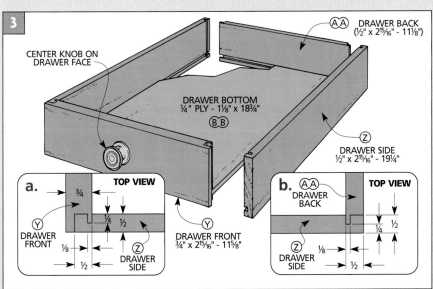

3

CENTER KNOB ON DRAWER FACE

DRAWER BACK (AA)
($^1/_2$" x $2^{15}/_{16}$" - $11^1/_8$")

DRAWER BOTTOM
$^1/_4$" PLY - $11^1/_8$" x $18^3/_4$"
(BB)

DRAWER SIDE (Z)
$^1/_2$" x $2^{15}/_{16}$" - $19^1/_4$"

a. TOP VIEW
$^3/_4$
$^1/_4$ $^1/_2$
(Y)
DRAWER FRONT
$^1/_8$ (Z)
$^1/_2$
DRAWER SIDE

b. (AA)
DRAWER BACK
TOP VIEW
(Z) $^1/_8$ $^1/_4$ $^1/_2$
DRAWER SIDE
$^1/_2$

DRAWER FRONT (Y)
$^3/_4$" x $2^{15}/_{16}$" - $11^5/_8$"

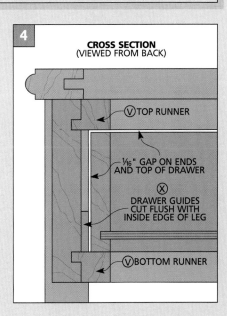

4

CROSS SECTION
(VIEWED FROM BACK)

(V) TOP RUNNER

$^1/_{16}$" GAP ON ENDS AND TOP OF DRAWER

(X) DRAWER GUIDES CUT FLUSH WITH INSIDE EDGE OF LEG

(V) BOTTOM RUNNER

Coffee Table

The diagonal grain patterns on the top of this Coffee Table create an interesting surface. Combined with a matching End Table this set becomes the focal point of a beautiful living room.

When I built this Coffee Table and its companion End Table (see page 24), I did something very different with the legs. Traditionally, table legs are square posts connected by stretchers with mortise and tenon joinery. The base on this table is solid, but it doesn't involve making square posts or cutting mortises and tenons.

BUILT-UP LEGS. Instead, the legs on the tables are built up from three pieces of 3/4"-thick oak. The first two pieces are glued together to form an outside corner. Then a third piece is beveled to fit behind the inside corner.

The beveled piece gives the leg its triangular shape. The design "traps" half-lap joints on the ends of the table aprons, giving each table added strength and the appearance of furniture made with traditional joinery. To add a shelf to the end table option, all I had to do was modify the inside corner block.

GRAIN DIRECTION. I paid close attention to wood grain when making the legs. I selected the mating pieces of each leg from the same section of stock (see the Cutting Diagram on the opposite page). Then when all the corners were rounded over, the color and grain

direction created the illusion that the built-up legs were solid.

TOP. The Coffee Table's top is made of three sections of oak plywood. I cut the panel so the grain runs diagonally. This way I can alternate the grain direction from one panel to the next (see inset photo above). To add contrast to the End Table, I positioned the shelf so the grain runs 90° to the top.

FINISH. I lightly stained the table and then I finished it with three coats of polyurethane for protection (see the Finishing Tip on page 22).

EXPLODED VIEW

OVERALL DIMENSIONS:
16¹/₄H x 23D x 47L

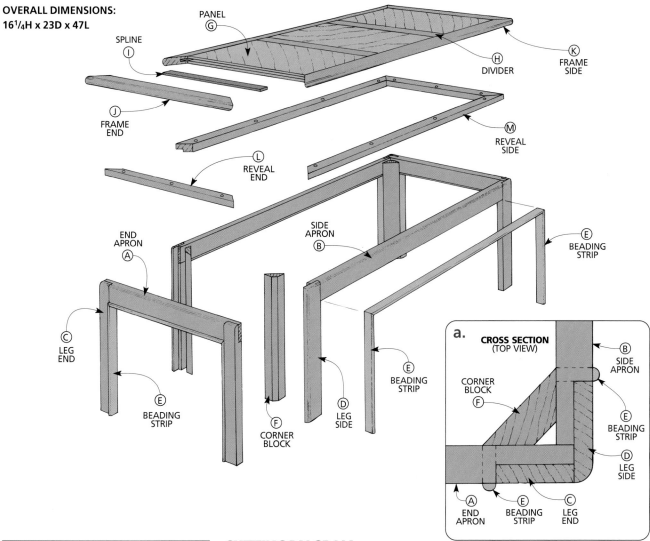

PANEL
G

SPLINE
I

H
DIVIDER

K
FRAME
SIDE

J

FRAME
END

M
REVEAL
SIDE

L
REVEAL
END

END
APRON
A

SIDE
APRON
B

E
BEADING
STRIP

C
LEG
END

E
BEADING
STRIP

F
CORNER
BLOCK

D
LEG
SIDE

E
BEADING
STRIP

a.

CROSS SECTION
(TOP VIEW)

B
SIDE
APRON

CORNER
BLOCK
F

E
BEADING
STRIP

D
LEG
SIDE

A
END
APRON

E
BEADING
STRIP

C
LEG
END

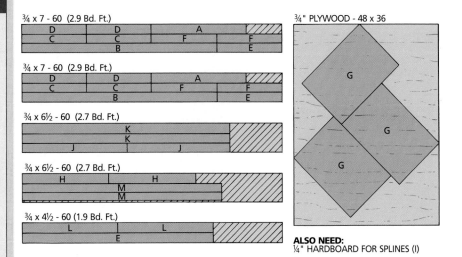

MATERIALS LIST

TABLE BASE

A	End Aprons (2)	³/₄ x 2 - 21³/₄
B	Side Aprons (2)	³/₄ x 2 - 45³/₄
C	Leg Ends (4)	³/₄ x 1⁵/₈ - 15
D	Leg Sides (4)	³/₄ x 2 - 15
E	Beading Strips	¹/₄ x ⁷/₈ - 26' rough
F	Corner Blocks (4)	³/₄ x 2³/₁₆ - 14³/₄

TABLE TOP

G	Panels (3)	³/₄ ply - 13 x 19
H	Dividers (2)	³/₄ x 2 - 19
I	Splines	¹/₄ x ¹⁵/₁₆ - cut to fit
J	Frame Ends (2)	³/₄ x 2 - 23
K	Frame Sides (2)	³/₄ x 2 - 47
L	Reveal Ends (2)	³/₄ x 1³/₈ - 23 rough
M	Reveal Sides (2)	³/₄ x 1³/₈ - 47 rough

HARDWARE SUPPLIES
(14) No. 8 x 1¹/₄" Fh woodscrews

CUTTING DIAGRAM

³/₄ x 7 - 60 (2.9 Bd. Ft.)

D	D	A	
C	C	F	F
B			E

³/₄ x 7 - 60 (2.9 Bd. Ft.)

D	D	A	
C	C	F	F
B			E

³/₄ x 6¹/₂ - 60 (2.7 Bd. Ft.)

K	
K	
J	J

³/₄ x 6¹/₂ - 60 (2.7 Bd. Ft.)

H	H	
M		
M		

³/₄ x 4¹/₂ - 60 (1.9 Bd. Ft.)

| L | L | |
| E | | |

³/₄" PLYWOOD - 48 x 36

G

G

G

ALSO NEED:
¹/₄" HARDBOARD FOR SPLINES (I)

TABLE BASE

There are two main parts to the Coffee Table — the table base and the top. I built the base first, then made the top to fit. But instead of just building four legs and connecting them with aprons, I began by building four individual "U-shaped" assemblies *(Figs. 1 and 2)*. Then the asssemblies are glued together to form the base, (refer to *Fig. 4*).

APRONS. Start by ripping two apron ends (A) and two apron sides (B) to the same width (2") from $^3/_4$" stock *(Figs. 1 and 2)*. Then trim all four aprons to finished lengths ($21^3/_4$" and $45^3/_4$").

LEGS. Now the legs can be added to the aprons to complete the four assemblies. For the best grain match when the assemblies are joined later, try to cut the mating pieces for each leg (C, D) from the same section of $^3/_4$" stock (refer to Cutting Diagram on page 17).

Note: Mark the mating pieces so they can be assembled into the same leg unit later.

First, I cut four blanks to rough width (4") and finished length (15"). Next, rip these four blanks to produce four leg ends (C) $1^5/_8$" wide *(Fig. 1)*, and four leg sides (D) 2" wide *(Fig. 2)*.

HALF LAPS. The legs are joined to the aprons by means of half-lap joints. To end up with the cleanest cuts possible, I used a straight bit in the router.

To make routing the half laps easier, I made an edge guide for my router. (For details on this, see the Shop Jig on page 23.)

Note: Half laps are cut half the thickness of the mating pieces ($^3/_8$" deep).

Using an edge guide to rout half laps involves two different fence setups. First, the lap on the top of each leg piece is routed 2" wide (to accept the 2"-wide aprons) *(Figs. 1 and 2)*. Then, $1^5/_8$"-wide laps are routed on the ends of each apron, (refer to *Figs. 1 and 2*).

U-SHAPED ASSEMBLIES. When the half laps have been cut on all twelve base pieces, they can be glued up into four U-shaped assemblies.

Note: The side aprons (B) will not lap completely over the leg sides (D) *(Fig. 2a)*. That's okay because the legs and ends of the aprons are rabbeted next.

RABBETS. Now the four U-shaped leg assemblies are joined with rabbet joints to form the table base. Rabbets are cut only on the legs of the side assemblies — not the end assemblies *(Fig. 3)*. Again, I used the edge guide with the router.

ASSEMBLY. When the rabbets have been cut on the side assemblies, all four assemblies can be glued together to form the table base *(Fig. 4)*.

ROUNDOVERS. To help the leg pieces blend together, round over the outside corner of each leg side *(Figs. 5 and 5a)*. I also rounded over the top outside edge of each apron.

EDGE BEADING. After the legs and aprons are rounded over, beading strips are attached to the inside edges of the legs to soften the look *(Fig. 6)*. The beading strips (E) start out as 2"-wide blanks of $^3/_4$"-thick stock.

Cut two blanks to a rough length of

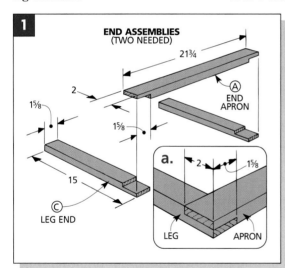

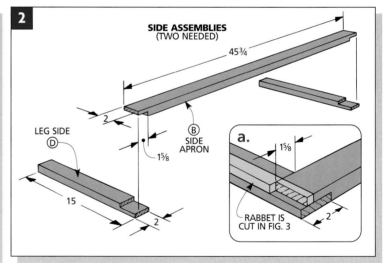

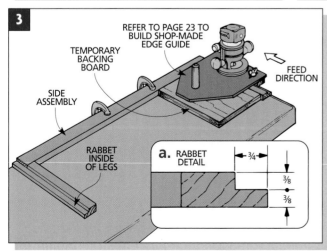

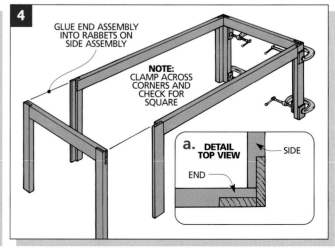

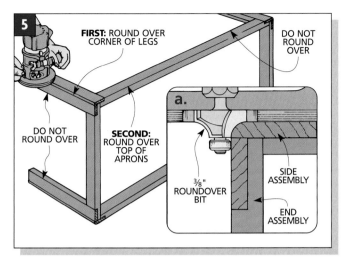

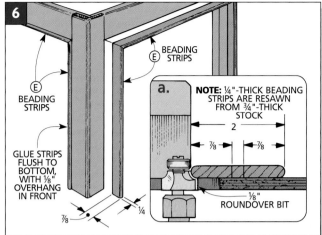

14" for the legs. Then cut another blank to a rough length of 42" for the end and side aprons. (You'll get four strips from each leg blank and two strips from the apron blank.)

With the blanks on edge, resaw them to produce $\frac{1}{4}$"-thick strips (2" wide). Round over both edges of the beading strips on the router table, (refer to *Fig. 6a*). Then rip the strips to produce the final width of $\frac{7}{8}$".

ATTACH BEADING. To mount the beading strips, miter one end of each short strip to fit on the inside edge of each leg *(Fig. 6)*. Glue the strip in place so the square edge is flush to the back of the leg. (The front edge sticks out $\frac{1}{8}$".)

Finally, miter both ends of the long beading strips. Sneak up on their length to fit between the upright beading

strips. Then glue them to the bottom edges of the aprons *(Fig. 6)*.

CORNER BLOCKS. To complete the legs, I cut corner blocks (F) to give the legs their triangular shape. To make the blocks, first cut four pieces of $\frac{3}{4}$" stock to a width of $2\frac{1}{2}$". Cut the blocks to final length — $\frac{1}{4}$" *shorter* than the table legs *(Fig. 7)*.

The corner blocks can now be beveled to fit behind each leg assembly (refer to

Fig. 7 and the Shop Tip below).

To glue the blocks in place, I used a V-block and C-clamps *(Fig. 7a)*.

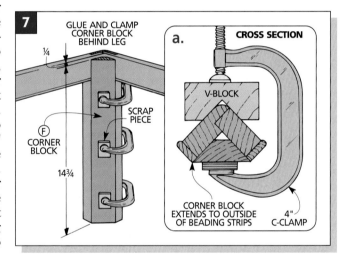

SHOP TIP . . . . *Safe Bevel Ripping*

Bevel ripping both edges of a narrow workpiece using the table saw is a delicate operation. In order to make this procedure safer, I like to use a narrow,

shop-made push stick, and the eraser end of a pencil as a hold-down.

The procedure that I used to make the corner blocks for the coffee table

was to start by ripping a 45° bevel along one edge of each block (see left drawing below).

Then I ripped another bevel on the opposite edge

(see right drawing below).

I carefully sneak up on the final width until the triangular block just fits in the back corner of each leg (refer to *Fig. 7a* above).

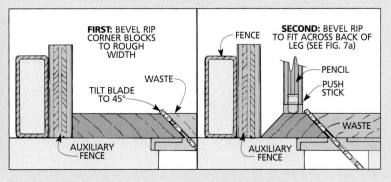

Once the table base is assembled, work can begin on the table top. The top consists of three plywood panels and two dividers surrounded by an oak frame. The parts are joined with spline and groove joints.

The panels for the top can be cut from less than half a sheet (4' x 4') of hardwood plywood. I used $3/4$" oak plywood for the panels (refer to the Cutting Diagram on page 17).

PLYWOOD PANELS. To make the top more interesting to look at, I cut the panels with the grain oriented 45° to the outside frame.

The problem was finding the best way to cut a piece of plywood into the three panels with diagonal grain. The procedure I used involved following a number of steps.

LAY OUT PANELS. The first thing I do is draw a pencil line at a 45° angle across one of the corners (*Fig. 9*). This line indicates one edge of each of the panels. Then I used a framing square to lay out all three panels, working off the first pencil line.

Note: Lay out the panels oversize (14" wide x 20" long) (*Fig. 9*). This allows extra room for cleaning up any rough cuts left by the jig saw.

JIG SAW ROUGH. Start cutting out the panels by making a single straight cut along the first layout line. To do this, I used a jig saw guided by a straightedge (*Fig. 9*). After this first cut, use the jig saw freehand to cut out each panel, carefully following the pencil lines.

SAW A CLEAN EDGE. Next I moved to the table saw. The goal of the first cut on the table saw is simply to get a clean, straight edge. (The jig saw probably left some splinters.) So run each panel

through the table saw with the straightest edge against the rip fence, making a straight cut along the opposite edge (*Fig. 10*).

Note: When cutting plywood on the table saw, use a good sharp blade designed for cutting plywood. Also make all the cuts with the good sides facing up. This way any chipout will be on the bottom side of each panel where it won't be visible after assembly.

SAW ADJACENT EDGE. The next step is to establish one square corner on each panel. Here I switched to the miter gauge and squared up a corner by holding the table-sawn edge against the miter gauge (*Fig. 11*).

Note: If you have a panel-cutting jig for the table saw, it will make this step go a little smoother.

You should now have one clean, straight, long edge and one clean, straight, short edge on each panel, with a square corner in between.

SAW TO SIZE. Now the panel can be cut to finished width (*Fig. 8*). Set the rip fence 13" from the blade and trim the jig sawn edge off each piece.

After the panels are cut to width, they

can be cut to length. Here I set the rip fence to cut the panels a little long (19$1/2$"). This extra $1/2$" will allow room for trimming the uneven edges after the panels are assembled (refer to *Fig. 13*). Once they're cut to rough length, all three panels should be the exact same width and length.

PANEL DIVIDERS

After the panels have been cut to rough size, the next step is to cut two panel dividers (H). The dividers are ripped from $3/4$"-thick hardwood to a width of 2", and crosscut to the same length as the plywood (19$1/2$") (*Fig. 8*).

INSIDE SLOTS. Now slots can be cut on both edges of the dividers and the panels (*Fig. 12*). I used a $1/4$" slot cutter, centering them on the thickness of the dividers (*Fig. 12a*).

Note: The routing direction for the slots on all the panels, dividers, and framing pieces should be counterclockwise (*Fig. 14*), or opposite the direction of the rotation of the bit. This gives greater control of the router during the cutting process.

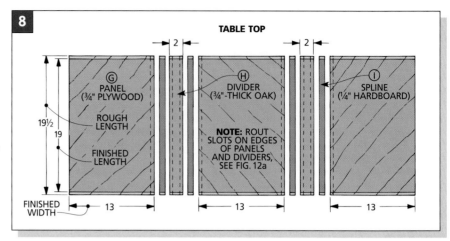

8

TABLE TOP

G PANEL ($3/4$" PLYWOOD)
H DIVIDER ($3/4$"-THICK OAK)
I SPLINE ($1/4$" HARDBOARD)

ROUGH LENGTH
FINISHED LENGTH
19$1/2$
19

NOTE: ROUT SLOTS ON EDGES OF PANELS AND DIVIDERS, SEE FIG. 12a

FINISHED WIDTH
13   13   13
2   2

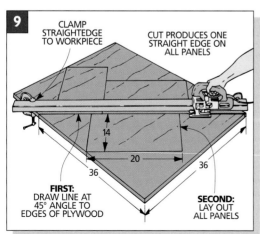

9

CLAMP STRAIGHTEDGE TO WORKPIECE
CUT PRODUCES ONE STRAIGHT EDGE ON ALL PANELS
14
20
36   36
FIRST: DRAW LINE AT 45° ANGLE TO EDGES OF PLYWOOD
SECOND: LAY OUT ALL PANELS

10

NOTE: CUT ALL PANELS OVERSIZE
WITH STRAIGHTEST EDGE AGAINST FENCE, CUT A CLEAN EDGE ON EACH PANEL

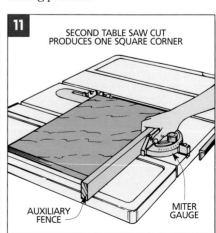

11

SECOND TABLE SAW CUT PRODUCES ONE SQUARE CORNER
AUXILIARY FENCE
MITER GAUGE

The important thing here is that all slots are cut with the router riding on the *top* face of each piece. The reason for this is that the dividers and panels may not be the exact same thickness. But by indexing off the top face, they will all be flush at the top *(Fig. 12b)*.

So I marked the top face of each piece in advance, then always routed with the marked face up *(Fig. 12)*.

Note: Once you've got the router adjusted for this, don't change the setup of the router — you'll need it later.

SPLINES. Next, cut the splines for attaching the panels to the dividers (and also the outside frame). I made the splines (I) from 1/4"-thick hardboard. To

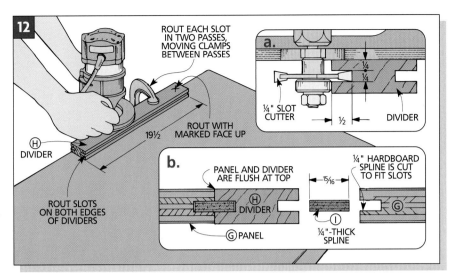

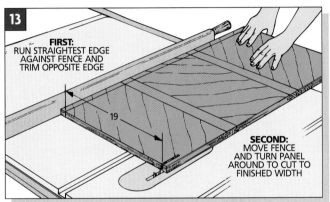

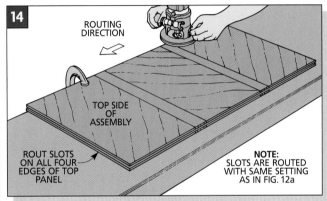

allow for easier assembly in the two 1/2"-wide slots, rip the splines to a width of 15/16" *(Fig. 12b)*.

You'll need six splines 19 1/2" long for the long edges of the plywood panels. Later, you'll use two splines 43 3/4" long for attaching the long outside frame sections. So it's easiest to cut all the splines at one time from the end of a single four-foot-wide sheet.

ASSEMBLY. When the slots have been routed on both the dividers and plywood panels, the pieces can be glued together as a unit.

After the assembly is dry, trim it to finished width in two passes on the table saw *(Fig. 13)*. The first cut gives you one straight edge. Turn the piece around for the second cut. This cut produces the finished width, and another straight edge.

OUTSIDE SLOTS. Now slots are cut along all four of the outside edges for attaching the outside frame *(Fig. 14)*. Again, I cut these slots with the router and a slot cutter adjusted the same as before *(Fig. 12a)*. Remember to keep the face side of the table up so you're always routing along the top side.

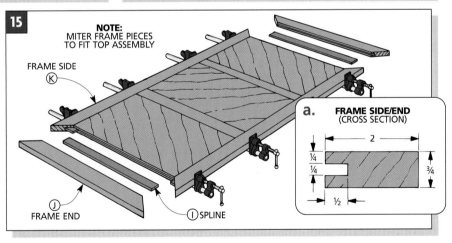

OUTSIDE FRAME

There are just a few more steps to complete the table. First, the top is surrounded by an oak frame. Then a "reveal" frame is made for attaching the top to the base.

TOP FRAME. The frame around the plywood top hides the edges of the panels. It's attached to the edges with splines glued into slots *(Fig. 15)*.

To make the frame, start by ripping two pieces for the frame ends (J) and

two frame sides (K) the same width as the panel dividers (2" wide) *(Fig. 15a)*.

Now miter both ends of each frame piece so the finished length (long-point to long-point) equals the distance along the plywood edge plus the width of two frame pieces (4").

Next, rout a slot on the inside edge of each frame piece to align with the slot around the plywood assembly. Then glue splines into the slots in the panels, and glue the frame pieces onto the splines *(Fig. 15)*.

ROUND OVER EDGES. Before attaching the top to the base, I softened the top and bottom edges of the frame with a $3/8$" roundover bit *(Fig. 16)*.

Note: I used my shop-built edge guide to rout the roundovers on both edges of the frame. There's a good reason for doing this — the fence on the edge guide keeps the bit cutting uniform roundovers on the top and bottom edges of the frame *(Fig. 16a)*. Without the fence, the router bit would cut deeper on the second pass, since some of the surface the pilot bearing runs against is removed on the first pass.

REVEAL FRAME

The next step is to build the reveal frame. This visually "lifts" the table top from the base *(Fig. 17)*. To build this frame, first rip the ends (L) and sides (M) to finished width ($1^3/8$") and rough length from $3/4$" stock *(Fig. 17a)*.

Next, you'll cut an $11/32$"-wide rabbet on the lower outside edge of each frame section to fit on the top edges of the aprons *(Fig. 17a)*.

To determine the length of the pieces, measure the *inside* dimensions of the top of the table base and add $11/16$". Now miter the pieces to length.

Before gluing the reveal frame to the base, I drilled a series of $3/16$" countersunk shank holes in each frame section for attaching the top.

SCREW TOP TO FRAME. Once the reveal frame sections are glued in place, turn the table top upside down on a flat surface to attach the top to the base *(Fig. 18)*. Center the base on the top.

Then, drill $1/8$" pilot holes into the underside of the top frame through the holes in the reveal frame. Now screw the base unit to the top *(Fig. 18a)*.

FINISH. The final step is to apply the finish (see the Finishing Tip below). ■

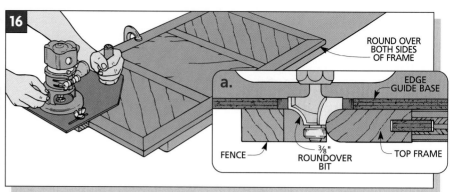

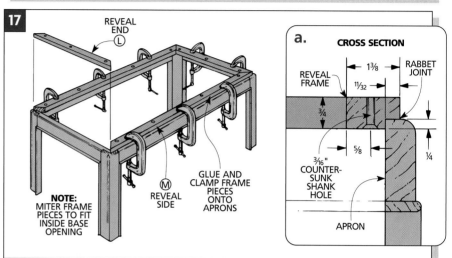

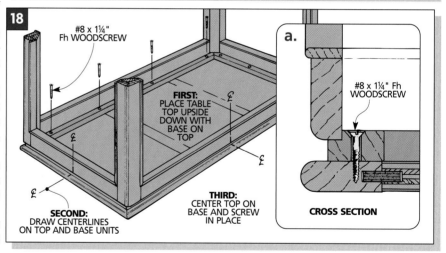

FINISHING TIP . . . . *Custom Oil*

I wanted to bring out just a bit of color when I finished the tables, so I stained them using a homemade stain. I mixed a teaspoon of burnt umber artists' oil color into a quart of boiled linseed oil.

The tables will take a lot of abuse, so I use a finish that can be built up, such as polyurethane.

I brush on at least three coats of finish to all surfaces of the tables and allow it to dry fully. Lightly

sand with 320-grit sandpaper between coats.

I like to top it off with a coat of paste wax applied with 0000 steel wool and buffed with a clean rag. This smoothes the surface and protects it.

SHOP JIG . . . . Edge Guide

To cut the half laps easily on the ends of the long aprons on the Coffee Table, I built an edge guide for a hand-held router (see photo). The guide is similar to one bought in a store, but I think it's more versatile.

HALF LAPS. The aprons on the Coffee Table connect to the legs with half-lap joints. But the aprons are too long to stand on end on the table saw and be cut easily. With this edge guide, I was able to clamp the aprons to my bench and run the router over the workpiece (see photo).

RABBETS. Another thing I liked about this edge guide is that it can be used to cut the 3/4"-wide rabbets on the Coffee Table's leg units after they're assembled. For that matter, the edge guide can be adjusted to cut just about any size rabbet on any workpiece.

ROUNDOVERS. This edge guide also came in handy when I was routing roundovers on the edges of the frame that surrounds the Coffee Table top. Using this jig made the job safer than balancing the assembled top on the router table. It allowed me to uniformly round over the top and bottom edges.

BUILDING THE GUIDE

The edge guide has two main parts. There's a base of 1/4" hardboard with a hole at one end for a router bit, and a handle at the other end for controlling the jig. Also, there's an adjustable fence with a notch in the middle that lets you rout with a bit recessed into the fence.

BASE. After the base has been cut to size *(Fig. 1)*, bore a 1"-dia. hole through one end for the router bit to extend through. Then, remove the existing base from your router and use it as a template to locate the mounting holes on the new router base.

After drilling and countersinking holes for the mounting screws, bore a series of holes in the base to form two slots for adjusting the fence *(Fig. 1)*. Then screw a dowel handle to the other end. Finally, attach the base to the router.

FENCE. I made the fence from a piece of 3/4"-thick hardwood with a notch in the center and holes in both ends for countersunk bolts *(Fig. 1)*. Two machine bolts with wing nuts hold the fence to the base.

USING THE GUIDE

To use the edge guide, adjust the distance between the fence and the *outside* edge of a straight router bit *(Fig. 2)*.

This distance determines the width of the cut. The depth of the cut is determined by the height of the router bit.

To rout a half-lap with this guide, make the first cut (to establish the shoulder) with the fence butted to the end of the workpiece *(Fig. 3)*.

Then to finish the half-lap, clean out the waste between the shoulder and the end of the workpiece by making several freehand passes *(Fig. 4)*.

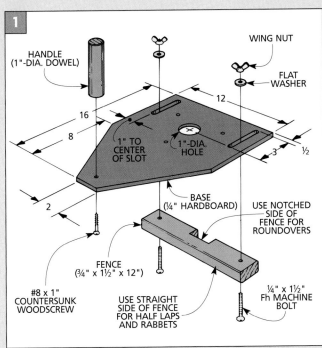

1

HANDLE (1"-DIA. DOWEL)

WING NUT

FLAT WASHER

16

8

12

1" TO CENTER OF SLOT

1"-DIA. HOLE

3

1/2

2

BASE (1/4" HARDBOARD)

USE NOTCHED SIDE OF FENCE FOR ROUNDOVERS

FENCE (3/4" x 1 1/2" x 12")

#8 x 1" COUNTERSUNK WOODSCREW

USE STRAIGHT SIDE OF FENCE FOR HALF LAPS AND RABBETS

1/4" x 1 1/2" Fh MACHINE BOLT

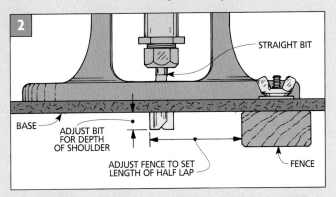

2

STRAIGHT BIT

BASE

ADJUST BIT FOR DEPTH OF SHOULDER

ADJUST FENCE TO SET LENGTH OF HALF LAP

FENCE

3

FIRST CUT ESTABLISHES SHOULDER

RUN FENCE ALONG END OF WORKPIECE

4

WASTE

CLEAN OUT WASTE TO COMPLETE HALF LAP

DESIGNER'S NOTEBOOK

This End Table is a nice companion piece to the Coffee Table, but with its own challenges in building it. It's taller and not as long as the Coffee Table, but the most noticeable change is the added shelf.

CONSTRUCTION NOTES:

■ The End Table is taller than the Coffee Table, but not as long. Besides the differences in overall dimensions, there are four main design changes on the End Table.

■ The most notable change from the Coffee Table to the End Table is the addition of a shelf made from the same $^3/_4$" plywood used for the top *(Fig. 1)*. It's installed with the grain running at 90° to the grain of the top.

■ To mount the shelf to the table, the corner blocks located behind each leg are modified.

■ Then hardwood edging is added all around to hide the exposed edges of the plywood shelf.

■ There's one more not-so-obvious difference with the End Table. I've relocated the rabbeted corner joint on the legs. What you want is a joint line that's not visible from the front. So the rabbets on the End Table will be cut on the *end* leg assemblies, instead of the *apron* leg assemblies.

■ To build this End Table, begin with the directions for the base that start on page 18. But use the dimensions in the Materials List below and *Fig. 1* on the next page. (Don't forget to rabbet just the end units.) When you get to the corner blocks, don't install the lower

END TABLE

blocks (T) until you're ready to attach the shelf.

■ As you're building the base for the End Table and you're ready to glue in the corner blocks, stop — the shelf comes next. First, cut the shelf (U) oversize from a sheet of $^3/_4$" plywood. (Refer to *Fig. 9* on page 20 for informa-

MATERIALS LIST

NEW PARTS

N	End Aprons (2)	$^3/_4$ x 2 - 18$^3/_4$
O	Side Aprons (2)	$^3/_4$ x 2 - 24$^3/_4$
P	Leg Ends (4)	$^3/_4$ x 2 - 22
Q	Leg Sides (4)	$^3/_4$ x 1$^5/_8$ - 22
R	Beading Strips	$^1/_4$ x $^7/_8$ - 20 rough
S	Upp.Cor. Blks. (4)	$^3/_4$ x 2$^3/_{16}$ - 14$^3/_4$
T	Low.Cor. Blks. (4)	$^3/_4$ x 2$^3/_{16}$ - 6$^1/_4$
U	Shelf (1)	$^3/_4$ ply - 16 x 22
V	Shelf Edging	$^3/_4$ x $^3/_4$ - 20
W	Table Top (1)	$^3/_4$ ply - 16 x 22
X	Frame Ends (2)	$^3/_4$ x 2 - 20
Y	Frame Sides (2)	$^3/_4$ x 2 - 26
Z	Reveal Ends (2)	$^3/_4$ x 1$^3/_8$ - 20 rough
AA	Reveal Sides (2)	$^3/_4$ x 1$^3/_8$ - 26 rough

HARDWARE SUPPLIES

(16) No. 8 x 1$^1/_4$" Fh woodscrews

CUTTING DIAGRAM

$^3/_4$ x 7 - 60 (2.9 Bd. Ft.)   **ALSO NEED: 48" x 48" SHEET OF $^3/_4$" PLYWOOD**

Q	Q	S
P	P	S
O	N	

$^3/_4$ x 7 - 60 (2.9 Bd. Ft.)

Q	Q	S
P	P	S
O	N	

$^3/_4$ x 6$^1/_2$ - 60 (2.7 Bd. Ft.)

Y	X	T	T
Y	X	T	T

$^3/_4$ x 5$^1/_2$ - 60 (2.3 Bd. Ft.)

AA	Z	
AA	Z	
R		

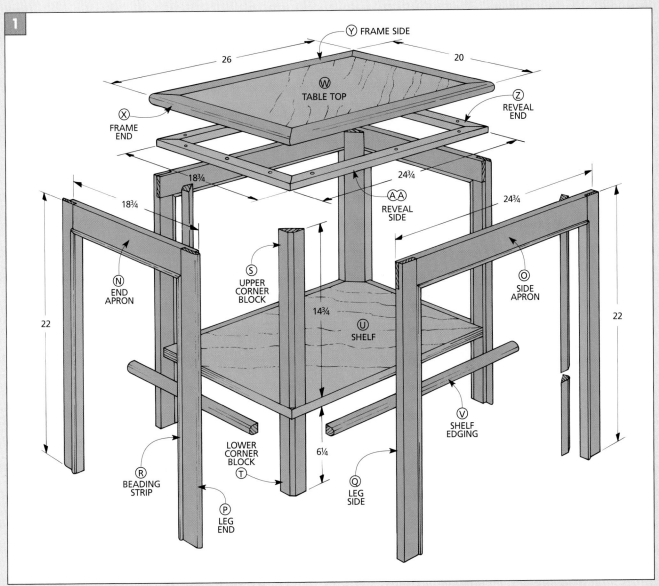

1

Y FRAME SIDE

26

20

W
TABLE TOP

X
FRAME
END

Z
REVEAL
END

18¾

18¾

24¾

AA
REVEAL
SIDE

24¾

N
END
APRON

S
UPPER
CORNER
BLOCK

O
SIDE
APRON

22

22

14¾

U
SHELF

R
BEADING
STRIP

LOWER
CORNER
BLOCK
T

6¼

V
SHELF
EDGING

P
LEG
END

Q
LEG
SIDE

tion on cutting the piece at an angle.) Then you can measure inside the corners of the legs to determine the finished size of the plywood panel.

■ Now, turn the table base upside down and glue in the upper corner blocks (S) *(Fig. 2)*. Place the shelf with the good side down inside the base and screw the shelf to the blocks *(Fig. 3a)*. (The screws will pull the shelf tight to the corner blocks so there's no gap when the table sits right side up.)

■ Now the lower corner blocks (T) can be cut to finished length and then glued in place *(Fig. 3)*. Make sure the blocks are flush at the bottoms of all of the legs.

■ Finally, I cut edging strips (V) and rounded over the edges with a ³⁄₈" roundover bit on the router table. Then the strips can be cut to length to fit between the legs, and glued to the edges of the shelf *(Fig. 3a)*.

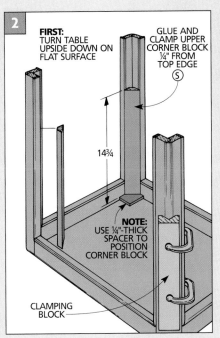

2

FIRST:
TURN TABLE
UPSIDE DOWN ON
FLAT SURFACE

GLUE AND
CLAMP UPPER
CORNER BLOCK
¼" FROM
TOP EDGE
S

14¾

NOTE:
USE ¼"-THICK
SPACER TO
POSITION
CORNER BLOCK

CLAMPING
BLOCK

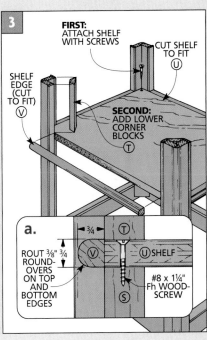

3

FIRST:
ATTACH SHELF
WITH SCREWS

CUT SHELF
TO FIT
U

SHELF
EDGE
(CUT
TO FIT)
V

SECOND:
ADD LOWER
CORNER
BLOCKS
T

a.

¾

T

ROUT ³⁄₈" ¾
ROUND-
OVERS
ON TOP
AND
BOTTOM
EDGES

V

U SHELF

#8 x 1¼"
Fh WOOD-
SCREW

S

Queen Anne End Table

This graceful, formal-looking walnut end table features cabriole legs and a dovetailed drawer. With challenging techniques and a timeless appearance, it's sure to be appreciated by all.

There are a few pieces of furniture that every woodworker would love to build — someday. This Queen Anne End Table is one of those pieces. Besides the beauty of the design, the attraction of this table seems to be related to the skill required to build it.

I'm not saying that you have to be a master craftsman to build it. You don't. But there is the challenge of learning several woodworking techniques and pulling them all together to produce one piece of heirloom furniture.

The primary technique, of course, is making the cabriole legs. They're not as difficult as you might imagine. No turning on the lathe. No carving. They can be cut easily with a band saw and finished off with a little hand filing. (Okay, I did use a spokeshave, but you could use a file or rasp.) The step-by-step details of this technique are described starting on page 33.

There are a number of other techniques to building this table as well. For the drawer, I cut half-blind dovetail joints by hand. The aprons and legs are assembled with traditional mortise and tenon joinery. In addition, there are interesting chamfers cut around the top of the table.

WOOD. I think a formal-looking project like this should be built from a dark wood such as walnut. Mahogany and cherry would also work, but you may want to consider staining them dark.

I used 3" x 3" turning squares to make the legs (see Sources, page 126).

FINISH. To finish the table, I started with a paste wood filler to fill the pores. Then I used a high gloss varnish as a top coat. Start with a thinned coat (50/50) to seal the surface. Then finish it off with four full-strength coats. Finally, I rubbed it out to a glass-smooth surface with some 600-grit sandpaper, pumice, and rottenstone.

EXPLODED VIEW

OVERALL DIMENSIONS:
20W x 24D x 22H

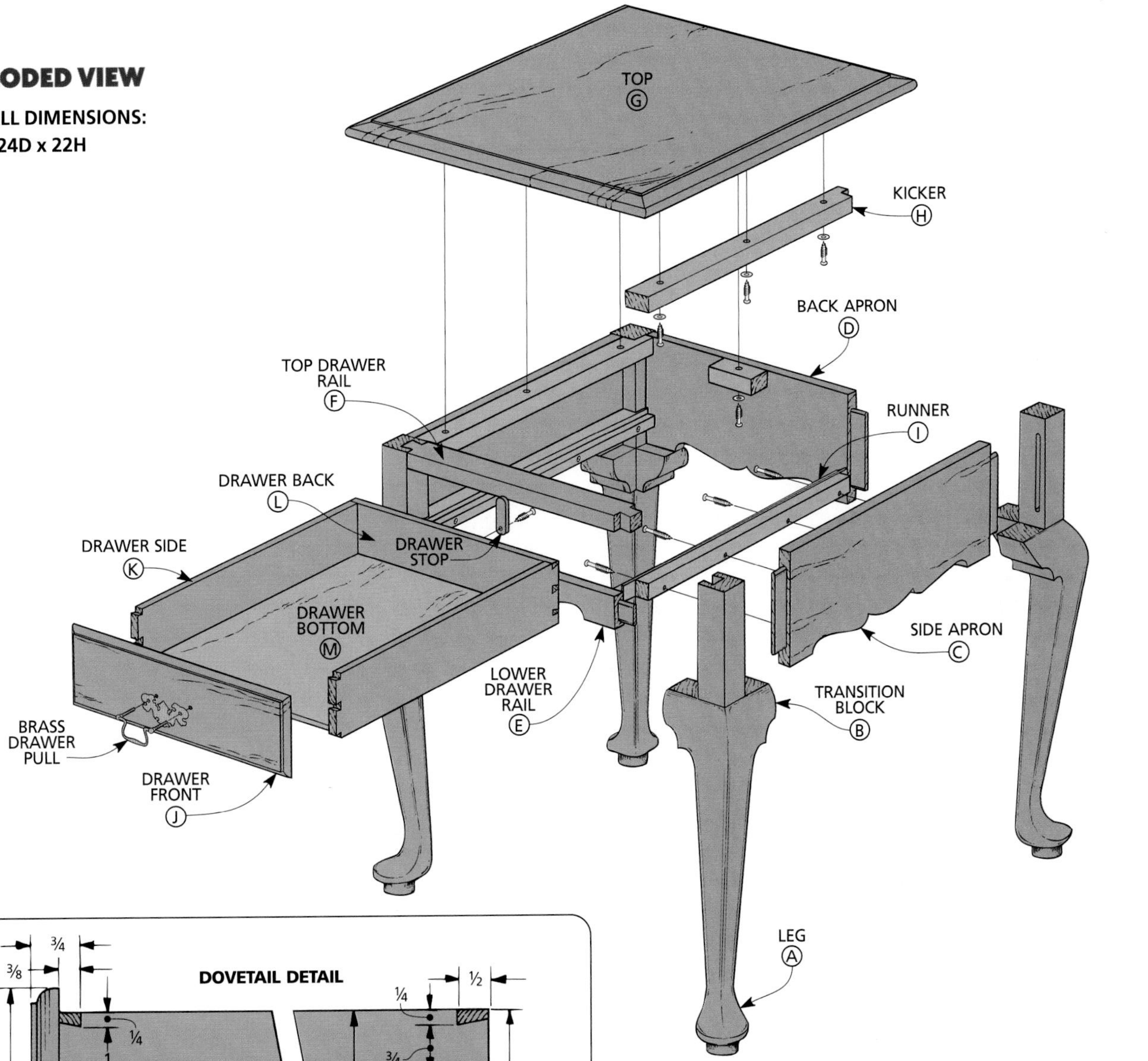
TOP
G
KICKER
H
BACK APRON
D
TOP DRAWER
RAIL
F
RUNNER
I
DRAWER BACK
L
DRAWER SIDE
K
DRAWER
STOP
DRAWER
BOTTOM
M
SIDE APRON
C
LOWER
DRAWER
RAIL
E
TRANSITION
BLOCK
B
BRASS
DRAWER
PULL
DRAWER
FRONT
J
LEG
A

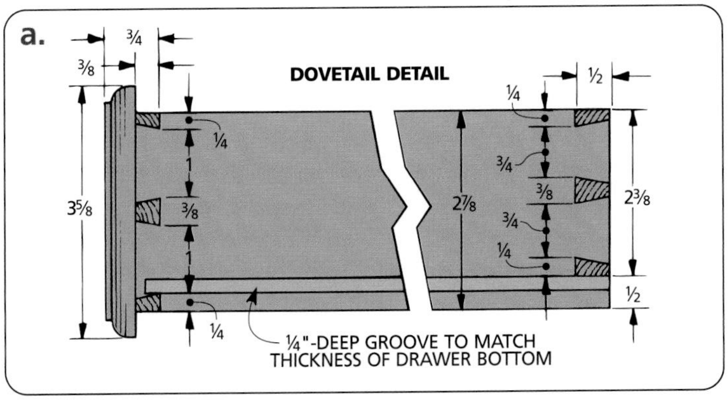
a.
DOVETAIL DETAIL
3/4
3/8
1/4
1
3/8
1
1/4
3 5/8
2 7/8
1/2
1/4
3/4
3/8
3/4
1/4
2 3/8
1/2
1/4"-DEEP GROOVE TO MATCH
THICKNESS OF DRAWER BOTTOM

MATERIALS LIST

WOOD

A	Legs (4)	2¾ x 2¾ - 21¼
B	Transition Blocks (8)	2¾ x 2¾ - 2
C	Side Aprons (2)	¾ x 5¼ - 20
D	Back Apron (1)	¾ x 5¼ - 16
E	Lwr. Drwr. Rail (1)	¾ x 1½ - 16
F	Top Drwr. Rail (1)	¾ x 1¾ - 15½
G	Top (1)	¾ x 20 - 24
H	Kickers (2)	¾ x 1½ - 18 13/16
I	Runners (2)	¾ x 1½ - 19¾
J	Drawer Front (1)	¾ x 3⅝ - 14½
K	Drawer Sides (2)	½ x 2⅞ - 18
L	Drawer Back (1)	½ x 2⅜ - 13¾
M	Drawer Bottom (1)	¼ ply - 17⅞ x 13¼

HARDWARE SUPPLIES

- (1) 3" smooth-face cast plate handle
- (1) No. 6 x ¾" Fh woodscrew
- (8) No. 8 x 1¾" Fh woodscrews
- (8) No. 8 x 1" Rh woodscrews
- (8) No. 8 (7/16" O.D.) washers
- (2) ¾" wire brads

CUTTING DIAGRAM

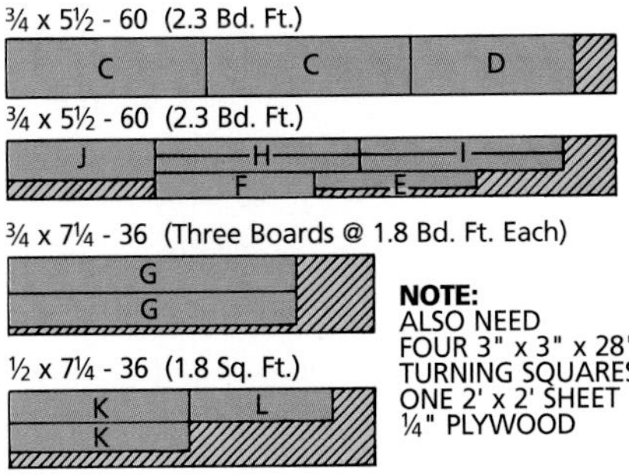
¾ x 5½ - 60 (2.3 Bd. Ft.)
C
C
D
¾ x 5½ - 60 (2.3 Bd. Ft.)
J
H
I
F
E
¾ x 7¼ - 36 (Three Boards @ 1.8 Bd. Ft. Each)
G
G
½ x 7¼ - 36 (1.8 Sq. Ft.)
K
L
K

NOTE:
ALSO NEED
FOUR 3" x 3" x 28"
TURNING SQUARES,
ONE 2' x 2' SHEET
¼" PLYWOOD

CABRIOLE LEGS

Each leg starts out as a block of walnut $2^3/_4$" square by roughly 28" long. This length includes enough for one leg (A) plus the two transition blocks (B) that are glued on near the knee *(Fig. 1)*.

Note: You can also buy pre-made cabriole legs (see mail order sources on page 126). But I like to make my own.

If you decide to make your own legs,

I don't recommend gluing them up from four pieces of $3/_4$"-thick stock. The glue lines will become very obvious when the leg is shaped. Instead, I like to start with a 3" x 3" turning square and trim it down to the $2^3/_4$" square size. Again, this is all explained in the article starting on page 33.

After squaring the stock to $2^3/_4$" (see the Shop Tip on the opposite page), cut off two 2" lengths for the transition

blocks and a $21^1/_4$" length for the leg.

PATTERN. Before gluing the transition blocks on, first mark the pattern on two adjacent faces of the leg blank.

To do this, make a pattern from the grid drawing in *Fig. 1*. (You can also order a cabriole leg pattern. See *Woodsmith Project Supplies* on page 126.) It's best to use carbon paper to trace this pattern onto a piece of posterboard or hardboard. Then cut out the shape and lay it over the printed pattern to make sure the shapes are the same.

Now use the cut-out pattern to mark the outline on the legs (refer to *Step 1* on page 34). Since I was working with walnut, it was difficult to see a pencil line. Instead, I used a felt-tip marker to draw the pattern on the leg blank.

REFERENCE LINES. After the pattern is marked, use a square to mark a reference line right where the corner post meets the top of the knee *(Fig. 1)*.

Mark this line around all four faces of the leg. These lines are used later when cutting the leg to shape and when gluing on the transition blocks (refer to *Fig. 13* on page 30).

MORTISES IN THE LEGS

Before cutting the legs to shape, the mortises are laid out. The mortises are marked on the two inside faces of the legs — the faces with the patterns marked on them.

However, because the mortise layout is different on the front legs and back legs, it helps to mark each leg to indicate the position it will be in when the table is assembled (refer to *Fig. 6*).

MORTISES ON BACK LEGS. The mortises on the back legs are the same on both faces — $1/_4$" wide by $3^3/_4$" long by $1^1/_{16}$" deep and centered $1^1/_4$" from the inside corner *(Fig. 2)*. This position (centered $1^1/_4$" from the corner) makes for a small shoulder ($1/_8$" wide) between the face of the apron and the face of the corner post of the leg *(Fig. 5)*.

MORTISES ON FRONT LEGS. The mortises on the two front legs are a little trickier because the two mortises are different sizes and positioned differently. One side has a $3^3/_4$"-long mortise for the side apron (that's positioned the same as on the back legs) *(Fig. 3)*.

But the other side has a mortise only 1" long for the lower drawer rail (E) (refer to *Fig. 6*). This mortise is also positioned differently — it's centered

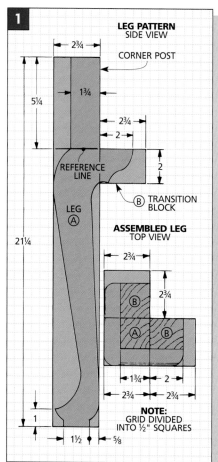

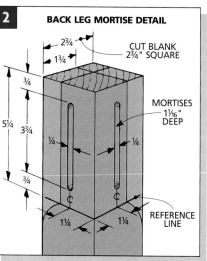

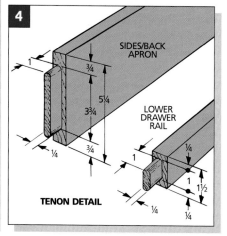

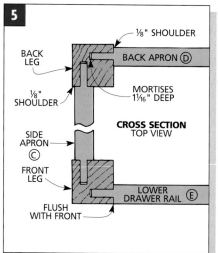

$1^3/_8$" from the inside corner instead of $1^1/_4$" *(Fig. 3)*. This way the rail will be flush with the front of the corner post.

After the mortises were marked on all four legs, I drilled them out on a drill press by drilling a series of overlapping holes. Then I cleaned up the cheeks with a sharp chisel.

APRONS

When the mortises were complete, I proceeded to make the three aprons and the lower drawer rail out of $3/_4$"-thick stock. The two side aprons (C) and the back apron (D) are all cut to a common width of $5^1/_4$" *(Fig. 4)*.

Then the side aprons (C) are trimmed to a length of 20". This allows a shoulder-to-shoulder length of 18", and 2" for the 1"-long tenon on each end *(Fig. 6)*. The back apron (D) is 16" long (this apron has a shoulder-to-shoulder

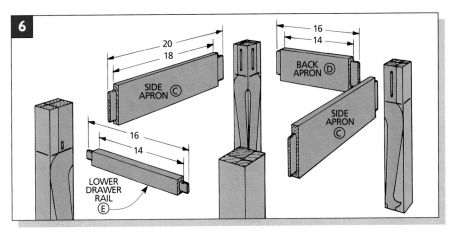

length of 14").

DRAWER RAIL. Next, the lower drawer rail (E) is cut $1^1/_2$" wide and to a length of 16". This length should match the back apron (D) *(Fig. 6)*.

TENONS. After all four pieces have been cut to size, cut tenons centered on the ends of each piece to fit the mortises

cut earlier in the legs *(Fig. 4)*.

When the tenons fit, dry-assemble the table and check to see that the top edges of the three aprons are flush with the top ends of the corner post. Also, the bottom edges of these aprons and the lower drawer rail should be aligned on the reference lines on the legs.

SHOP TIP . . . . *Squaring Up Leg Blanks*

I used turning squares to make the cabriole legs for the Queen Anne End Table. But even though they're called turning squares, I've rarely seen one with two square (90°) faces over its entire length. The easiest way to square one up is with a jointer. But it can also be done on a table saw.

To cut the leg blanks square using the table saw, I built a jig out of a couple pieces of scrap. The jig keeps the blank from rocking and twisting while it's being ripped.

To make the jig, nail a piece of hardboard at 90° to a scrap of $3/_4$" stock. The hardboard should be about as long as the blank.

After the jig is nailed together, position the turning square in the inside corner of the jig and tack it in place *(Fig. 1)*.

Note: Remember to tack toward the ends where the nail holes can

be cut off when cutting out the leg profiles.

Next, I followed a sequence of four cuts until the four sides were 90° to one another. First, place the jig on the table saw with the jig against the rip fence *(Step 1 in Fig. 3)*.

Now set the fence so the blade will make a cut along face A. For a clean cut, I ripped this face in

increments, raising the blade slightly between each pass.

A 10" blade can't be raised high enough to cut all the way through a 3" turning square. So I removed the square from the jig and planed down the extra lip *(Fig. 2)*.

Next, turn the square *(Step 2)*, nail it to the jig, and adjust the rip fence to

cut the next surface (B).

Once again, make the cut in increments and plane it flat. At this point surfaces A and B should be square to one another.

To make the final two cuts, the jig won't be needed. Just set the rip fence for the finished width and cut surface C *(Step 3)*, and finally surface D *(Step 4)*.

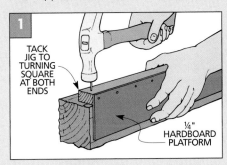

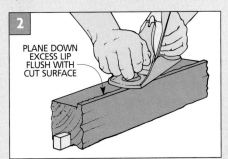

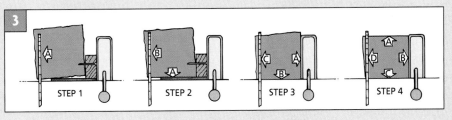

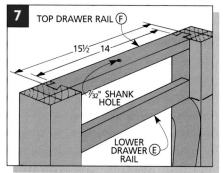

7 TOP DRAWER RAIL F

15½ 14

⁷⁄₃₂" SHANK HOLE

LOWER DRAWER RAIL E

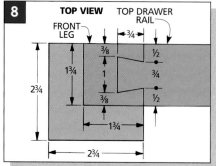

8 TOP VIEW

TOP DRAWER RAIL

FRONT LEG

¾

⅜

1

⅜

½

¾

½

1¾

2¾

1¾

2¾

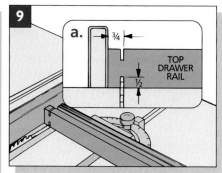

9

a. ¾

TOP DRAWER RAIL

½

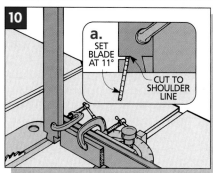

10

a. SET BLADE AT 11°

CUT TO SHOULDER LINE

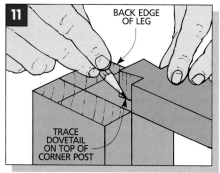

11 BACK EDGE OF LEG

TRACE DOVETAIL ON TOP OF CORNER POST

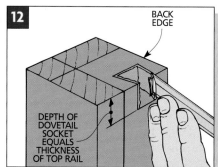

12 BACK EDGE

DEPTH OF DOVETAIL SOCKET EQUALS THICKNESS OF TOP RAIL

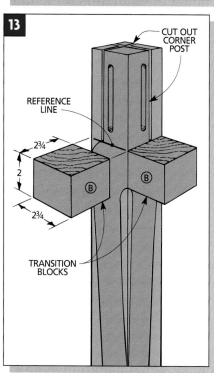

13 CUT OUT CORNER POST

REFERENCE LINE

2¾

2

2¾

B B

TRANSITION BLOCKS

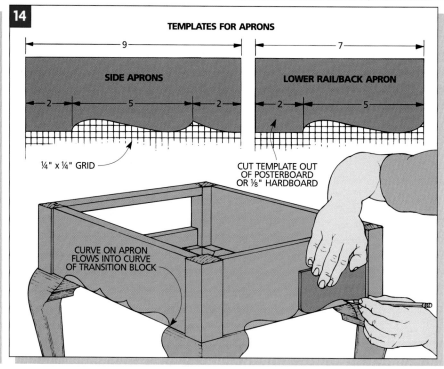

14 TEMPLATES FOR APRONS

9

SIDE APRONS

2 5 2

7

LOWER RAIL/BACK APRON

2 5

¼" x ¼" GRID

CUT TEMPLATE OUT OF POSTERBOARD OR ⅛" HARDBOARD

CURVE ON APRON FLOWS INTO CURVE OF TRANSITION BLOCK

TOP DRAWER RAIL

There's one more rail to add to the end table — a top drawer rail (F) *(Fig. 7)*. This rail will be mounted with a single dovetail joint.

Start by cutting the rail from ³⁄₄"-thick stock to a width of 1³⁄₄" and a length of 15¹⁄₂" *(Figs. 7 and 8)*.

CUT DOVETAILS. To make the dovetails on a table saw, first make ¹⁄₂"-deep shoulder cuts, ³⁄₄" in from each end

(Fig. 9). These cuts will establish a shoulder-to-shoulder length of 14" (equal to that of the lower rail). Then, just make 11° cuts with the rail standing on end *(Fig. 10)*.

CUT SOCKET. Now use the dovetails to mark the sockets on the corner posts of the two front legs *(Fig. 11)*. Then chop out the socket *(Fig. 12)*.

Also, drill a counterbored shank hole at the center of the rail *(Fig. 7)*. (It's the same size as the one in *Fig. 15a*.)

CUT CABRIOLE LEGS

The basic parts of the table are completed, so now comes the challenging part — cutting the cabriole legs to shape. (See the technique section starting on page 33.)

The procedure is to make the two face cuts for the corner posts first. Then glue the transition blocks (B) to the legs *(Fig. 13)*. Finally, cut and file the cabriole legs to shape.

SHAPE THE APRONS

After the cabriole legs have all been shaped, dry-assemble the table to mark the curved pattern on the bottoms of the aprons *(Fig. 14)*.

Position the pattern so the curve of the apron blends into the curve of the transition block on the leg. After the pattern is marked, remove the aprons and cut them to shape on a band saw.

ASSEMBLY. To assemble the table, I glued the side aprons to their corresponding legs first. Then I joined these units to the back apron and front rails.

DRAWER RUNNERS

When the table is assembled, drawer runners and kickers can be added.

KICKERS. First, kickers (H) are glued to the inside of the aprons. Cut them to length to fit between the front leg and the back apron *(Fig. 15)*.

Notch out the back end of the kicker to fit around the post. But before mounting it, drill oversized shank holes for the screws that hold the top in place *(Fig. 15a)*. (The oversized holes allow the top to expand and contract.)

RUNNERS. Next, cut the runners (I) to fit between the front rail and the back apron *(Fig. 15)*. Notch the ends to fit around the posts *(Step 1 in Fig. 16)*.

Also, rabbets are cut in the runners to guide the drawer *(Step 2)*. To prevent the drawer side from rubbing against the post, cut the rabbet so its shoulder sticks out $^1/_{16}$" from the face of the corner post *(Fig. 17)*.

Now trim off the small sliver next to the front notch *(Step 3)*. Then screw (don't glue) the runner to the aprons so the bottom of the rabbet is flush with the lower drawer rail.

SCREW BLOCK. The last piece to add is a screw block centered on the top edge of the back apron *(Fig. 15)*.

DRAWER

The drawer is built the old-fashioned way: with half-blind dovetails on the front, and through dovetails on the back *(Fig. 18* and detail 'a' in the Exploded View on page 27)*.

Note: Other types of joinery could be used, but this might change the length of the drawer parts.

FRONT. Start by cutting the drawer front (J) to size. To determine its length,

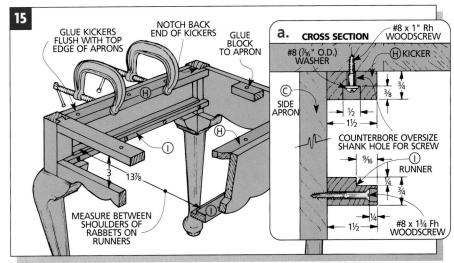

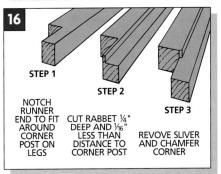

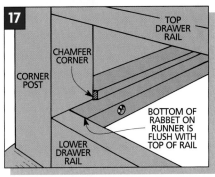

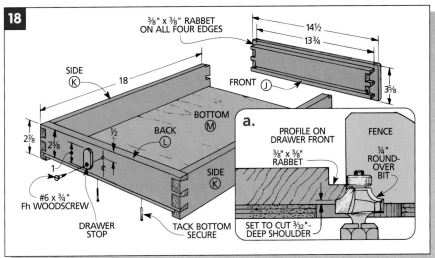

measure the distance between the shoulders of the rabbets on the runners, less $^1/_8$" (for clearance), plus $^3/_4$" (for the $^3/_8$"-wide lipped edges). The width is equal to the height of the opening, less $^1/_8$", plus $^3/_4$".

Now cut $^3/_8$" x $^3/_8$" rabbets on all four edges of the drawer front. Then the pins (sockets) of the dovetail can be cut. To complete the drawer front, rout a profile on the front face *(Fig. 18a)*.

SIDES. Next, cut the drawer sides (K) to size out of $^1/_2$"-thick stock. Then cut

dovetails on the ends to fit the sockets in the drawer front. Also, cut grooves for the $^1/_4$" plywood drawer bottom in the front and sides *(Fig. 18)*.

BACK. The drawer back (L) is joined to the sides with through dovetails. I also made a turnbutton from scrap wood to extend above the drawer back as a stop *(Fig. 18)*.

BOTTOM. Finally, you can glue the drawer together. Then cut the plywood bottom (M) to fit in the grooves and slip it in place *(Fig. 18)*.

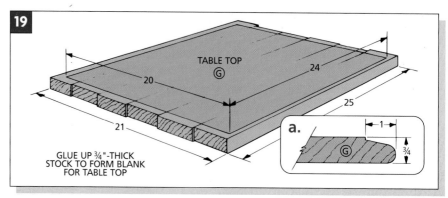

The table is complete now except for the top (G). To make the top, glue up ³/₄"-thick stock to get a blank that's roughly 21" by 25" *(Fig. 19)*.

Once the glue is dry on the blank, sand or plane both faces down so they're smooth and flat.

When it's flat, trim the blank to a final size of 20" wide by 24" long. (This produces a 1¹/₄" lip on all four sides of the assembled table.)

PROFILE THE EDGES. After the table top was trimmed to final size, I cut the edge profiles.

Note: It's best to cut the profiles immediately after planing the top smooth. If you wait overnight or a few days, the top will have a chance to warp. Even if the warp is very slight, it will cause problems when cutting the profiles to shape.

CHAMFER CUT. The first cut to make is a wide chamfer. To do this, tilt the saw blade to 11° and raise the height to 1" *(Fig. 20)*. Then adjust the fence so the saw blade cuts a chamfer that leaves a ³/₃₂" shoulder.

SQUARE SHOULDER CUT. After making the 11° chamfer cut on all four edges, reset the saw blade to 90° and lower the blade so it just barely cuts a square shoulder up to the chamfered surface *(Fig. 21)*.

ROUND THE EDGES. When the chamfer is complete, all four edges are rounded over with a ¹/₄" roundover bit on a router table. First, round over the bottom edge *(Fig. 22)*.

Next, round over the chamfered edge *(Fig. 23)*. Sneak up on this cut, raising the bit in small increments. What you're trying to do is round as much of the corner as possible without allowing the corner of the bit to hit the chamfered surface *(Fig. 23a)*. Then smooth the edge with sandpaper.

MOUNT THE TOP. When the top is complete, you can mount it to the table. First, remove the drawer runners so they're not in the way. Then, to ensure that the top is centered on the table, mark a centerline on the underside of the top and on the aprons and top drawer rail *(Fig. 24)*.

With the table centered on the top, drill pilot holes in the top, and temporarily screw the top in place with 1" roundhead screws. Then remove the screws so the table can be finished. ■

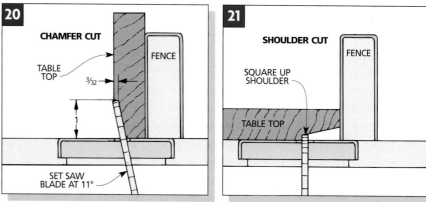

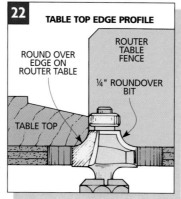

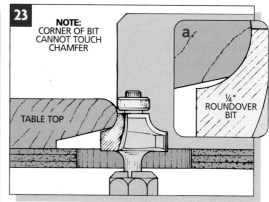

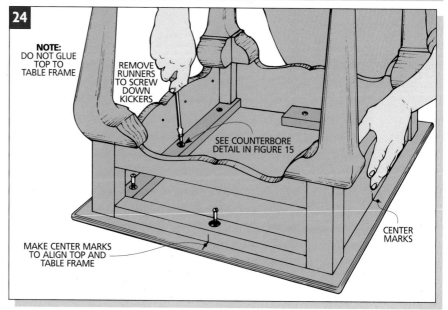

It's easy to be convinced that making a cabriole leg is a form of sculpture — that you have to visualize the leg in a block of wood, then carve away everything that isn't a leg.

But the truth is that a cabriole leg almost evolves by itself. As an experiment, try gluing up some scraps of 2x4 to get a block with a rough size of 3" x 3". Then draw the leg profile on two adjacent sides of this stock, and cut along the lines with the band saw.

When the waste falls away, you have the basic shape of a cabriole leg (as shown on the left in the photo). Okay, it's a little rough maybe — but all it takes from there is some filing and sanding to refine the shape of the leg.

LEG HEIGHT. One thing I particularly like about this method for making a cabriole leg is that you can use it no matter how tall the leg is. Sure, you will need a different pattern for the taller legs on a dining table than you would for an end table or a footstool. But the steps to make the leg are the same. The section between the knee and the ankle is just "stretched" out for a taller leg.

Note: You might have noticed that the photo above and the drawings on the next few pages are for a shorter leg than is needed on the Queen Anne End Table featured on page 26 of this book. But there is a reason for this. It was easier to show the steps in the drawings clearly and accurately on a shorter leg. Again, the procedure is the same no matter the length.

START WITH A BLANK. Basically, a cabriole leg starts out as a square piece

There are three basic stages in making a cabriole leg. In Stage 1, the blank is cut to basic shape on the band saw. In Stage 2, the corners are filed off. Finally, the corners are rounded over and the leg sanded smooth in Stage 3.

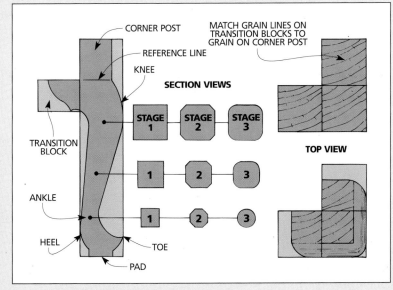

of stock. Depending on the pattern you decide to use, this leg blank is usually a 3" x 3" square.

To get a blank this size, you can glue four pieces of $^3/_4$"-thick stock together. However, the glue lines will show when the leg is formed. Also, because of changes in the grain patterns, there may be some problems during the shaping process.

What works much better is to use a 3" x 3" "turning" square (the kind used for turning on the lathe). If you can't find them locally, they're available through several mail order catalogs (see page 126). I buy the squares extra

long so I can also cut transition blocks from the blank.

EARLY WORK. Even before any cutting starts, there is some preparatory work to be done. Usually, there are mortises that have to be cut in the blank to attach aprons or rails that run between the cabriole legs.

Also, the curved transition blocks are glued in place.

STAGE ONE. Once all the preliminary work is completed, the leg blank goes through three stages to become the finished leg. First, the blank is bandsawn to the basic cabriole leg shape. (This is shown on the left in the photo above.)

Although the leg has a lot of curves at this point, the cross sections at various points along the leg are all squares. (This is shown in the three Section Views labeled "Stage 1" in the diagram at left.)

SECOND STAGE. In the second stage, the corners of the squares at the cross sections are filed or rasped to a 45° angle to give the leg blank an eight-sided cross section (see Section Views labeled "Stage 2" at left).

THIRD STAGE. In the third stage, the corners are rounded over to produce the final shape of the cabriole leg. In its finished form, the ankle cross section is a circle, and the cross sections at other points are just squares (with their corners rounded to the same radius as at the ankle).

Although it certainly doesn't look like when you see the finished leg, all you're really doing to make the cabriole leg is making a square leg that has rounded corners.

The process of making a cabriole leg should always start with a good squared-up blank. If you're using a rough turning square, see the Shop Tip on page 29 to square it up.

The next step is to make a full-size pattern of the cross section of the leg. (I cut the pattern out of hardboard.) The same pattern is used for laying out two adjacent faces of the leg *(Step 1)*.

CUT MORTISES. After the pattern is drawn on the blank and reference lines for the corner post *(Step 2)*, mortises for aprons are cut in the two sides of the blank marked with the patterns. I cut the mortises on the drill press *(Step 3)*.

CUT CORNER POST. Next, make two cuts to form the faces of the post *(Step 4)*.

TRANSITION PIECES. Here I break with tradition. The method traditionally shown is to cut the legs first and glue on the transition blocks later. I've found that gluing curved transition blocks to a curved leg is very awkward. Instead, I glue square transition blocks to the square legs *(Step 5)* and then bandsaw the whole thing to final shape at once.

Note: For best appearance, turn the blocks so the end grain on the blocks looks like it flows into the end grain on the leg (see Top View on page 33).

FINAL LAYOUT. The final steps before cutting are to lay out cuts on the transi-

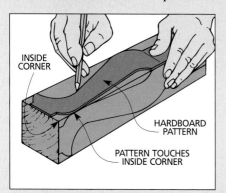

1 To draw the leg pattern, position template so back edge of corner post and heel align with inside corner of stock. Flip template and repeat on adjacent side.

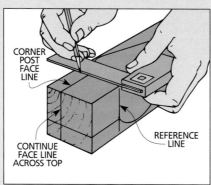

2 Draw reference lines around all four sides where the corner post meets knee. Also draw lines on top end that continue the face lines of the corner post.

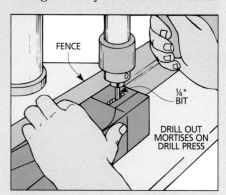

3 Cut mortises on two faces of the corner post. Drill a series of overlapping holes to rough out the mortise. Then clean up the cheeks with a sharp chisel.

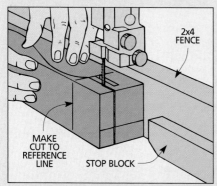

4 Set up band saw to make the face cuts on the corner post. Use a fence to guide the leg and clamp a stop block to the fence to stop the cut at reference line.

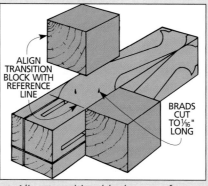

5 Align transition blocks on reference lines and glue and clamp in place. To keep block from shifting when clamped, drive in brads and cut off to ¹/₁₆" long.

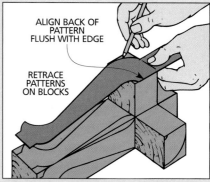

6 Trace the curve of the knee on the outer surfaces of the transition blocks. The reference line on the pattern should align with the top of the transition block.

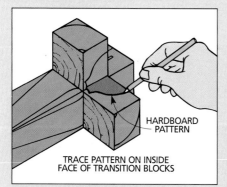

7 A second pattern is used to trace the profile on the inner surface of the transition blocks. Place the small pattern tight in the corner and mark outline.

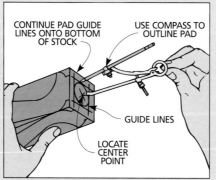

8 Use a square to draw lines across the bottom of the leg that continue the outline of the pad. Then use a compass to draw a circle that fits inside the square.

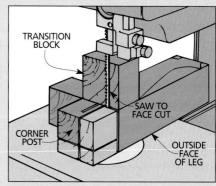

9 Start sawing at the corner post by aligning blade with top of transition block. Saw to the cut made in Step 4. Repeat the cut on the adjacent face.

tion blocks *(Steps 6 and 7)* and the pad at the bottom of the leg *(Step 8)*.

BANDSAW TO SHAPE. The cutting begins at the corner post *(Step 9)*. After the corner post is sawed to shape, saw the profile of the knee *(Step 10)*.

From this point on, save all the scraps that fall away. They're needed to cut the profile on the adjacent surface.

Now cut from the knee down to the foot *(Step 11)*. Next, the bottom of the foot and the pad are sawn in two steps. First make a short, straight cut on the bottom end of the blank to define the front of the pad. Then cut the curved part on the bottom by starting at the point of the toe and sawing down to the cut just made to define the pad.

Once the front face is cut, the process is repeated to cut the back *(Step 12)*.

Now all of the scraps can be put back in place (I use carpet tape or hot-melt glue), and the profiles cut on the adjacent face *(Step 13)*. Finally remove the taped-on scraps *(Step 14)*.

FLATTEN THE SURFACES. The band saw will leave some bumps, so the next step is to smooth these out with a spokeshave or rasp *(Step 15)*. The section between the knee and the ankle should be worked until it's flat *(Step 16)*. Then the curved sections can be smoothed with a plane and file *(Steps 17 and 18)*.

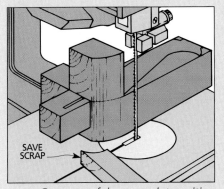

10 *Cut top of knee and transition block with blade guide raised. Saw from tip of knee back to corner post. Be careful not to nick corner post.*

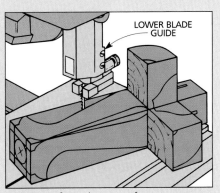

11 *Saw from knee to foot to remove waste on front of leg. Lower blade guide as soon as it clears transition block. Be sure to save waste pieces.*

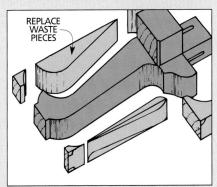

12 *The cut-away pieces are needed to support the leg blank in the next step. Use carpet tape to fasten cut-away pieces back in their original positions.*

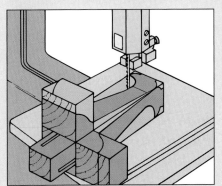

13 *After pieces are taped on, cut out the adjacent profile by flipping the workpiece and sawing along lines. Work in any direction that feels comfortable.*

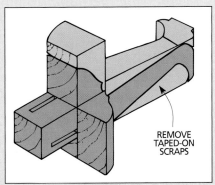

14 *Remove the taped-on pieces to reveal basic shape of a cabriole leg. Complete each leg to this point before proceeding so scraps don't get mixed up.*

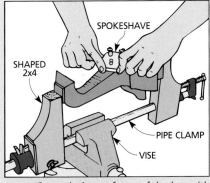

15 *Smooth the surfaces of the leg with a spokeshave or rasp. To hold the leg while working, mount it in a carver's cradle made from pipe clamp and 2x4s.*

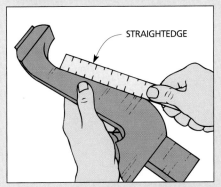

16 *The area between curve of knee and curve of ankle should be a straight line. Use a straightedge to check progress on all four sides of leg.*

17 *To smooth the leg, use whatever tools seem to do the job best. With a sharp block plane, plane carefully across the grain to smooth outside of the knee.*

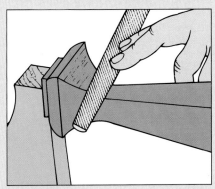

18 *Remove the marks left by the band saw and smooth the inside contour of the ankle with the rounded side of a rasp or wood file.*

At this point the leg has been smoothed, but it's still square. The next step is to knock off all the corners at 45°.

LAYOUT LINES. To do this, first draw layout lines to mark the limits of how much is to be removed. First divide the ankle into quarters *(Step 19)*. Then draw centerpoint lines *(Step 20)* and quarterpoint lines *(Step 21)* up each leg.

CHANGE CROSS SECTION. The next step is to take the leg from a square leg to an eight-sided leg. This is simply a matter of removing the corners at 45° to create a flat surface down to the quarterpoint layout lines.

Start on the front, removing the corners of the straight "shin." I'm most comfortable using a spokeshave on these sections *(Step 22)*, but I will switch to a rasp or file when working around the curved areas *(Steps 23 and 24)*. On these curved areas, taper the corners so they end in a point.

The back is shaped like the front and also comes to a point *(Step 25)*. The sides are also similar, but stop the taper where the transition block begins *(Step 26)*.

FOOT. Now you can switch your attention to the bottom of the foot. Start by marking each side of the foot into quarters. Then cut off the front and side corners between the marks *(Step 27)*.

After the foot is shaped, the pad is cut

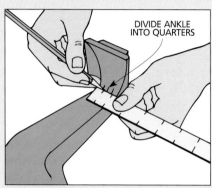

19 *Divide the narrowest part of the ankle into quarters. These marks position the layout lines used when shaping the square to its final contour.*

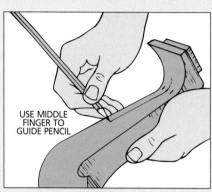

20 *Draw layout lines on both sides of each corner by marking lines from the centerpoints on the ankle. Use middle finger to maintain distance from edge.*

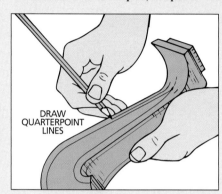

21 *Draw another set of layout lines extending from quarterpoint marks on the ankle. Again, draw two lines on each corner from knee to the ankle.*

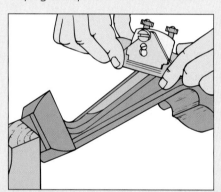

22 *To start forming the leg, remove the corners on the straight parts down to the quarterpoint layout lines. A spokeshave or flat side of a rasp works.*

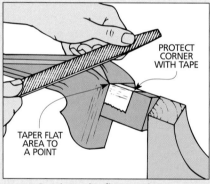

23 *Continue the flattened corner over the top of the knee so it forms a point at the corner post. Protect corner post with several layers of duct tape.*

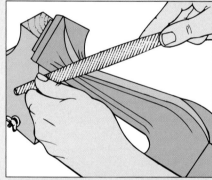

24 *Flatten corner of the front of the ankle with the rounded side of the rasp. Continue this surface over the top of the foot to form a point almost to the toe.*

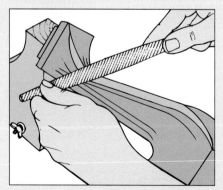

25 *Use a rasp or file to blend the flattened corner on the back of the leg down over the heel. This surface tapers to a point where the heel meets the pad.*

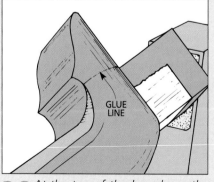

26 *At the top of the leg, shape the inside corners on the back of the knee to a tapered point that ends about where the transition block begins.*

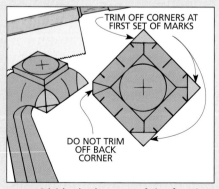

27 *Divide the bottom of the foot into quarters. Then use these marks to cut off the front corner and both side corners. Don't cut off the corner at the heel.*

to an eight-sided shape. Undercut the corners, then remove the corners by sawing down to the undercuts *(Step 28)*.

FINAL SHAPING. Now that the entire leg has eight flat surfaces, the shaping can begin. This is just a process of rounding over all the corners.

Start by rounding over the pad until it's a circle *(Step 29)*. Then move on to the foot using the edge of the pad as a visual guide *(Step 30)*. The edge of the pad and the edge of the foot should be two concentric circles, but the foot doesn't get rounded at the heel.

Next rasp the high spots on the bottom of the foot *(Step 31)*. Then finish off by contouring the heel *(Step 32)*.

ROUND THE LEG. With the foot done, you can move back to the upper part of the leg. Rounding these areas is just a matter of filing from the centerpoint layout lines and blending the corner into a smooth arc *(Steps 33 and 34)*.

Now the top of the foot can be brought to its final shape. To do this, file the ridge on the top of the foot to get a nice smooth curve from the ankle to the perimeter of the foot *(Step 35)*.

The last rounding to do is to ease over the top of the transition block so it flows into the apron *(Step 36)*.

SANDING. Once everything has been filed to shape, just sand the whole leg.

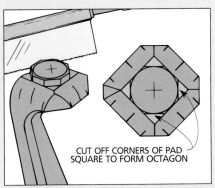

28 *To shape the pad, undercut the four corners first. Then, use the edge of the circle as a guide and cut down to the undercuts to remove the corners.*

CUT OFF CORNERS OF PAD SQUARE TO FORM OCTAGON

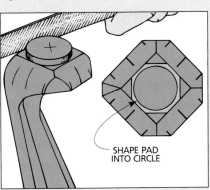

29 *Use the flat side of a rasp or file to round the pad to the edge of the traced circle. Be careful not to score the bottom of the foot with the rasp edge.*

SHAPE PAD INTO CIRCLE

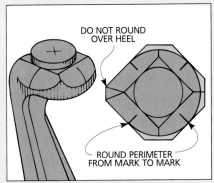

30 *Shape the perimeter of the foot from mid-point to mid-point to form a circle that's concentric with edge of pad. Do not round over area at heel.*

DO NOT ROUND OVER HEEL

ROUND PERIMETER FROM MARK TO MARK

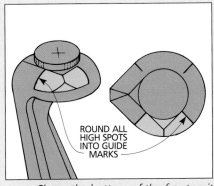

31 *Shape the bottom of the front so it curves from the pad up to the edge of the foot. Don't rasp over guide marks until the high spots have been smoothed.*

ROUND ALL HIGH SPOTS INTO GUIDE MARKS

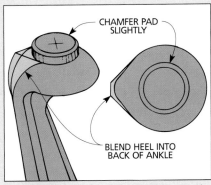

32 *Shape back of the heel by continuing the curve on the foot bottom and blending it into the back of ankle. Also, chamfer pad to prevent chipping.*

CHAMFER PAD SLIGHTLY

BLEND HEEL INTO BACK OF ANKLE

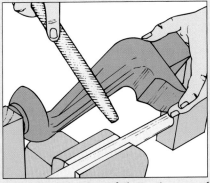

33 *Final shaping of the main part of the leg and the knee is just a matter of rounding over the corners. Use the centerpoint layout lines as a guide.*

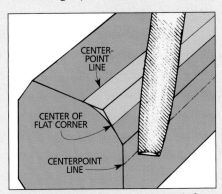

34 *To shape the corners, work from the centerpoint layout lines on one side to center of the flat area. Complete the arc by working from the other side.*

CENTER-POINT LINE

CENTER OF FLAT CORNER

CENTERPOINT LINE

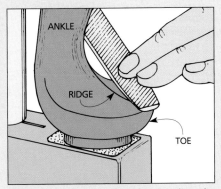

35 *Complete the foot by standing the leg upright. Use a file to smooth the ridge that extends from the ankle, blending curve of the ankle into the foot.*

ANKLE

RIDGE

TOE

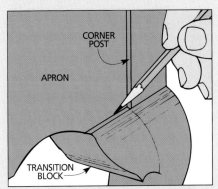

36 *Temporarily put apron in place and trace edge on transition block. Then remove apron and use a chisel to round transition block to marked line.*

CORNER POST

APRON

TRANSITION BLOCK

Dining Table

Clean and understated, this full-size oak Dining Table looks simple at first glance. But what you don't see are the special pull-out extension leaves hidden underneath the table top.

The biggest problem with this table is trying to explain how it works. I had such a hard time explaining the design to everyone that I finally went to the shop and just built it.

When I finished, everyone said, "That's nice, but I thought you said this table had leaves?" I couldn't resist showing off; I lifted one end of the free-floating top and pulled the leaf from underneath. I didn't get a chance to pull out the other leaf before someone lifted the table top off to see how it worked.

HOW IT WORKS. On most extension tables, the table top is cut in half and each half is attached to some sort of runners. To extend the table, you pull the halves apart and the leaves drop in — on top of the runners.

With this table both *leaves* are attached to the runners. When you want to extend the table, lift up one end of the top and pull out a leaf. When the leaf is fully extended, the top drops down and rests on top of the runners.

WOOD. I built the legs and main parts of the table with solid red oak. The top and leaves were cut from a single sheet of ³/₄″ oak plywood. To make the grain of the top match the leaves, I laid out my cuts as if the leaves were part of the top (see detail 'a' in the Exploded View).

Since the leaves fit under the table top when stored, they are slightly narrower than the top.

LEGS. Another interesting feature is the legs. They're mounted with corner blocks and hanger bolts so they stand at a 45° angle to the aprons. This makes them removable, and they can also be tightened with a wrench if they loosen.

FINISH. To provide the table with extra protection, I used two coats of polyurethane, sanding between coats.

OTHER PROJECTS. To build the chairs shown in the photo above, see page 92. Also, a simpler, square version of the table is shown on page 45.

EXPLODED VIEW

OVERALL DIMENSIONS:
35W x 97³/₄L x 29H

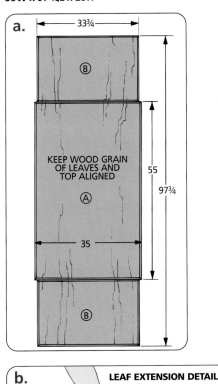

a.

33¾

KEEP WOOD GRAIN
OF LEAVES AND
TOP ALIGNED

Ⓑ
Ⓐ
Ⓑ

55
97¾
35

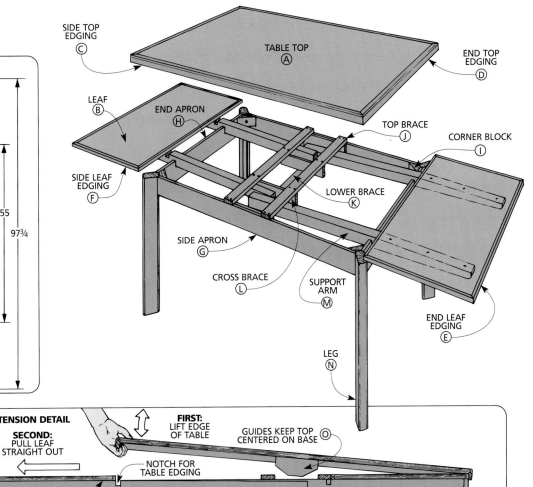

SIDE TOP
EDGING Ⓒ

TABLE TOP Ⓐ

END TOP
EDGING Ⓓ

LEAF Ⓑ

END APRON Ⓗ

TOP BRACE Ⓙ

CORNER BLOCK Ⓘ

SIDE LEAF
EDGING Ⓕ

LOWER BRACE Ⓚ

SIDE APRON Ⓖ

CROSS BRACE Ⓛ

SUPPORT
ARM Ⓜ

END LEAF
EDGING Ⓔ

LEG Ⓝ

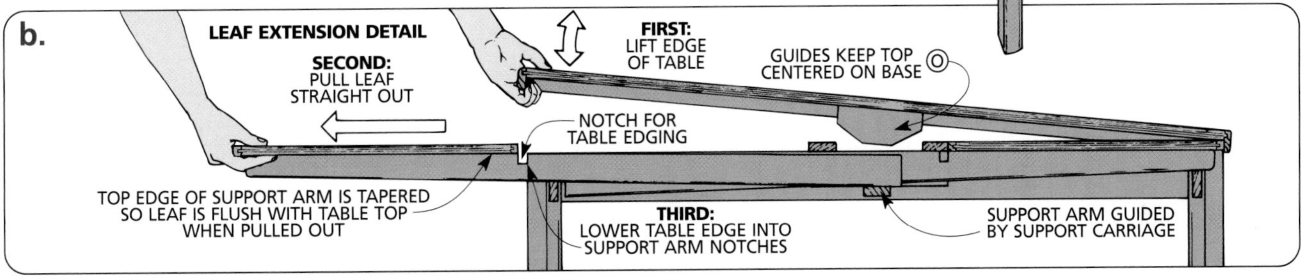

b.

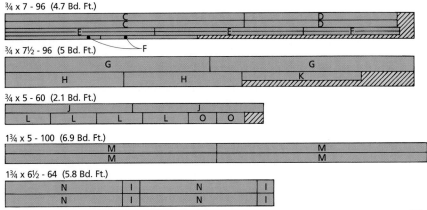

LEAF EXTENSION DETAIL

SECOND: PULL LEAF STRAIGHT OUT

FIRST: LIFT EDGE OF TABLE

GUIDES KEEP TOP CENTERED ON BASE Ⓞ

NOTCH FOR TABLE EDGING

TOP EDGE OF SUPPORT ARM IS TAPERED SO LEAF IS FLUSH WITH TABLE TOP WHEN PULLED OUT

THIRD: LOWER TABLE EDGE INTO SUPPORT ARM NOTCHES

SUPPORT ARM GUIDED BY SUPPORT CARRIAGE

MATERIALS LIST

WOOD

A	Top (1)	¾ ply - 34¼ x 54¼
B	Leaves (2)	¾ ply - 33 x 20⅝
C	Side Top Edging (2)	½ x 1⅝ - 56 rough
D	End Top Edging (2)	½ x 1⅝ - 36 rough
E	End Leaf Edging (4)	½ x ⅞ - 35 rough
F	Side Leaf Edging (4)	½ x ⅞ - 22½ rough
G	Side Aprons (2)	¾ x 3½ - 47¾
H	End Aprons (2)	¾ x 3½ - 27¾
I	Corner Blocks (4)	1¾ x 3 - 4
J	Top Braces (2)	¾ x 2 - 29¾
K	Lower Brace (1)	¾ x 2 - 28¼
L	Cross Braces (4)	¾ x 2½ - 10¾
M	Support Arms (4)	1¾ x 2¼ - 49½
N	Legs (4)	1¾ x 3 - 27½
O	Guides (2)	¾ x 2½ - 6⅝

HARDWARE SUPPLIES

(32) No. 8 x 1¼" Fh woodscrews
(12) No. 8 x 1½" Fh woodscrews
(4) ⅜"-16 x 5" hanger bolts
(4) ⅜"-I.D. washers
(4) ⅜" nuts

CUTTING DIAGRAM

¾ x 7 - 96 (4.7 Bd. Ft.)

C C D
E E F
F

¾ x 7½ - 96 (5 Bd. Ft.)

G G
H H K

¾ x 5 - 60 (2.1 Bd. Ft.)

J J
L L L L O O

1¾ x 5 - 100 (6.9 Bd. Ft.)

M M
M M

1¾ x 6½ - 64 (5.8 Bd. Ft.)

N I N I
N I N I

NOTE: ALSO NEED ONE 4' x 8' SHEET OF ¾" PLYWOOD FOR TABLE TOP AND LEAVES, HARDBOARD SCRAP FOR SPLINES.

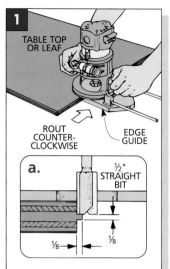

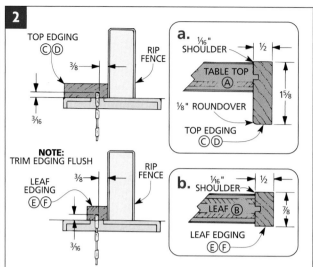

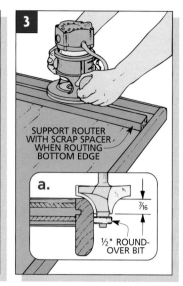

TOP & LEAVES

The table begins with a top and two leaves. They're just pieces of $^3/_4$" oak plywood framed with $^1/_2$"-thick stock.

LAY OUT PIECES. I wanted the grain to flow from one end of the table to the other, so the top piece (A) had to be cut from between the two pieces for the leaves (B) (refer to detail 'a' in the Exploded View on page 39).

CUT TO SIZE. So begin by ripping a $34^1/_4$"-wide piece off the sheet of plywood.

Note: The top is 35" wide, but it's cut $^3/_4$" less to allow for edging and joinery.

Then cut a $54^1/_4$"-long piece for the top (A) from the *exact middle* of the workpiece. And cut the two leftover end pieces $20^1/_8$" long for the leaves (B).

Finally, trim $^5/_8$" off both edges of each leaf so the leaves will end up $1^1/_4$" less in width (33") than the top.

Note: I trimmed *both* edges so the grain would still align with the grain on the top when the leaves are extended.

ROUT TONGUE. The edging pieces are attached to the plywood with tongue and groove joinery. So rout tongues on the edges of the plywood. To do this, mount an edge guide and a $^1/_2$" straight bit in the router *(Fig. 1)*. Then rout rabbets on the top and bottom faces to produce $^1/_8$"-thick tongues *(Fig. 1a)*.

EDGING. When the tongue is routed, you can cut the four top edging pieces (C, D). They're resawn to $^1/_2$" thick, ripped $1^5/_8$" wide *(Fig. 2a)*, and cut to rough length (about 2" longer than the top sides and ends). Also cut the eight $^7/_8$"-wide leaf edging pieces (E, F) *(Fig. 2b)*.

GROOVE IN EDGING. The edging is joined to the plywood by cutting a $^1/_8$"-

wide groove (to match the tongue) on the inside face *(Fig. 2)*. Position the groove so when the edging is mounted, the top edge extends about $^1/_{16}$" above the plywood. (It's trimmed flush later.)

ROUND INSIDE EDGE. Before mounting the top edging pieces (C, D), I softened the *inside* bottom edge by rounding it over with a $^1/_8$" roundover bit *(Fig. 2a)*.

APPLY EDGING. Now the edging is glued and clamped to the plywood. Miter the ends of the top edging pieces (C, D) and glue them to the top (A).

Note: If you don't have long enough clamps, try taping the edging tight while the glue dries. I used filament packaging tape that is strong and won't stretch.

Also miter and glue the leaf edging (E, F) to the leaves (B).

When the glue is dry, trim the edging flush with the plywood. (I used a flush trim bit in the router.) The edging on the leaves (B) is trimmed flush with both the top and the bottom faces.

ROUND OVER EDGING. To complete

the edging on the top, use a $^1/_2$" roundover bit and rout the outside top and bottom edges *(Fig. 3)*. On the leaves, use a $^1/_8$" roundover bit.

APRONS

The next phase is to make four aprons to hold the legs together. The side aprons (G) are easy — just cut two pieces of $^3/_4$"-thick stock $3^1/_2$" wide by $47^3/_4$" long (refer to *Fig. 9*). The end aprons (H) are also $3^1/_2$" wide, but only $27^3/_4$" long.

NOTCH END APRONS. After the end aprons are cut to length, the next step is to lay out the locations of two notches *(Fig. 4)*. These notches allow the leaf supports to be pulled out (refer to the Exploded View on page 39).

The notches in the end aprons are in different positions so the leaf supports will bypass each other under the table. To make the notches, raise the table saw blade to cut $1^9/_{16}$" deep. Make repetitive passes to waste out the notches.

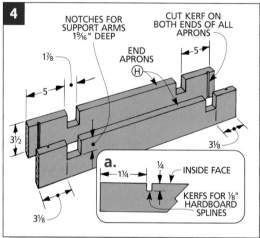

After the notches are cut, use a rasp to form slight bevels on the bottoms of the notches *(Fig. 5)*. This bevel should slope toward the *inside* face of the end aprons so the leaf support arms will smoothly pull out from under the table.

KERFS FOR SPLINES. To complete the aprons, kerfs are cut at both ends of all four aprons. These kerfs match up with kerfs in the corner blocks (I) so splines can be used to align the aprons to the blocks. Cut these kerfs $1^1/4$" from the end of each apron, $1/4$" deep *(Fig. 4a)*.

CORNER BLOCKS

The aprons are held at the corners with corner blocks (I) (refer to *Fig. 9*).

CUT THE BLOCKS. Since the corner blocks are cut from the same $1^3/4$" stock as the legs (N), I made the leg blanks longer than needed and cut a corner block off the end of each leg blank (refer to the Cutting Diagram on page 39). To do this, start by cutting four leg blanks from $1^3/4$"-thick stock. Cut the blanks to a width of 3" and $31^3/4$" long.

Then, to make the corner blocks, set the saw blade at 45° and cut a bevel off one end of each leg blank *(Fig. 6)*. Now turn the blank over and cut it again to form a triangular-shaped piece so one corner has a $1/2$"-wide flat face *(Fig. 6a)*.

KERF THE BLOCKS. The corner blocks are kerfed to accept $1/8$" hardboard splines. These splines align the corner blocks to the kerfs in the aprons.

First, position the saw fence $1^1/2$" from the blade, and set the blade height to $1/4$" *(Fig. 7a)*. Then cut kerfs in both beveled sides of the corner blocks *(Fig. 7)*.

Note: The kerfs in the aprons are only $1^1/4$" from the end of the apron so the corner block is set back a little from the ends of the aprons (refer to *Fig. 8a*).

SHANK HOLE. Later, the legs are mounted to the blocks with hanger bolts. So drill a $3/8$"-dia. shank hole through the block. I used my drill press, centering the hole on the inside face *(Fig. 8)*.

ASSEMBLE APRONS. Now the aprons are assembled by gluing corner blocks in place (with hardboard splines) flush with the tops of the aprons *(Figs. 8a and 9)*.

Note: To keep the corners square, I made some special clamping blocks (see the Shop Tip below).

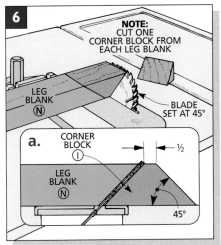

6 NOTE: CUT ONE CORNER BLOCK FROM EACH LEG BLANK

LEG BLANK (N)
BLADE SET AT 45°

a. CORNER BLOCK (I) $1/2$
LEG BLANK (N) 45°

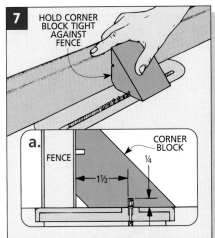

7 HOLD CORNER BLOCK TIGHT AGAINST FENCE

a. FENCE $1^1/2$ CORNER BLOCK $1/4$

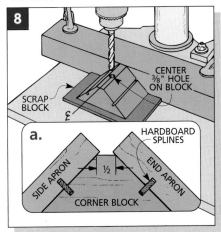

8 CENTER $3/8$" HOLE ON BLOCK
SCRAP BLOCK

a. HARDBOARD SPLINES
SIDE APRON $1/2$ END APRON
CORNER BLOCK

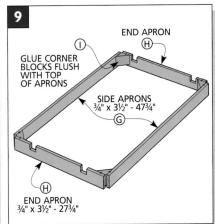

9 END APRON (H)
GLUE CORNER BLOCKS FLUSH WITH TOP OF APRONS
SIDE APRONS $3/4$" x $3^1/2$" – $47^3/4$" (G)
END APRON $3/4$" x $3^1/2$" – $27^3/4$" (H)

SHOP TIP .... *Corner Clamping Blocks*

To keep the corners of the Dining Table's apron assembly square, I made some special clamping blocks for use with C-clamps *(Fig. 2)*.

I made the clamping blocks from scrap pieces of 2x4 and cut them to shape with a band saw *(Fig. 1)*. The relief area will then direct the pressure directly over the splines *(Fig. 2a)*.

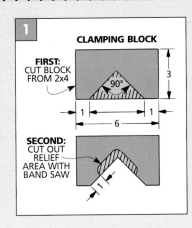

1 CLAMPING BLOCK
FIRST: CUT BLOCK FROM 2x4 90° 3
1 1 6
SECOND: CUT OUT RELIEF AREA WITH BAND SAW 1

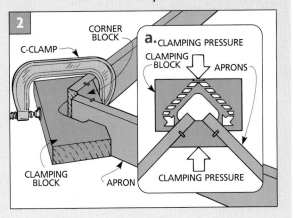

2 CORNER BLOCK
C-CLAMP
a. CLAMPING PRESSURE
CLAMPING BLOCK APRONS
CLAMPING BLOCK
APRON CLAMPING PRESSURE

The next step is to cut and shape the legs (N). First, cut them to a finished length of 27$\frac{1}{2}$".

CHAMFER THE LEGS. The inside edges of each leg (N) are then chamfered so the leg can butt up against the table aprons at a 45° angle.

Begin by setting the table saw blade to 45° and positioning the rip fence 1" from the blade (*Fig. 10b*).

With the saw set up, cut a chamfer on one edge of each piece, then turn the piece around and cut a matching chamfer on the other edge. This should leave a $\frac{1}{4}$"-wide flat on the inside face of the leg (*Fig. 10a*).

ROUND THE EDGES. After the legs are chamfered, I routed both outside edges with a $\frac{1}{2}$" roundover bit in the router table (*Fig. 10c*).

DRILL PILOT HOLES. The legs are joined to the corner blocks with $\frac{3}{8}$"-dia. hanger bolts. To do this, just drill a pilot hole 1$\frac{1}{2}$" down from the top and centered on the $\frac{1}{4}$" flat on the inside face of each leg (*Fig. 11*).

ASSEMBLY. Now, the table base can be assembled. First, screw a hanger bolt in from the outside of each leg (see the Shop Tip below). Then fit the hanger bolt through the hole in the corner block and tighten on a washer and nut (*Fig. 12*).

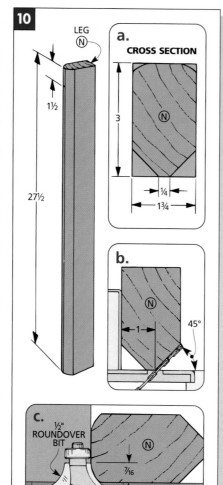

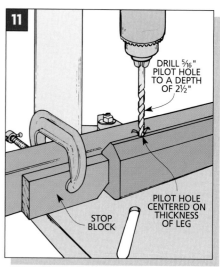

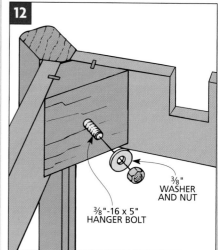

SHOP TIP .... *Hanger Bolts*

The dining table uses almost no hardware. The only metal pieces in the table are woodscrews and four hanger bolts. A hanger bolt has threads like a lag screw on one end and machine threads on the other (*Fig. 1*).

Hanger bolts come in a variety of sizes, and for the dining table I used one of the largest ($\frac{3}{8}$"-16 x 5").

You could use a lag screw to attach the leg to the corner block, but I used a hanger bolt for two reasons. First, the machine thread of the bolt allows you to easily remove the

nut, then remove the leg. That's handy if you're moving, or have to replace or repair a leg.

The other benefit is if the leg becomes loose, you can tighten the nut.

To screw in a hanger bolt I start by turning two nuts onto the bolt until the top nut is flush with the end.

After the nuts are tight, place a socket wrench over the top nut only and

tighten the hanger bolt into the leg (*Fig. 2*).

Then remove the nuts, fit the bolt through the block, and tighten a washer and nut against the block (see *Fig. 12* above).

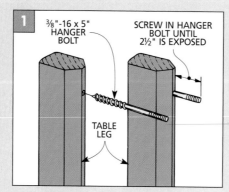

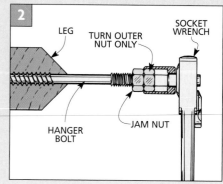

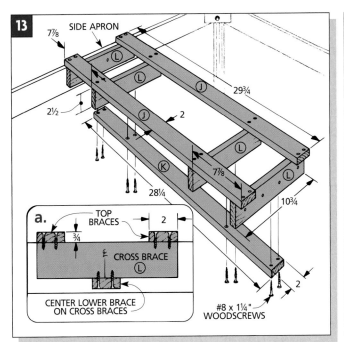

13

SIDE APRON

7⅞

2½

L

L

J

J

29¾

2

L

L

L

K

7⅞

28¼

10¾

2

#8 x 1¼"
WOODSCREWS

2

a. TOP
BRACES

¾

2

CROSS BRACE
L

CENTER LOWER BRACE
ON CROSS BRACES

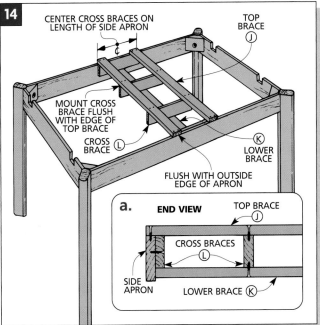

14

CENTER CROSS BRACES ON
LENGTH OF SIDE APRON

TOP
BRACE
J

MOUNT CROSS
BRACE FLUSH
WITH EDGE OF
TOP BRACE

CROSS
BRACE
L

K
LOWER
BRACE

FLUSH WITH OUTSIDE
EDGE OF APRON

a. **END VIEW**

TOP BRACE
J

CROSS BRACES
L

SIDE
APRON

LOWER BRACE
K

SUPPORT ARM CARRIAGE

With the legs attached to the aprons, I started working on the support carriage that guides the support arms.

CUT PIECES TO SIZE. All the pieces for the carriage are made from ³⁄₄" stock. First, cut four cross braces (L) 2¹⁄₂" wide by 10³⁄₄" long *(Fig. 13)*. Then cut two top braces (J) 2" wide by 29³⁄₄" long, and a lower brace (K) 2" wide by 28¹⁄₄" long.

ATTACH CROSS BRACES. When all the pieces are cut to size, screw two of the cross braces (L) to the inside faces of the side aprons *(Fig. 13)*. Center the brace on the length of the apron and make sure the top edges are flush *(Fig. 14a)*.

LOWER BRACE. With the outside cross braces attached, turn the table over and

screw the lower brace (K) to the center of the cross braces (L) *(Fig. 13a)*.

TOP BRACES. Now turn the table upright and screw the two top braces (J) to the tops of the aprons. They should be flush with the outside of the aprons and the ends of the cross braces (L) *(Fig. 14)*.

Next, slide the remaining two cross braces between the top braces and the lower brace and screw them in place.

SUPPORT ARMS

The four support arms (M) are the key to making this table work. Since I wanted the leaves to slide up to be level with the main top, I tapered the top edge of each arm so that the leaves are level with the top when extended.

CUT THE BLANKS. To make the support arms (M), cut 1³⁄₄"-thick stock 2¹⁄₄" wide by 49¹⁄₂" long *(Fig. 15)*.

CUT NOTCHES. The top of each arm is notched so the edging (D) on the table top can fit into it. Locate the 1"-deep notches 20¹⁄₂" in from the ends of the arms *(Fig. 15)*. Cut the notch the same as on the aprons, but leave the bottom flat.

TAPER SUPPORT ARMS. After cutting the notch, lay out the taper on the top edge of each arm *(Fig. 15)*. I cut it oversize on the band saw *(Fig. 16)* and then planed it smooth with a hand plane.

SOFTEN THE END. Next, file the bottom corner of each arm to a ³⁄₈" radius *(Fig. 15b)*. Then you can finish the supports by routing ¹⁄₈" roundovers on both bottom edges *(Fig. 15a)*.

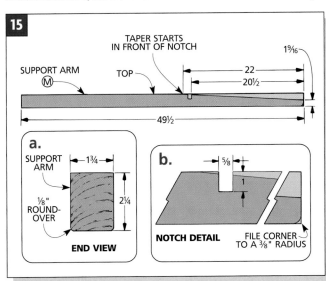

15

SUPPORT ARM
M

TOP

TAPER STARTS
IN FRONT OF NOTCH

22

20½

1⁹⁄₁₆

49½

a. SUPPORT
ARM

1¾

2¼

¹⁄₈"
ROUND-
OVER

END VIEW

b.

⅝

1

NOTCH DETAIL

FILE CORNER
TO A ³⁄₈" RADIUS

16

CUT TAPER
SLIGHTLY
OVERSIZE
AND PLANE
TO LINE

TAPER RUNS
⅞" BEYOND
NOTCH

ATTACHING THE LEAVES

Once the tapers have been cut on the support arms, screw holes are drilled on the bottom side of each arm so the arm can be fastened to the leaves.

DRILLING THE ARMS. First, locate three shank holes on the bottom side of each support arm. The first hole is $2^1/2$" from the narrow end, and then two more holes are $8^1/2$" apart *(Fig. 17)*.

With the hole locations marked, place the tapered side of the support arm face down on the drill press table. Now, at the marked locations, drill $3/8$" holes centered on the thickness of each arm for the counterbore so the screws can reach up into the leaf.

Note: To get the correct counterbore depth, set the depth stop on the drill press so the bottom of the bit stops 1" from the table *(Fig. 17a)*.

Once the counterbores are complete, drill the rest of the way through with a $3/16$" bit for the shank holes.

POSITION THE LEAVES. After the screw holes are drilled, the leaves are positioned on the support arms. Begin by putting the arms in place in the table, so that the inside of the notches in the arms are flush with the outside edge of the apron *(Fig. 18a)*.

Next place a leaf on top of the arms so the inside edge of the leaf is flush with the outside edges of the notches.

ATTACH THE LEAVES. Now, adjust the leaf so it's centered on the support arms. Using No. 8 x $1^1/2$" woodscrews, attach the leaf to the support arm at the deepest counterbores only. This allows for adjusting the arm.

With the leaf in place, slide it all the way into the table. Now, adjust the tapered end of the arm so it's centered in the apron notch *(Fig. 18b)*. With the arm centered, reach under the table and screw in the rest of the screws through the arms and into the leaves.

TOP GUIDES

Now that the leaves have been attached to the support arms, the last step on the table is to attach two guides (O) to the bottom of the table top. These guides are what keep the table top from moving around.

CUT TO SIZE. Beginning with $3/4$" stock, cut two pieces $2^1/2$" wide by $6^5/8$" long *(Fig. 21)*. With the guides cut to length and width, cut a tapered notch off

each end. The taper is cut to leave a 2"-long flat on the guide bottom *(Fig. 21)*.

Now rout $1/8$" roundovers on the bottom and end edges of both guides.

POSITION GUIDES. With the guides completed, I located their position on the bottom side of the table top. First locate the guides so they're centered on the length of the table top *(Fig. 19)*.

Then, measuring from the inside of the side top edging, mark lines $3^7/8$" in from either side *(Fig. 20)*.

Since the guides must fit between

the top braces, I tested their location before I glued them in place by sticking them on with double-sided carpet tape. Once everything fit, I marked their location and glued them in place.

Now the leaves should slide out when the top is lifted up.

That brings up one more point that may be confusing. The top is not fastened to the aprons. It's held down simply by gravity, but won't move around because of the way the guides and top edging fit over the base. ■

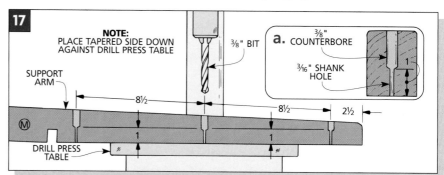

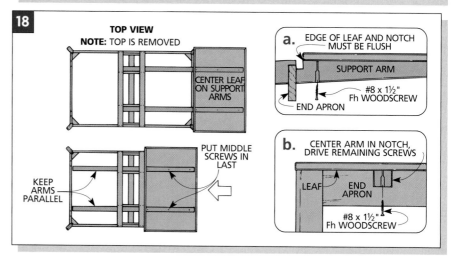

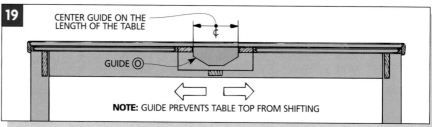

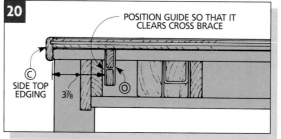

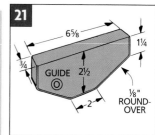

DESIGNER'S NOTEBOOK

Making a square, informal version of the Dining Table is actually very simple. By changing the top and removing the leaf extension system, you have a project that's easy to make and good for many uses.

CONSTRUCTION NOTES:

■ Making a square version of the Dining Table is actually much simpler, because there is no leaf extension system.

■ Start with the top (A), cutting the plywood to width and length (see drawing below). Both dimensions are the same as the width for the Dining Table.

■ Cut a sheet of plastic laminate slightly oversize and glue it to the top with contact cement. Then use a flush trim bit to trim the laminate flush with the plywood.

   Note: As an option, you could use plywood for the top without the laminate.

■ Now use a straight bit to rout rabbets on the edges of this top assembly (refer to *Fig. 1* on page 40). This leaves a $1/8$" x $1/8$" centered tongue to hold the edging.

■ Cut four $1^5/8$"-wide edging pieces (D) to rough length. Then add a groove on the inside face of each edging piece to accept the tongues. Again, position the groove so the edging extends slightly above the top (refer to *Fig. 2* on page 40).

■ Glue the edging to the plywood, let it dry, and trim it flush with the top.

■ Next, build four of the short (end) aprons (H), but *don't* cut notches in them this time. Use the same corner block assembly as shown on page 41.

■ The rest of the table is the same, except you don't make the leaves or any of the sliding parts (see the Materials List below). Fasten the top to the base with figure 8 fasteners (see detail 'a').

KITCHEN TABLE

MATERIALS LIST

CHANGED PARTS

A	Top (1)	$3/4$ ply - $34^1/4$ x $34^1/4$
D	End Top Edging (4)	$1/2$ x $1^5/8$ - 36 rough
H	End Aprons (4)*	$3/4$ x $3^1/2$ - $27^3/4$

* Aprons are not notched.
Note: Do not need parts B, C, E, F, G, J, K, L, M, O.

HARDWARE SUPPLIES

(4) No. 8 x $1/2$" Fh woodscrews
(4) No. 8 x 1" Fh woodscrews
(8) Figure 8 fasteners
(4) $3/8$"-16 x 5" hanger bolts
(4) $3/8$"-I.D. washers
(4) $3/8$" nuts
(1) Plastic laminate, 36" x 36" rough

PLASTIC LAMINATE (OPTIONAL)

PLYWOOD PANEL

SEE DETAIL a

3

a.

FIGURE 8 FASTENER

#8 x 1" Fh WOODSCREW

#8 x $1/2$" Fh WOODSCREW

DESKS

Whether it's in the home or in an office, a desk serves the same purpose a workbench does in the shop. As with a bench, you should choose a desk that suits the type of work to be done and the tools you use to do it. This trio of desks provides a broad selection of styles and functions. Plus, each one offers options that let you customize it to the way you work.

The contemporary computer desk fits neatly into a corner. Optional wings let you add as much work surface as you need, where you need it. And changing the look is as easy as selecting a laminate that suits you.

The classic appearance of the oak desk may date from the early 1900s, but we've included an optional keyboard tray to allow it to accommodate today's technology.

For an even more traditional piece, the roll-top desk was inspired by writing desks from colonial times. Its tapered legs, tambour door, and slide-in organizer evoke a more relaxed, elegant era.

Computer Desk

A modular design and knock-down hardware allow you to tailor the components of this computer desk to suit your needs. Choose a laminate for the top that will complement your work space's decor.

Whether they're used for work, play, or both, computers have become fixtures at home and at the office. While computers might save you work, all the components take a fair amount of desk space.

So when designing this computer desk, I wanted it to be large enough for a regular computer monitor and other desk accessories. But I didn't want to make it so big that it took over the whole room. The answer came in two parts. First, I designed the desk to fit in a corner. This allows you to make the desk deep enough for the monitor. And because it sits in a corner, it won't take up much more space than an ordinary writing desk.

MODULAR DESIGN. The second thing I did was design the desk to be modular. You can build just the basic corner unit (see photo at right), or if you need more space, you can expand the desk by adding an optional extension wing as shown above. And because the wings can be added to either end of the desk, you can configure it to your size and space requirements. A couple of variations are shown on page 56.

MODERN MATERIALS. To go along with the modern design of the computer desk, I used some modern materials as well, like plastic laminate and medium-density fiberboard (MDF) for the top. Using plastic laminate allows you to choose from hundreds of colors and patterns and build a desk that matches your decor.

And instead of traditional joinery, the

major components of the desk are assembled with knock-down hardware. This makes it easy to assemble, but also helps when taking the desk apart for moving or changing its configuration.

HARDWARE KIT. *Woodsmith Project Supplies* offers separate hardware kits for the desk and the extension wing. See page 126 for more information.

EXPLODED VIEW

OVERALL DIMENSIONS:
52³/₄W x 52³/₄D x 30H

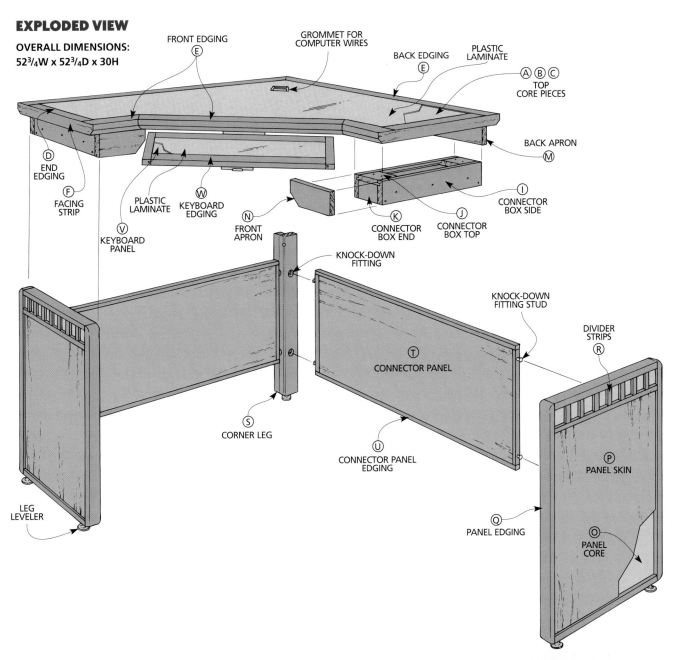

FRONT EDGING (E)

GROMMET FOR COMPUTER WIRES

BACK EDGING (E)

PLASTIC LAMINATE

(A)(B)(C) **TOP CORE PIECES**

(D) **END EDGING**

(F) **FACING STRIP**

PLASTIC LAMINATE

(W) **KEYBOARD EDGING**

(V) **KEYBOARD PANEL**

(N) **FRONT APRON**

BACK APRON (M)

(I) **CONNECTOR BOX SIDE**

(K) **CONNECTOR BOX END**

(J) **CONNECTOR BOX TOP**

KNOCK-DOWN FITTING

KNOCK-DOWN FITTING STUD

DIVIDER STRIPS (R)

(T) **CONNECTOR PANEL**

(S) **CORNER LEG**

(U) **CONNECTOR PANEL EDGING**

(P) **PANEL SKIN**

(Q) **PANEL EDGING**

(O) **PANEL CORE**

LEG LEVELER

MATERIALS LIST

(For Corner Unit shown in detail photo at left)

TOP

A	Lg. Core Piece (1)	³/₄ MDF - 19 x 47³/₄
B	Sm. Core Piece (1)	³/₄ MDF - 19 x 28³/₄
C	Crnr. Core Piece (1)	³/₄ MDF - 21¹/₄ x 21¹/₄
D	End Edging (2)	1¹/₂ x 2³/₈ - 19
E	Ft./Bk. Edging	1¹/₂ x 2¹/₂ - 14 ft. rgh.
F	Facing Strips (2)	¹/₈ x 1¹/₂ - 24
G	Corner Block (1)	2¹/₂ x 5 - 5
H	Block Filler (1)	³/₄ x 5 - 5
I	Conn. Box Sides (4)	³/₄ x 3³/₈ - 20
J	Conn. Box Tops (4)	³/₄ x 2⁵/₈ - 5
K	Conn. Box Ends (4)	³/₄ x 2⁵/₈ - 4¹/₂
L	Box Fillers (2)	³/₄ x 5 - 19
M	Back Aprons (2)	³/₄ x 3³/₈ - 47¹¹/₁₆
N	Front Aprons (2)	³/₄ x 3³/₈ - 8¹/₂

END PANELS/CORNER LEG

O	Panel Cores (2)	³/₄ MDF - 21³/₈ x 26¹/₂
P	Panel Skins (4)	¹/₄ ply - 21³/₈ x 26¹/₂
Q	Panel Edging	³/₄ x 1¹/₂ - 18 ft. rgh.
R	Divider Strips	¹/₄ x ⁵/₈ - 7 ft. rough
S	Corner Leg (1)	3 x 3 - 28

CONNECTOR PANELS

T	Panels (2)	³/₄ ply - 46³/₁₆ x 16¹/₂
U	Edging	³/₄ x ³/₄ - 22 ft. rough
V	Keyboard Panel (1)	³/₄ ply - 7¹/₂ x 24¹/₂
W	Keyboard Edging	¹³/₁₆ x 1¹/₂ - 6 ft. rgh.

Note: Also need 38 lin. ft. of ¹/₄ x ¹⁵/₁₆ hardboard spline for top and end panel assemblies.

HARDWARE SUPPLIES

(8) No. 8 x 1¹/₄" Fh woodscrews
(10) No. 8 x 2" Fh woodscrews
(2) No. 8 x 3¹/₂" Fh woodscrews
(7) ¹/₄"-20-I.D. threaded inserts
(6) ¹/₄" x 1¹/₄" hex bolts
(1) ¹/₄" x 2" hex bolt
(7) ¹/₄" washers
(8) Knock-down fittings
(1) 4" x 2" rectangular grommet
(1) Keyboard tray slide
(5) Leg levelers, 1⁵/₈"-dia. with ³/₈"-dia. shaft

CUTTING DIAGRAM

¾ x 7 - 96 (4.6 Bd. Ft.)

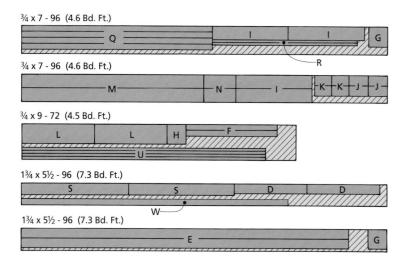

¾ x 7 - 96 (4.6 Bd. Ft.)

¾ x 9 - 72 (4.5 Bd. Ft.)

1¾ x 5½ - 96 (7.3 Bd. Ft.)

1¾ x 5½ - 96 (7.3 Bd. Ft.)

¼" PLYWOOD - 48 x 72

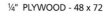
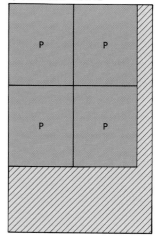

¾" PLYWOOD - 48 x 48

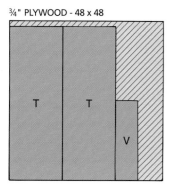

PLASTIC LAMINATE - 48 x 48

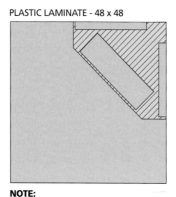

NOTE:
ALSO NEED SMALL PIECE OF
¼" HARDBOARD FOR SPLINES

¾" MDF - 48 x 96

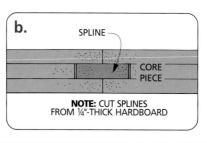

1

ALL CORE PIECES
ARE ¾"-THICK MDF

19

47¾

LARGE CORE
PIECE
Ⓐ

28¾

SMALL CORE
PIECE
Ⓑ

19

¼" x ¹⁵⁄₁₆"
HARDBOARD
SPLINE
(38" LONG)

21¼

CORNER CORE
PIECE
Ⓒ

SPLINE
(20" LONG)

a.

½

CENTER GROOVE
ON THICKNESS
OF CORE PIECE

CORE
PIECE

¼" SLOT-
CUTTING BIT

b.

SPLINE

CORE
PIECE

NOTE: CUT SPLINES
FROM ¼"-THICK HARDBOARD

DESK TOP CORE

Whether you're building the entire computer desk complete with a couple of wings or just the corner unit, it's best to start by building the desk top for the corner unit. That's because most of the other components of the desk are fastened to it in some way.

CORE PIECES. The top consists of a ³/₄"-thick MDF core topped with plastic laminate. Instead of trying to wrestle with a heavy, single sheet of MDF, I made the top out of three separate core pieces (A, B, C) *(Fig. 1)*. This also solves the problem of trying to cut the inside miters for the front of the desk.

The two rectangular pieces can be

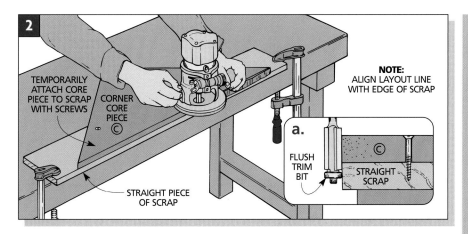

2

TEMPORARILY ATTACH CORE PIECE TO SCRAP WITH SCREWS

CORNER CORE PIECE ©

STRAIGHT PIECE OF SCRAP

NOTE: ALIGN LAYOUT LINE WITH EDGE OF SCRAP

a.

FLUSH TRIM BIT

© STRAIGHT SCRAP

cut easily on the table saw. But when it came to the triangular piece, I used a little different approach.

I started with a 21$\frac{1}{4}$"-square blank, and laid out a diagonal line between two corners. But instead of trying to find a way to cut the piece on the table saw, I used a hand-held jig saw, staying on the waste side of the line.

The jig saw leaves a rough edge, but this can be cleaned up with a router and a flush trim bit. Just screw the MDF down to a straight piece of scrap. (The screw holes are covered by laminate later.) Then let the bearing of the router bit ride on the scrap as you trim the edge *(Figs. 2 and 2a)*.

CORE ASSEMBLY. When it comes to gluing the core pieces together, there are a couple of things to consider. First, the pieces need to be kept aligned. And second, the porous edges of MDF don't make for a very strong edge-glued joint. The solution to these problems is simple. I used $\frac{1}{4}$"-thick hardboard splines inserted into grooves along the edges of the pieces.

I cut the grooves for the splines with

a router and a slot-cutting bit *(Fig. 1a)*. And since splines will also be used later to attach hardwood edging around the desk top, I cut grooves on all the edges of the core pieces.

Note: Run the router on the same (top or bottom) face of all three pieces so the grooves will align.

To glue up the three core pieces, I had to find a way to clamp the triangular piece to the two rectangular pieces. Because of the angles involved, there isn't a convenient place to apply clamping pressure. The solution I came up with is shown in the Shop Tip below.

PLASTIC LAMINATE

Once the core pieces are glued up, they can be covered with plastic laminate. I used a single, oversize piece because I didn't want any seams in the top.

The laminate is glued to the core with contact cement. After the cement has been applied to both the core and the laminate, set a row of scrap pieces on the core to keep the two surfaces apart while you position the laminate.

SHOP TIP

Laminate Bit

The offset cutter of this special carbide bit allows it to trim through the middle of a sheet of laminate. The tight radius trims all the way up to the inside corners of the desk top. The guide on the bottom lets it trim the laminate flush with the core. (For sources, see page 126.)

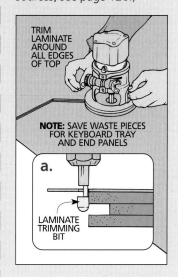

TRIM LAMINATE AROUND ALL EDGES OF TOP

NOTE: SAVE WASTE PIECES FOR KEYBOARD TRAY AND END PANELS

a.

LAMINATE TRIMMING BIT

Then, once the laminate is situated above the desk top, pull out the scraps starting on one side, pressing the laminate in place as you go.

Finally, I trimmed the edges of the laminate with a hand-held router and a special, solid-carbide bit (see the Shop Tip above).

SHOP TIP . . . . *Corner Clamping Block*

One challenge to gluing up the top is finding a way to clamp the triangular piece to the two rectangular pieces.

The answer is to build a simple clamping block to provide a parallel clamping surface (see drawing). The block is notched to fit over the back corner of the desk.

Use this block again when clamping on the front edging.

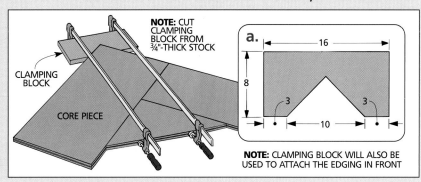

CLAMPING BLOCK

CORE PIECE

NOTE: CUT CLAMPING BLOCK FROM ¾"-THICK STOCK

a.

16

8

3   3

10

NOTE: CLAMPING BLOCK WILL ALSO BE USED TO ATTACH THE EDGING IN FRONT

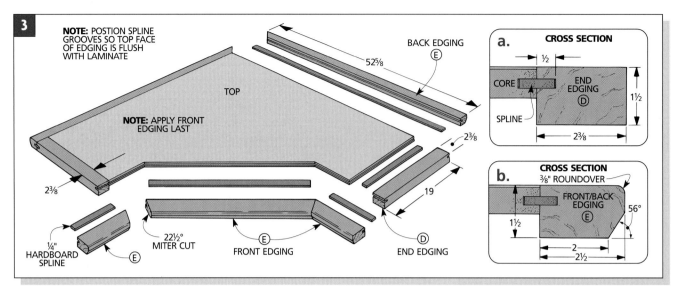

3

NOTE: POSTION SPLINE GROOVES SO TOP FACE OF EDGING IS FLUSH WITH LAMINATE

BACK EDGING
E

52⅝

TOP

NOTE: APPLY FRONT EDGING LAST

2⅜

2⅜

19

2⅜

¼" HARDBOARD SPLINE

E

22½° MITER CUT

FRONT EDGING

E

END EDGING

D

a. CROSS SECTION

½

CORE

SPLINE

END EDGING
D

1½

2⅜

b. CROSS SECTION
⅜" ROUNDOVER

FRONT/BACK EDGING
E

56°

1½

2

2½

EDGING

To hide the edges of the MDF on the top pieces, I added hardwood edging around all sides *(Fig. 3)*.

END EDGING. I started with the end edging (D). This is just a piece of 1½"-thick stock cut to align with the front and back edges of the top. Grooves are cut on the ends and one edge of each piece for splines *(Fig. 3a)*.

Note: I used the laminate-covered top as a gauge to set the depth of the bit.

Once the grooves are cut, the edging can be glued and clamped in place.

FRONT AND BACK EDGING. The front and back edging (F) are also made from 1½"-thick stock, but their profiles are different *(Fig. 3b)*. I cut the grooves for the splines first. Then I routed a ⅜" roundover on the top edge and ripped a 56° bevel on the bottom outside edge of each piece *(Fig. 4)*.

To cut the edging to length, miter

the ends of the two back pieces at the back corner *(Fig. 3)*. The front ends are cut flush with the end edging.

To fit the three front pieces, start with the center piece and miter the ends at 22½°. The finished length of the piece should equal the diagonal edge of the front of the desk.

The other two front pieces are then mitered at 22½° on only one end. The other end is square (refer to *Fig. 6)*.

GLUING ON EDGING. To help align the edging when gluing, again I used hardboard splines. And here there was another challenging clamping problem.

This time, the solution was to screw a block to the front edge *(Fig. 5)*. (The screw holes will be covered by edging later.) This block has two triangles attached to it *(Fig. 5a)*.

FACING STRIPS. To conceal the splines and the exposed end grain at the ends of the top, I glued a ⅛"-thick facing strip (F) to each end *(Fig. 6)*.

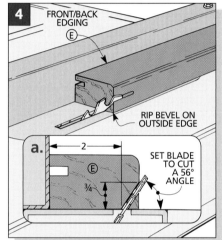

4

FRONT/BACK EDGING
E

RIP BEVEL ON OUTSIDE EDGE

a.

2

E

¾

SET BLADE TO CUT A 56° ANGLE

I carefully removed the overlapping material at the lower corners of the facing strips with a small hand saw, then touched up the surface with some light sanding *(Fig. 6a)*. Then I rounded over the edges with a router and a ⅛" roundover bit *(Fig. 6b)*.

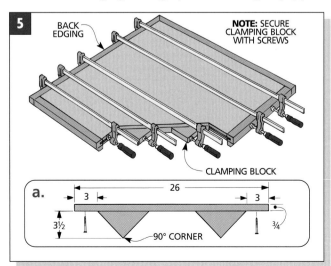

5

BACK EDGING

NOTE: SECURE CLAMPING BLOCK WITH SCREWS

CLAMPING BLOCK

a.

26

3

3

3½

¾

90° CORNER

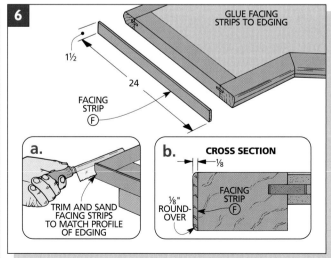

6

GLUE FACING STRIPS TO EDGING

1½

24

FACING STRIP
F

a.

TRIM AND SAND FACING STRIPS TO MATCH PROFILE OF EDGING

b. CROSS SECTION

⅛

FACING STRIP
F

⅛" ROUND-OVER

The top of the desk is supported by a corner leg at the back and two end panels on the sides. But the top isn't fastened directly to these pieces. Instead, there's a support "system" comprised of a corner block and a pair of connector boxes (refer to *Fig. 9*). Then the leg and panels are attached to these pieces with bolts and threaded inserts.

CORNER BLOCK. To attach the back corner leg to the top, I built a triangular-shaped corner block (G) *(Fig. 7)*. This $2\frac{1}{2}$"-thick block is made by laminating two pieces of wood (a $1\frac{3}{4}$"-thick piece and a $\frac{3}{4}$"-thick piece) together to form a 5" x 5" square. Then the square is cut diagonally to leave a 7"-long front edge.

Next, drill five holes through the edges and the face to allow the block to be screwed under the desk and to the leg *(Fig. 7)*. Finally, cut a notch out of the back corner of the block for the leg to fit into.

Since the top edging is thicker than the core, a block filler (H) creates a level surface for mounting the corner block *(Fig. 9)*. This filler is simply glued to the top core. Then the corner block is screwed in place *(Fig. 10b)*.

CONNECTOR BOXES. In addition to the corner block, a pair of connector boxes are mounted under the desk top *(Fig. 9)*. These are used to join the end panels with the top.

Each connector box consists of two sides (I), two tops (J), and two ends (K) *(Fig. 8)*. The tops are attached to the sides with $\frac{1}{4}$" x $\frac{1}{4}$" tongue and groove joints. But the ends are simply cut to fit between the sides and then glued and screwed in place.

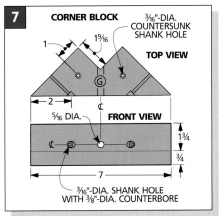

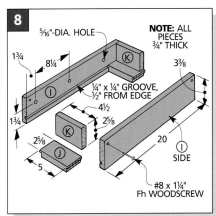

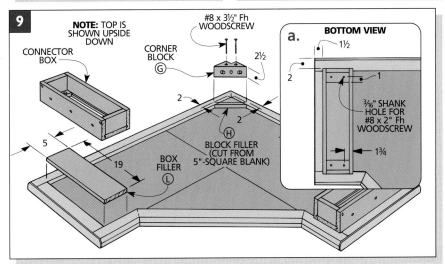

As with the corner block, I glued a couple of box fillers (L) to the underside of the top, then screwed the connector boxes to the fillers *(Figs. 9 and 9a)*.

APRONS. To conceal the connector boxes and corner block, I added $\frac{3}{4}$"-thick aprons to the front and back of the desk *(Fig. 10)*.

Note that there are $\frac{3}{8}$" roundovers on the lower front edges of the front aprons (N), but only $\frac{1}{8}$" roundovers on the back aprons (M) *(Fig. 10c)*. Also, the lower corners of the front aprons are lopped off so you don't hit your knees on them *(Fig. 10a)*.

The front aprons are simply glued to the connector boxes and the top. But with the back aprons, I also drove a couple of screws through the corner block into the aprons *(Fig. 10b)*.

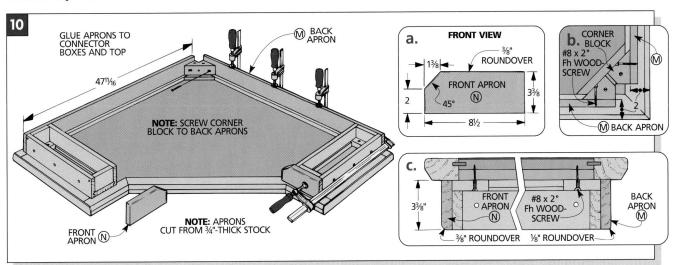

With the top of the desk completed, you can begin work on the two end panels.

BASIC PANEL. Like the top, each end panel starts off as a $^3/_4$"-thick MDF core (O) ($21^3/_8$" x $26^1/_2$") *(Fig. 11)*. But this time, I laminated both sides with $^1/_4$"-thick plywood. These plywood skins (P) are cut oversize and flush-trimmed after they're glued on with contact cement.

PLASTIC LAMINATE. The outside face of each panel has a band of plastic laminate at the top to match the desk top *(Fig. 11)*. To position this laminate, I drew a layout line $2^1/_8$" down from the top edge. Using contact cement, I glued an oversized piece of laminate flush with the line and then flush-trimmed the other three sides.

EDGING. Next, I applied some $^3/_4$"-thick edging (Q) to the panel *(Fig. 12)*. This edging is wider than the thickness of the panel to create an overhang around the outside face *(Fig. 13b)*. To attach the edging, I cut grooves in both the panels ($^1/_2$" deep) and the edging ($^1/_4$" deep) and inserted hardboard splines *(Figs. 11a and 12)*.

DIVIDER STRIPS. After the edging was glued in place, I added wood divider strips (R) to the plastic laminate on each panel to create "windows" *(Fig. 12)*.

The trick to making these strips is getting them to the correct thickness. They should end up flush with the edging. But because the horizontal strip is glued to the plywood instead of the laminate, it needs to be a little thicker than the vertical strips.

The horizontal strip is glued to the plywood, just below the laminate. The vertical strips are glued in place using a "super glue" adhesive *(Fig. 12a)*.

To soften the look of the panels, a $^3/_8$" radius is routed on each of the four corners *(Fig. 12a)*. Then $^1/_8$" roundovers are routed on the edges.

HARDWARE. Next, holes for the hardware can be drilled on the inside face of each panel *(Figs. 13a and 13b)*. First, drill two 25mm holes and install the knock-down cams. Make sure the line on the cam is in the vertical position and the "screw" is toward the inside of the desk *(Fig. 15c)*.

Then, if you'll be building the extension wings (see page 56), drill a double row of $^1/_4$"-dia. holes, $^3/_8$" deep for shelf support pins.

Finally, holes are drilled for threaded inserts and they're installed near the top of each panel. (Refer to the Shop Tip on page 58 for more about this.)

To complete the end panels, install leg levelers on the bottom of each panel *(Fig. 13a)*. (I painted my leg levelers black to match the laminate.)

CORNER LEG

The end panels alone are not enough to support the top. To support the back of the desk, I added a V-shaped corner leg (S). This leg starts out as a 3" x 3" post glued up from $1^1/_2$" stock *(Fig. 14)*.

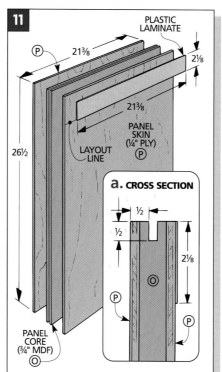

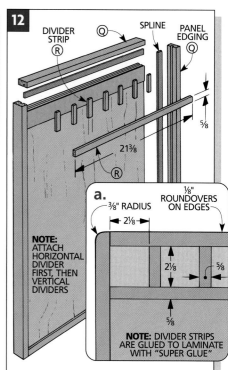

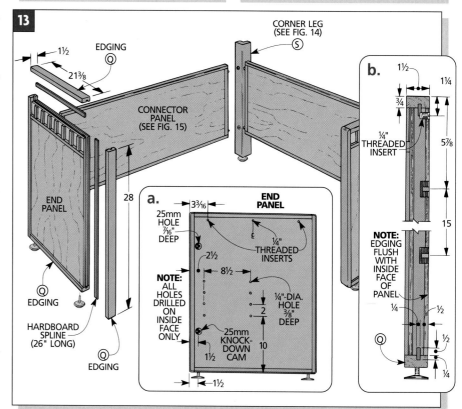

Next, I drilled the holes for the knock-down fittings. Once these are drilled, the back corner of the leg can be cut away on the table saw to create the "V" shape *(Figs. 14 and 14b)*.

To get the corner leg to match the profile of the end panels, round over the corners and edges of the leg *(Figs. 14 and 14b)*. Then to complete the leg, add a threaded insert toward the top of the leg and a leg leveler at the bottom *(Figs. 14 and 14b)*.

CONNECTOR PANELS

The connector panels serve an important purpose in the design. They join the end panels with the leg, bracing the desk to prevent it from racking.

Each connector panel starts as a $^3/_4$"-thick plywood panel (T) *(Fig. 15)*. Then the panels are framed with hardwood edging (U). I found it easiest to rip the edging a little wider than the thickness of the panels. Then after gluing it on, I routed it flush with a flush trim bit.

After trimming the edging flush, I rounded over the top and bottom edges only (not the side edging) with a $^1/_8$" roundover bit *(Fig. 15a)*. Then I added the knock-down fitting studs *(Fig. 15b)*.

FINAL ASSEMBLY

With all the parts made, the corner unit can be assembled with knock-down hardware. Start by joining the connector panels to the end panels and the corner leg *(Fig. 15c)*. Then secure the top to this base assembly by tightening $^1/_4$" bolts through the connector boxes into the threaded inserts in the end panels *(Fig. 15d)*.

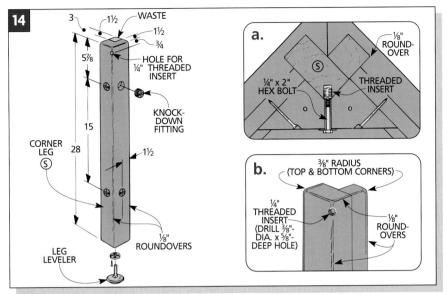

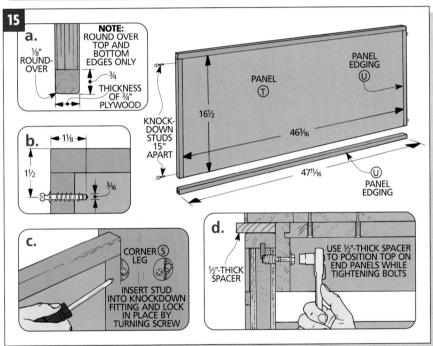

DESIGNER'S NOTEBOOK

Combining different woods with other styles of laminates offers plenty of design options for the desk.

ALTERNATE LOOKS

■ Laminate is available in dozens of colors and patterns.
■ The left photo shows a less formal appearance by using solid red oak, oak plywood, and a dark green laminate.
■ In the photo on the right, solid maple and maple plywood were used. The cherry-colored laminate (with a wood grain pattern) appears to be real wood.

The corner unit of the computer desk is designed so that it can be used alone. But for more space and storage, you might want to consider building one or two extension wings to fit on the ends of the corner unit. The wings are designed so that they can fit on either side of the corner unit (see the left photo below). Or they can be placed alongside each other to fit against a long wall (see the right photo below).

The number of extension wings you build and how you arrange them will not only affect the look, but also the usefulness of the desk. Maybe you want one wing to hold a printer or scanner, and another on the other side to use as a writing surface.

DRAWER AND SHELF. There are a couple of additional features on the extension wings that aren't on the basic corner unit. First of all, each extension wing has a convenient drawer that pulls out on full-extension slides (see photo above). When the drawer is pushed

back into the wing, the drawer front blends in nicely with the apron.

Each wing also has an optional, adjustable storage shelf underneath for storing books and extra paper. If you want more leg room under the wing, simply leave the shelf off.

CONSTRUCTION. After building the corner unit, the extension wing is a snap. That's because the construction of the two units is almost identical.

Note: The cutting diagram and materials list on the opposite page are for a single extension wing. If you plan on making two wings (or more), be sure to purchase enough material.

TOP

I started building the extension wing by working on the top. It's built the same as the corner unit top, but it's smaller and there are no odd angles *(Fig. 16)*.

CONSTRUCTION. The top consists of a rectangular MDF core (X) covered with plastic laminate. Once the laminate is trimmed flush with the core, slots are routed around all four edges of the core. Just like with the corner unit, these slots accept splines that help attach and align the end edging (Y) and front and back

edging (Z) *(Fig. 16)*. The profiles of the edging strips match the corner unit (refer to *Figs. 3a and 3b* on page 52).

After the edging strips have been glued in place, facing strips (AA) are applied to both ends to cover the splines and the exposed end grain on the front and back edging.

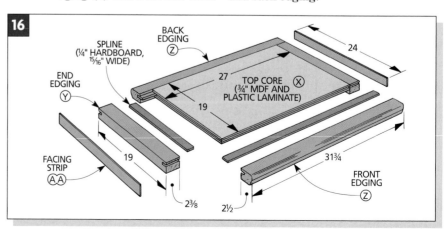

16

SPLINE (¼" HARDBOARD, ¹⁵⁄₁₆" WIDE)
BACK EDGING (Z)
END EDGING (Y)
TOP CORE (X) (¾" MDF AND PLASTIC LAMINATE)
27
24
19
19
FACING STRIP (AA)
2⅜
2½
31¾
FRONT EDGING (Z)

MATERIALS LIST

(For one Extension Wing)

WING TOP
X	Top Core (1)	¾ MDF - 19 x 27
Y	End Edging (2)	1½ x 2⅜ - 19
Z	Ft./Bk. Edging (2)	1½ x 2½ - 31¾
AA	Facing Strips (2)	⅛ x 1½ - 24
BB	Conn. Box Sides (4)	¾ x 3⅜ - 20
CC	Conn. Box Tops (4)	¾ x 2⅝ - 5
DD	Conn. Box Ends (4)	¾ x 2⅝ - 4½
EE	Box Fillers (2)	¾ x 5 - 19
FF	Back Apron (1)	¾ x 3⅜ - 30½
GG	Inside Apron (1)	¾ x 3⅜ - 7½
HH	Outside Apron (1)	¾ x 3⅜ - 6

SUPPORT PANEL/CONNECTOR PANEL
II	Support Panels (2)	¾ ply - 12 x 26½
JJ	Spacers (8)	1/16 x 2 - 12
KK	Supp. Panel Edg.	¾ x 1½ - 7 ft. rough
LL	Conn. Panel (1)	¾ ply - 16½ x 29
MM	Conn. Panel Edg.	¾ x ¾ - 8 ft. rough

DRAWER/SHELF
NN	Shelf Panel (1)	¾ ply - 10 x 30⅜
OO	Shelf Edging (1)	¾ x 1½ - 30⅜
PP	Drwr. Ft./Back (2)	½ x 2⅝ - 17½
QQ	Drwr. Sides (2)	½ x 2⅝ - 15⅝
RR	Drwr. Bottom (1)	¼ ply - 15½ x 17
SS	Drwr. False Ft. (1)	¾ x 3 5/16 - 18½

Note: Also need 8 lin. ft. of ¼ x 15/16 hardboard for splines

HARDWARE SUPPLIES
(12) No. 8 x 1¼" Fh woodscrews
(8) No. 8 x 2" Fh woodscrews
(2) No. 8 x 1" washerhead screws
(6) ¼"-20 - I.D. threaded inserts
(4) ¼" brass shelf pins
(6) ¼" x 1¼" hex bolts
(6) ¼" washers
(4) Knock-down fittings
(1) 2"-dia. grommet
(1 pair) 16" drawer slides
(2) Leg levelers, 1⅝"-dia. with ⅜"-dia. shaft

EXPLODED VIEW

OVERALL DIMENSIONS:
31¾W x 24D x 30H

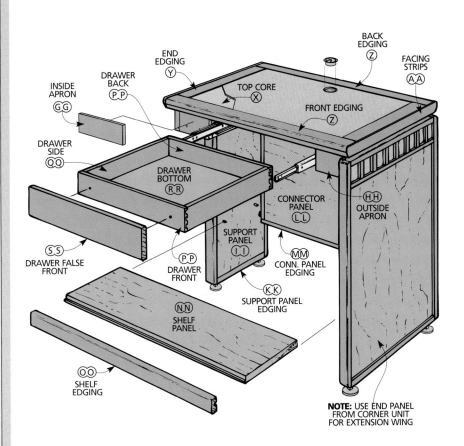

END EDGING Ⓨ
BACK EDGING Ⓩ
FACING STRIPS Ⓐ
INSIDE APRON Ⓖ
DRAWER BACK Ⓟ
TOP CORE Ⓧ
FRONT EDGING Ⓩ
DRAWER SIDE Ⓠ
DRAWER BOTTOM Ⓡ
CONNECTOR PANEL Ⓛ
OUTSIDE APRON Ⓗ
DRAWER FALSE FRONT Ⓢ
DRAWER FRONT Ⓟ
SUPPORT PANEL Ⓘ
CONN. PANEL EDGING Ⓜ
SUPPORT PANEL EDGING Ⓚ
SHELF PANEL Ⓝ
SHELF EDGING Ⓞ

NOTE: USE END PANEL FROM CORNER UNIT FOR EXTENSION WING

CUTTING DIAGRAM

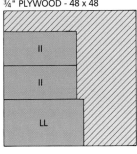

¾" PLYWOOD - 24 x 48 — NN

¾" MDF - 24 x 48 — X

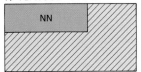

¾" PLYWOOD - 48 x 48 — II, II, LL

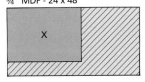

¼" PLYWOOD - 24 x 48 — RR

NOTE: CUT PARTS JJ FROM SCRAP. ALSO NEED 24" x 48" SHEET OF PLASTIC LAMINATE AND ¼" HARDBOARD FOR SPLINES.

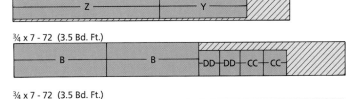

1¾ x 5½ - 60 (4.6 Bd. Ft.) — Z, Y

¾ x 7 - 72 (3.5 Bd. Ft.) — B, B, DD, DD, CC, CC

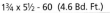

¾ x 7 - 72 (3.5 Bd. Ft.) — FF, HH, SS, GG, KK, MM, OO

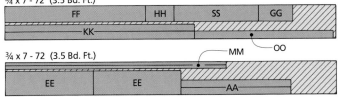

¾ x 7 - 72 (3.5 Bd. Ft.) — EE, EE, AA

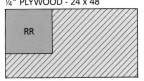

½ x 5½ - 36 (1.4 Sq. Ft.) — PP, QQ

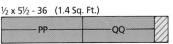

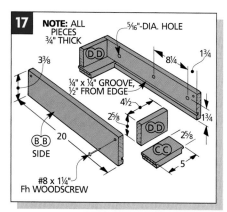

17 NOTE: ALL PIECES ¾" THICK

⁵⁄₁₆"-DIA. HOLE

DD

3⅜

8¼

1¾

¼" x ¼" GROOVE, ½" FROM EDGE

4½

1¾

2⅝

BB
SIDE

20

DD

2⅝

CC

5

#8 x 1¼" Fh WOODSCREW

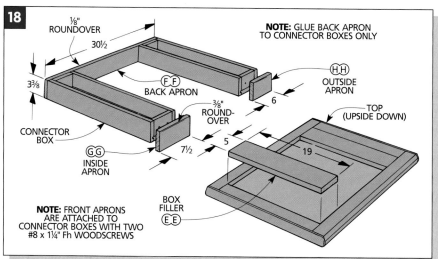

18 ⅛" ROUNDOVER

30½

NOTE: GLUE BACK APRON TO CONNECTOR BOXES ONLY

3⅜

FF
BACK APRON

HH
OUTSIDE APRON

6

TOP (UPSIDE DOWN)

CONNECTOR BOX

⅜" ROUND-OVER

GG
INSIDE APRON

7½

5

19

BOX FILLER
EE

NOTE: FRONT APRONS ARE ATTACHED TO CONNECTOR BOXES WITH TWO #8 x 1¼" Fh WOODSCREWS

SUPPORT SYSTEM

Under the top of the extension wing is a support system similar to the one on the basic corner unit. There are a pair of connector boxes and front and back aprons *(Fig. 18)*. By shifting the connector boxes to the left or right and switching the two front aprons, the extension wing can be used on either side of the corner unit *(Fig. 19)*.

CONNECTOR BOXES. The connector boxes are identical to the ones used on the corner unit. They consist of two box sides (BB) that are grooved to accept the box tops (CC) *(Fig. 17)*. Holes are drilled in the outer side (BB) before the two box ends (DD) are added.

Once the boxes are complete, the next things to make are a couple of box fillers (EE) to fit between the boxes and the top *(Fig. 18)*. When the fillers are in place, the boxes can be screwed to the underside of the top. Position them according to which side of the corner unit the wing will sit on *(Fig. 19)*.

APRONS. When it comes to making the back, inside, and outside aprons (FF, GG, HH), the profiles are identical to those used on the aprons of the corner unit, but the lengths are different *(Fig. 18)*. And, when cutting the front aprons to finished size, it's important to note they're different lengths — one is longer to span the gap between the corner unit and the extension wing.

The back apron is simply glued to the connector boxes. But be careful not to glue it to the top itself, since it will have to be shifted along with the connector boxes if you move the extension wing from one side of the desk to the other side. And since the front aprons have to be switched in order to move the wing, I attached them to the connector boxes with just screws rather than glue *(Fig. 18)*.

SUPPORT PANEL

Now that the top is assembled, you can begin working on the other elements of the extension wing.

The outer end of the extension wing will be supported by the end panel of the corner unit. (The end panel is removed from the corner unit and fastened to the end of the wing.)

To support the other end of the extension wing and to connect the wing with the corner unit, I built a support panel. This support panel is narrower

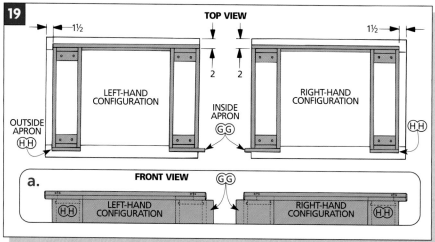

19 TOP VIEW

1½

2   2

1½

LEFT-HAND CONFIGURATION

INSIDE APRON
GG

RIGHT-HAND CONFIGURATION

OUTSIDE APRON
HH

HH

a. FRONT VIEW   GG

HH
LEFT-HAND CONFIGURATION

RIGHT-HAND CONFIGURATION
HH

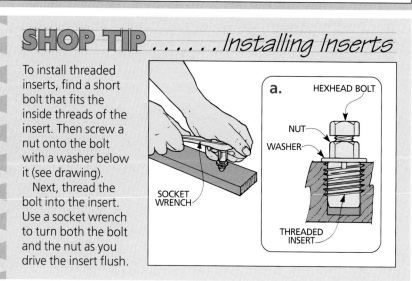

SHOP TIP .... Installing Inserts

To install threaded inserts, find a short bolt that fits the inside threads of the insert. Then screw a nut onto the bolt with a washer below it (see drawing).

Next, thread the bolt into the insert. Use a socket wrench to turn both the bolt and the nut as you drive the insert flush.

SOCKET WRENCH

a. HEXHEAD BOLT

NUT

WASHER

THREADED INSERT

than the end panel to allow for leg room underneath the desk.

PANEL CONSTRUCTION. I used two ³/₄" plywood panels (II) to make up the support panel. This creates a slight problem. The support panel needs to be the same thickness as the end panel (1½") in order to fit between the wing and corner unit. But most ³/₄" plywood is a little less than ³/₄" thick. So I cut several very thin spacers (JJ) to place between the two pieces of plywood to make their combined thickness 1½" *(Fig. 20)*. (You'll have to experiment a little. My spacers ended up a little more than ¹/₁₆" thick.)

PANEL EDGING. To conceal the edges of the plywood, I added hardwood edging (KK) all around the support panel *(Fig. 20)*. Unlike the edging on the corner unit end panels, the edging on the support panels is flush with both sides *(Fig. 20c)*. And this time, I didn't use any splines to attach the edging — it's simply glued in place.

Once the edging is attached, the corners can be rounded to a ³/₈" radius and ¹/₈" roundovers can be routed on all the edges *(Fig. 20b)*.

HARDWARE. I used threaded inserts to attach the support panel to the connector boxes *(Fig. 20a)*. But since there will be a connector box on both sides of the support panel (one for the wing and one for the corner unit), I installed inserts on each side.

Note: Since the support panel is narrower than the end panel, only two inserts are needed on each side.

I also installed knock-down fittings on both sides of the support panel to attach the connector panels (built next). Finally, I drilled holes on both sides of the panel for some shelf support pins and added a couple of leg levelers to the bottom of the panel *(Fig. 20a)*.

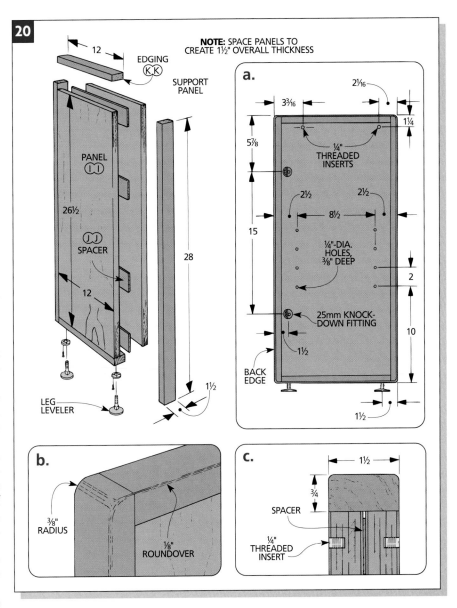

CONNECTOR PANEL

The extension wing connector panel is identical to the panels used on the corner unit except for its length (30½") *(Fig. 21)*. To build the panel, I just cut out a plywood panel (LL) and added some hardwood edging (MM) *(Figs. 21 and 21a)*. After rounding over the corners and edges of the panel, I added the studs for the knock-down fittings to both ends *(Fig. 21b)*.

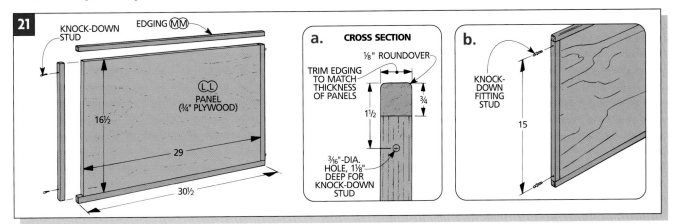

To complete the extension wing, I added a shelf and a drawer. The shelf provides a convenient area to store all those software manuals and other supplies. And the drawer makes a handy storage space for some old-fashioned "word processors" — pens and pencils.

SHELF. The shelf (NN) fits between the end panel and the support panel and sits on brass shelf pins. It's nothing more than a piece of $3/4$"-thick plywood cut to size (*Figs. 22 and 22a*).

To help strengthen the shelf and conceal the plywood edge, I added a strip of $1^1/2$"-wide hardwood edging (OO) to the front of the shelf. The edging is attached with a tongue and groove joint (*Fig. 22a*).

Note: I positioned the groove so the edging was just a hair proud of the top surface of the shelf. Then I sanded the edging flush.

DRAWER. The drawer fits in the opening between the two front aprons. I made it out of $1/2$"-thick poplar stock, with a $3/4$"-thick cherry false front to match the aprons (*Fig. 23*).

The drawer sides (QQ) are joined to the front and back (PP) with machine-cut dovetails. (I used a router and a dovetail jig to make these.) Then I cut $1/4$"-deep grooves on the inside faces of all four pieces to hold a $1/4$" plywood bottom (RR) (*Fig. 23a*).

DRAWER HARDWARE. Once the drawer is glued up, it can be mounted to the desk. To do this, I used full-extension drawer slides (*Fig. 23*). Mount the slides to the drawer first, centering them on the sides (*Fig. 23b*).

Then the drawer can be positioned in the opening and the slides attached to the connector boxes (*Fig. 22b*).

Note: The drawer should be positioned so that it hangs $1/4$" below the front edging of the top.

After the drawer is mounted and adjusted to fit, the $3/4$"-thick false front (SS) can be added. Before mounting the front to the drawer, round over the two bottom edges and the inside top edge (*Fig. 23b*). The outside top edge is left square to match the aprons on either side of the drawer. Then I stuck the

false front to the drawer with carpet tape while I attached it with a couple of screws from the inside (*Fig. 23a*).

ATTACH THE WING

To attach the wing to the desk, simply unbolt the end panel from the corner unit (you'll have to prop up the end of the desk) and fasten it to the end of the extension wing. Now attach the support panel to the desk where the end panel was. Finally, connect the wing to the support panel.

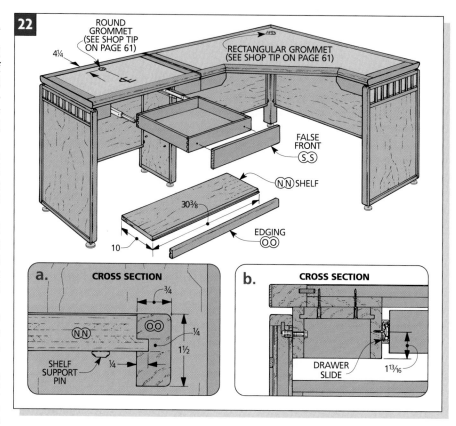

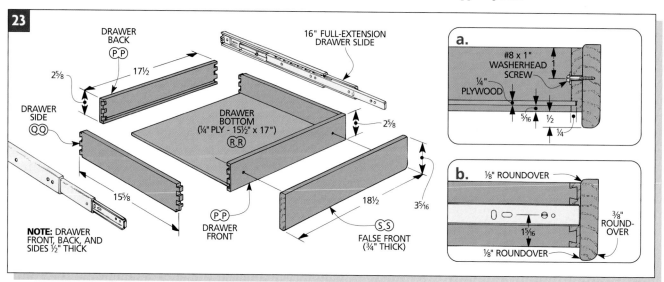

The next step is to add the keyboard tray to the corner unit. I started by cutting a keyboard panel (V) to size from ³/₄" plywood *(Fig. 24)*. Then I glued an oversized piece of laminate to the panel and flush-trimmed the edges.

EDGING. To complete the tray, I cut ¹/₄" x ¹/₄" tongues for edging (W) on all four edges *(Figs. 24 and 24a)*.

The keyboard edging is made from 1³/₄"-thick stock that has been resawn and planed to match the thickness of the laminated panel (in my case, ¹³/₁₆"). After cutting the pieces to size, the grooves and stub tenons can be cut.

Once the edging is glued to the panel, a ³/₈" radius can be rounded off each corner, as well as ¹/₈" roundovers on all the edges *(Figs. 24 and 24a)*.

HARDWARE. Now the panel can be mounted to the desk with some special hardware *(Fig. 25)*. This hardware allows the keyboard to slide out of the way under the desk top when it's not being used. (For hardware sources, see page 126.) Simply follow the instructions that come with the hardware.

GROMMET. The other piece of "computer" hardware to install is a plastic grommet for the wires to run through (see the Shop Tip below).

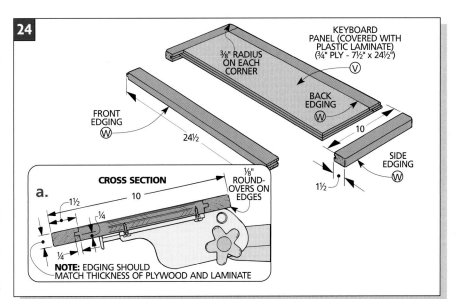

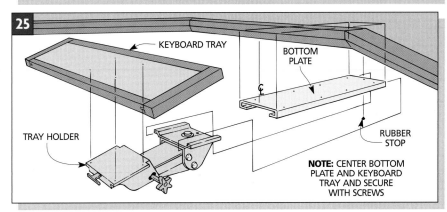

24

KEYBOARD PANEL (COVERED WITH PLASTIC LAMINATE) (³/₄" PLY - 7½" x 24½")
ⓥ

³/₈" RADIUS ON EACH CORNER

BACK EDGING
ⓦ

FRONT EDGING
ⓦ

24½

10

SIDE EDGING
ⓦ

1½

a. CROSS SECTION

1½

10

1/₄

1/₄

⅛" ROUND-OVERS ON EDGES

NOTE: EDGING SHOULD MATCH THICKNESS OF PLYWOOD AND LAMINATE

25

KEYBOARD TRAY

BOTTOM PLATE

TRAY HOLDER

RUBBER STOP

NOTE: CENTER BOTTOM PLATE AND KEYBOARD TRAY AND SECURE WITH SCREWS

SHOP TIP . . . . *Installing Grommets*

One thing to consider when building a computer desk is what to do with all the wires. Grommets let you feed the wires through the desk top.

The easiest grommet to install is a round one. I used this on the extension wings (refer to *Fig. 22* on page 60). All you need to install them is a hole saw.

On the corner unit, I used a rectangular grommet to accomodate additional wires.

To lay out the grommet, first tape over the area so you can see your layout lines. Then lay out the location using a combination square *(Fig. 1)*. Now to create the opening, drill a hole in each corner and cut out the waste with a jig saw. To prevent chipout, I used a special reverse-cut jig saw blade *(Fig. 2)*.

Finally, install the grommet and punch out tabs in the cover to create the openings *(Fig. 3)*.

For sources of grommets and reverse-cut blades, see page 126.

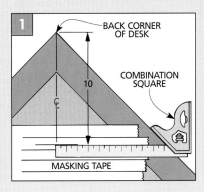

1

BACK CORNER OF DESK

COMBINATION SQUARE

10

MASKING TAPE

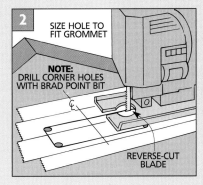

2

SIZE HOLE TO FIT GROMMET

NOTE: DRILL CORNER HOLES WITH BRAD POINT BIT

REVERSE-CUT BLADE

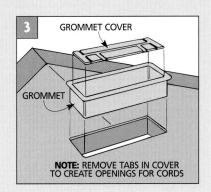

3

GROMMET COVER

GROMMET

NOTE: REMOVE TABS IN COVER TO CREATE OPENINGS FOR CORDS

Oak Desk

The symmetry of this desk simplifies construction — the pedestals are identical and so are the drawers.
An optional file drawer, vanity panel, and keyboard tray let you customize it to fit your style of work.

One of the things that makes a desk like this so appealing is its symmetry. The pedestals are identical, the side panels are identical, even the drawers are the same. For a woodworker, this means once you're set up to make a cut, the actual work is fairly easy and quick.

But it's not construction techniques that inspired me to make this desk. It's the classic design. Although this desk is typical of desks made in the early 1900s, some of the joinery techniques and materials I used are new.

JOINERY AND WOOD. For example, I used stub tenon and groove joinery to make the side and back frames. It looks like the frame and panel joinery of a hundred years ago. And the oak veneer plywood for the panels wasn't around that long ago either. But in combination with the solid oak base and frames, it has the traditional look, with greater dimensional stability.

OPTIONS. One of the things you're as likely to need today as a century ago is a file drawer. You can build this desk with one file drawer or as many as four.

Another option is a vanity panel. It encloses the knee space between the pedestals on the back of the desk. Adding the panel makes the desk seem more formal. Leaving the panel off makes the desk appear less bulky and more open (see the inset photo).

And to let this traditional desk accommodate today's technology, you can also add a hide-away tray for your computer keyboard. See the Designer's Notebook on pages 72-73 for more about adding this option.

FINISH. To give the desk an aged appearance, I applied a stain and two top coats of an oil/urethane finish.

HARDWARE KIT. *Woodsmith Project Supplies* offers the hardware needed to build the Oak Desk. See page 126 for more information and other sources.

EXPLODED VIEW

OVERALL DIMENSIONS:
61W x 30D x 30⅛H

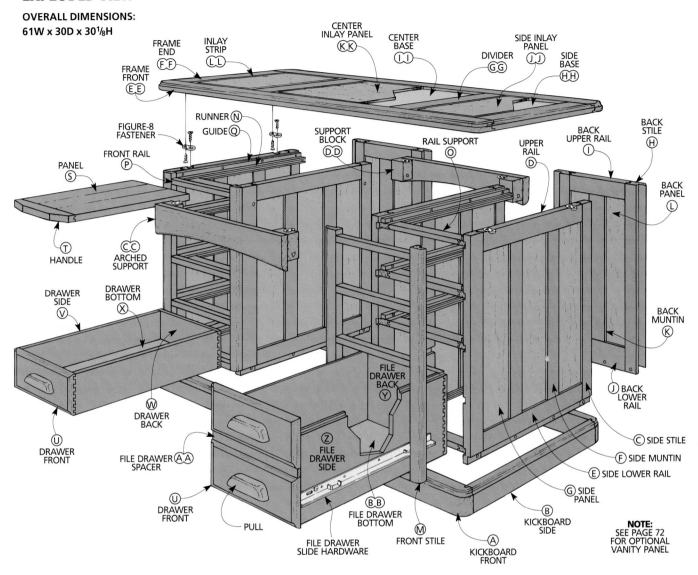

MATERIALS LIST

BASE

A	Kickboard Fr./Bk. (4)	1 x 3 - 17⅝
B	Kickboard Sides (4)	¾ x 3 - 27¼

SIDES

C	Stiles (8)	¾ x 2 - 27⅛
D	Upper Rails (4)	¾ x 2½ - 23½
E	Lower Rails (4)	¾ x 3½ - 23½
F	Muntins (8)	¾ x 2½ - 21⅝
G	Panels (12)	¼ ply - 6½ x 21⅝

BACKS

H	Stiles (4)	¾ x 2½ - 27⅛
I	Upper Rails (2)	¾ x 2½ - 12⅛
J	Lower Rails (2)	¾ x 3½ - 12⅛
K	Muntins (2)	¾ x 2½ - 21⅝
L	Panels (4)	¼ ply - 5¹/₁₆ x 21⅝

FRONTS/DRAWER GUIDES

M	Front Stiles (4)	¾ x 1¼ - 26⅛
N	Runners (18)	¾ x 1⅛ - 26⅜
O	Rail Supports (9)	¾ x 1¼ - 13⅝
P	Front Rails (9)	¾ x ¾ - 14⅛
Q	Guides (16)	⁹/₁₆ x ¾ - 26⅜
R	Stops (6)	¾ x ¾ - 2

WRITING SLIDES

S	Panels (2)	¾ x 14 - 26¼
T	Handles (2)	¾ x 2 -14

DRAWERS

U	Fronts (8)	¾ x 5¼ - 14
V	Sides (12)	½ x 5¼ - 23⅝
W	Backs (6)	½ x 5¼ - 14
X	Bottoms (6)	¼ ply - 13½ x 23½
Y	File Drwr. Fr./Bk. (2)	½ x 9¾ - 13
Z	File Drwr. Sides (2)	½ x 9¾ - 25⅝
AA	File Drwr. Spacer (1)	⅜ x ⅞ - 14
BB	File Drwr. Btm. (1)	¼ ply - 12½ x 25½
CC	Arched Supports *	¾ x 4 - 25¾
DD	Support Blocks (4)	1½ x 2 - 3

TOP

EE	Frame Fr./Bk. (2)	1 x 2½ - 61
FF	Frame Ends (2)	1 x 2½ - 26
GG	Dividers (2)	1 x 2½ - 26
HH	Side Base (2)	¾ ptbd. - 26 x 14⅝
II	Center Base (1)	¾ ptbd. - 26 x 24¾
JJ	Side Inlay Panel (2)	¼ ply - 24¾ x 13⅜
KK	Center Inlay Pnl. (1)	¼ ply - 24¾ x 23½
LL	Inlay Strips (12)	⅛ x ¼ - cut to fit

* Refer to note in text on page 70.

HARDWARE SUPPLIES

(110) No. 6 x 1" Fh woodscrews
(8) Wooden drawer pulls
     (or make from scrap)
(28 ft.) ½" nylon self-adhesive glide strip
(1 set) File drawer slide hardware (optional)
(4) ¼" x 3½" carriage bolts, nuts, washers
(8) Figure-8 fasteners

CUTTING DIAGRAM

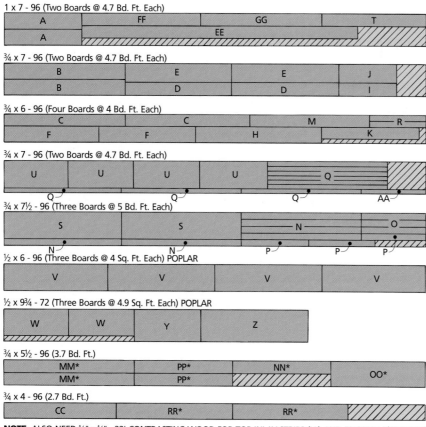

1 x 7 - 96 (Two Boards @ 4.7 Bd. Ft. Each)

| A | FF | GG | T |

| A | EE |

¾ x 7 - 96 (Two Boards @ 4.7 Bd. Ft. Each)

| B | E | E | J |
| B | D | D | I |

¾ x 6 - 96 (Four Boards @ 4 Bd. Ft. Each)

| C | C | M | R |
| F | F | H | K |

¾ x 7 - 96 (Two Boards @ 4.7 Bd. Ft. Each)

| U | U | U | U | Q |
| Q | Q | Q | AA |

¾ x 7½ - 96 (Three Boards @ 5 Bd. Ft. Each)

| S | S | N | O |
| N | N | P | P | P |

½ x 6 - 96 (Three Boards @ 4 Sq. Ft. Each) POPLAR

| V | V | V | V |

½ x 9¾ - 72 (Three Boards @ 4.9 Sq. Ft. Each) POPLAR

| W | W | Y | Z |

¾ x 5½ - 96 (3.7 Bd. Ft.)

| MM* | PP* | NN* | OO* |
| MM* | PP* |

¾ x 4 - 96 (2.7 Bd. Ft.)

| CC | RR* | RR* |

NOTE: ALSO NEED ⅛" x ¼" - 22' CONTRASTING WOOD FOR TOP INLAY STRIPS (LL) AND ENOUGH 1½" STOCK FOR SUPPORT BLOCKS (DD). PARTS WITH ASTERISK (*) ARE FOR OPTIONAL VANITY PANEL. SEE PAGE 72.

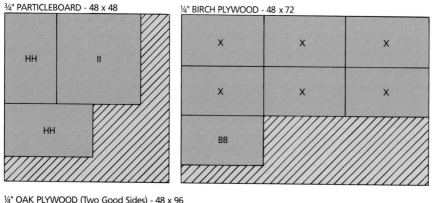

¾" PARTICLEBOARD - 48 x 48

| HH | II |
| HH |

¼" BIRCH PLYWOOD - 48 x 72

| X | X | X |
| X | X | X |
| BB |

¼" OAK PLYWOOD (Two Good Sides) - 48 x 96

G	G
G	G
G	G
G	G	JJ	KK	JJ
G	G
G	G
G	QQ*	L	QQ*
G	QQ*	L
		L
		L

I began work on the desk by making the bases for the pedestals. Each base is made up of four pieces: 1"-thick kickboard fronts/backs (A) and ¾"-thick kickboard sides (B) *(Fig. 1)*.

DADOES. The base pieces are joined with tongue and dado joints *(Fig. 1a)*. The dadoes are actually saw kerfs cut across the inside face of the kickboard fronts and backs (A). To do this, adjust the rip fence on the table saw so the distance from the *outside* of the blade to the fence equals the thickness of the side pieces (¾"). Now set the blade to cut ⅛" deep, and cut the dadoes using the fence as a stop.

CUT TONGUES. After the kerfs are cut in the front/back pieces (A), cut matching tongues on the ends of all the side pieces (B) *(Fig. 1a)*. Once the tongues are cut, the bases can be glued together *(Fig. 1)*.

ROUND CORNERS. A typical feature on a desk like this is large rounded corners. To round the corners, start by drawing a 1" radius arc on the corners *(Fig. 1a)*. Then rough cut the corners on the band saw and sand them smooth.

ROUT OGEE. The last step on the bases is to rout ogees on the top edges *(Fig. 1b)*. To do this, mount a ¼" Roman ogee bit in the router table. Then rout the ogees on the top, outside edges of all four sides.

PEDESTAL SIDES & BACKS

Once the pedestal bases are complete, the next step is to make the frame and panel units for the pedestal sides and backs. This is a systematic process — each of the panel units is made the same way, in a series of repetitive steps.

CUT TO LENGTH. Begin the process by cutting four pieces of ¾" stock for the back upper (I) and lower rails (J) to length *(Fig. 2)*. Then cut the eight pieces for the side upper (D) and lower rails (E) to length.

The twelve stiles (H, C) for all the frames are the same length (27⅛") *(Fig. 2)*. Each of the frames is divided by one or two vertical muntins (K, F). And all of these muntins are also the same length (21⅝") *(Fig. 2)*.

RIP TO WIDTH. With all the pedestal frame pieces cut to finished length, the next step is to rip the pieces to width. All the upper rails, muntins, and back panel stiles are ripped to the same width ($2\frac{1}{2}$") *(Fig. 2)*. The side panel stiles are ripped a little narrower (2"). And the lower rails are ripped $3\frac{1}{2}$" wide.

STUB TENONS AND GROOVES. After all the frame pieces have been cut to finished size, they can be joined together with stub tenon and groove joints.

To begin the joinery, first cut $\frac{1}{4}$"-deep grooves on the inside edges of all of the stiles and rails, and on both edges of the muntins *(Figs. 2a, 2b, and 2c)*.

Center the groove on the thickness of the workpiece, and cut the groove the same width as the thickness of the plywood to be used for the panels ($\frac{1}{4}$" plywood is usually less than $\frac{1}{4}$" thick).

All the stub tenons are cut the same way and at the same time. I used the table saw with the rip fence positioned $\frac{1}{4}$" from the outside of the blade. To determine the height of the blade, I used a test piece the same thickness as the actual workpieces. Sneak up on the height, cutting on both sides of the test piece until the tenon fits the groove.

Once the tenon on the test piece fits, stub tenons can be cut on the muntins *(Fig. 2b)* and the rails *(Fig. 2c)*.

PLYWOOD PANELS. After the stub tenons and grooves have been cut on the frame pieces, the next step is to cut the $\frac{1}{4}$" plywood panels (L, G) that fit inside the frames. The panels are all cut the same length as the muntins. To determine their width, I dry-assembled a side frame and back frame and cut the panels to fit between the bottoms of the grooves in each opening *(Fig. 2)*.

ASSEMBLY. With the plywood panels cut to size, the frame and panel units can be assembled. Make sure the four side units are identical in size, and that the two back units are identical as well.

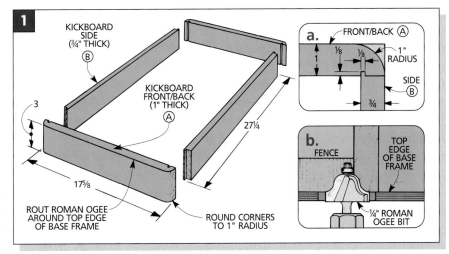

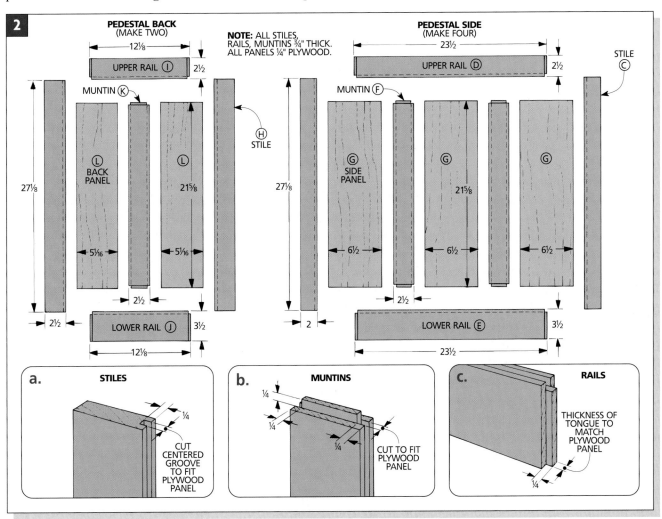

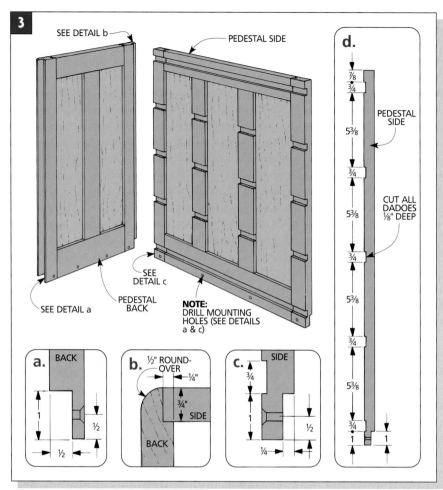

3

SEE DETAIL b

PEDESTAL SIDE

d.

PEDESTAL SIDE

CUT ALL DADOES 1/8" DEEP

⅞

¾

5⅜

¾

5⅜

¾

5⅜

¾

5⅜

¾

5⅜

¾

1 ← 1 →

SEE DETAIL c

SEE DETAIL a

PEDESTAL BACK

NOTE: DRILL MOUNTING HOLES (SEE DETAILS a & c)

a. BACK

1

½

½

b. ½" ROUND-OVER

¼"

¾"

SIDE

BACK

c. SIDE

¾

1

½

¼

4

SET ALL RUNNERS BACK ¼" FROM FRONT EDGE

¼

DRAWER RUNNER (N)

CUT 26⅜" LONG

a. PEDESTAL SIDE

1⅛

¾ ¼

¼

DRAWER RUNNER

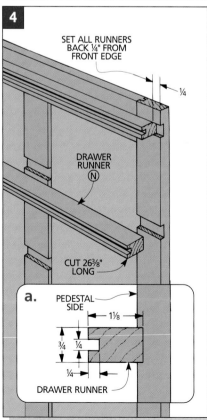

5

DRAWER GUIDE (Q)

SET END FLUSH WITH RUNNER

CUT SAME LENGTH AS RUNNER

a. 9/16

¾

DRAWER GUIDE

#6 x 1" WOOD-SCREW

RUNNER

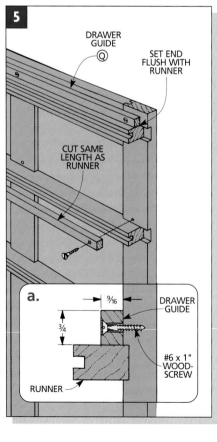

RABBETS. Before the base and panel units can be assembled to form the pedestals, joints are cut on each unit so they fit together and onto the base.

The side and back units fit inside the pedestal base by means of rabbets on their bottom edges *(Figs. 3a and 3c)*.

To cut the rabbet on the lower outside edge of each unit, I used a dado blade. (Note that the rabbet on the side unit is shallower than on the back unit.)

Then drill countersunk shank holes through the rabbets *(Figs. 3a and 3c)*. These are for the screws that will hold the units to the base.

Next, cut rabbets on the inside faces of the back units' stiles to join the back units to the side units *(Fig. 3b)*.

ROUNDOVERS. To complete the work on the back units, round over the outside edges of the back stiles *(Fig. 3b)*.

DADOES. Next, dadoes can be cut on the inside of the sides for the drawer runners. To cut these, first set up a ¾"-wide dado blade to cut ⅛" deep. Then lay out the dadoes on one of the side units *(Fig. 3d)*.

Now cut a dado on each side unit before moving the rip fence to cut the next set of dadoes. This way, each set of dadoes will align.

RUNNERS. Next I made the 18 drawer runners (N) to fit into the dadoes. Why 18 runners? I built the desk with six standard drawers requiring two runners each, plus two more for the file drawer, and four for the writing slides.

The runners are made from ¾" stock *(Fig. 4a)*. They are ⅝" shorter than the width of the side units. This way, they won't interfere with the back units when assembling the pedestals.

Before gluing the runners into the dadoes, cut a ¼"-deep groove in each runner for attaching rail supports (refer to *Fig. 7*). Center this groove on the thickness of the runner *(Fig. 4a)*.

Now the runners can be glued into the dadoes. Set the runners back ¼" from the front edge to leave room for front stiles added later *(Fig. 4)*.

DRAWER GUIDES. There's one more step before assembling the pedestals — installing drawer guides (Q) *(Fig. 5)*. These help the drawers track straight.

When the guides have been cut to finished size, screw them to the side units *(Fig. 5a)*.

Note: Don't glue the guides in place. That way they can be removed and custom fit later (if necessary).

PEDESTAL ASSEMBLY

Once the runners and guides are in place, the pedestals can be assembled.

SIDES AND BACK. First, screw two side units to a base from the inside *(Fig. 6a)*. Then, to install the back, spread glue along the rabbets in the stiles. Next, slip the bottom rabbet over the top of the base, and clamp the back between the sides. Now drive screws into the base.

FRONT STILES. To cover the front edges of each pedestal, cut four front stiles (M) to a width of $1\frac{1}{4}$" from $\frac{3}{4}$" stock *(Fig. 6)*. Then cut them to length to match the height of the sides.

Next, cut a rabbet on the back side of each stile and rout a $\frac{1}{2}$" roundover on the front edge *(Fig. 6b)*. Now glue the front stiles to the side units *(Fig. 6)*.

RAIL SUPPORTS. The desk drawers are separated by supports that stretch between the front stiles. Each support consists of two pieces: a rail support that fits between the runners, and a front rail *(Figs. 7 and 8)*.

Note: If you plan to build the file drawer (see page 69), you need only make nine supports.

Cut the rail supports (O) to length to fit between the grooves in the runners. Next, cut a centered tenon on each end of the supports to fit the grooves in the runners, and glue the supports in place.

FRONT RAILS. Now cut front rails (P) to length so they fit between the front stiles. Then glue the rails to the front of the supports *(Fig. 8)*.

DRAWERS

Each drawer is designed to fit in its opening with a $\frac{1}{16}$" gap all around. So, measure the openings and cut the $\frac{3}{4}$"-thick fronts (U) and backs (W) $\frac{1}{8}$" less than these dimensions. Next cut the $\frac{1}{2}$"-thick sides (V) $23\frac{5}{8}$" long.

FRONT OGEE. Now, rout ogees on the faces of the drawer fronts. I set the fence on the router table to decrease the width of the cut to $\frac{3}{8}$" *(Fig. 9a)*.

DRAWER JOINTS. I used half-blind dovetail joints cut with a router, $\frac{1}{2}$" dovetail bit, and a dovetail jig to join the drawer sides to the fronts and backs.

DRAWER BOTTOMS. Now, cut a groove for the plywood drawer bottom (X) *(Fig. 9b)*. Then, after cutting a bottom to fit, glue each drawer together.

PULLS. Finally, screw pulls to the front of each drawer (see page 68).

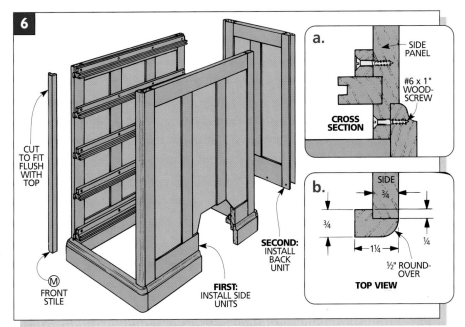

6

CUT TO FIT FLUSH WITH TOP

(M) FRONT STILE

FIRST: INSTALL SIDE UNITS

SECOND: INSTALL BACK UNIT

a.
SIDE PANEL
#6 x 1" WOOD-SCREW
CROSS SECTION

b.
SIDE
$\frac{3}{4}$
$\frac{3}{4}$
$\frac{1}{4}$
$1\frac{1}{4}$
$\frac{1}{2}$" ROUND-OVER
TOP VIEW

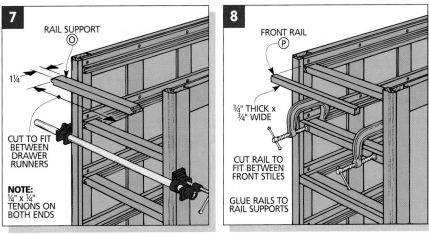

7

RAIL SUPPORT (O)

$1\frac{1}{4}$

CUT TO FIT BETWEEN DRAWER RUNNERS

NOTE: $\frac{1}{4}$" x $\frac{1}{4}$" TENONS ON BOTH ENDS

8

FRONT RAIL (P)

$\frac{3}{4}$" THICK x $\frac{3}{4}$" WIDE

CUT RAIL TO FIT BETWEEN FRONT STILES

GLUE RAILS TO RAIL SUPPORTS

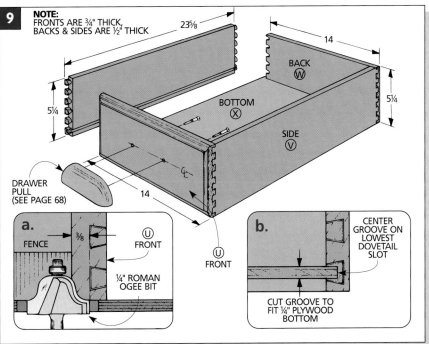

9

NOTE: FRONTS ARE $\frac{3}{4}$" THICK, BACKS & SIDES ARE $\frac{1}{2}$" THICK

$23\frac{5}{8}$

14

BACK (W)

BOTTOM (X)

SIDE (V)

$5\frac{1}{4}$

$5\frac{1}{4}$

14

DRAWER PULL (SEE PAGE 68)

(U) FRONT

a.
FENCE
$\frac{3}{8}$
(U) FRONT
$\frac{1}{4}$" ROMAN OGEE BIT

b.
CENTER GROOVE ON LOWEST DOVETAIL SLOT
CUT GROOVE TO FIT $\frac{1}{4}$" PLYWOOD BOTTOM

There's a good reason for making your own drawer pulls on a project such as the oak desk. If you use stock left over from making the drawer fronts, the pulls will match the drawers.

The drawer pulls I made for the desk started out as pieces of drawer stock that are cut to length and width, then routed to shape.

To make the routing operations safer, I built a simple jig to hold the blank while routing on the router table (see drawing at right). This also helps to produce pulls that are identical in shape and size.

The neat thing about this jig is that it's double-ended to serve two purposes. One end holds the blank for routing a cove for a finger slot. Then the workpiece is screwed to the other end of the jig for trimming the corners flush and rounding over the edges.

The jig is simply a pair of 3/4"-thick pieces of scrap cut to the desired length of the pulls

(6 1/4" was what I wanted for the oak desk). The pieces are then glued together with an equal amount of overhang at each end (see drawing). The width of the overhang matches the desired width of your pulls (for the oak desk, I made this overhang 1 3/8").

Next, drill two screw holes through the overhang so the workpiece can be secured while routing the edge (see

drawing). But don't worry about putting holes in your blanks. These holes serve another purpose later — they're used as mounting holes to fasten the pull to the drawer.

In order to keep the blank in place while routing the cove for the finger slot, screw a pair of 3/4"-thick cleats to the sides of the jig (*Step 1* below).

I cut and sanded a smooth radius on the front corners of the jig to serve as a pattern for the bearing on a flush trim router bit (*Step 5*).

Once the jig is built, it's simply a matter of following a series of steps to making the pulls (see below).

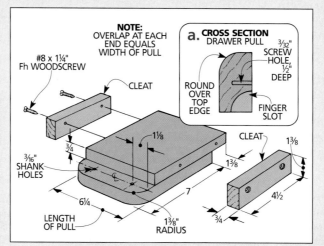

1 First, cut the blanks to length and width. Then, to rout a cove for a finger slot, slide one blank into the jig. It should fit snugly between the cleats.

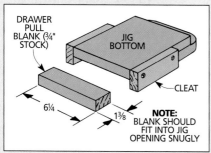

2 Clamp two stops to the router table an equal distance from the center of the bit. This determines the travel of the workpiece, and the slot length.

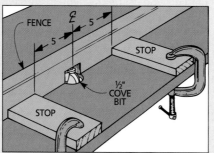

3 Now set the bit to cut full-depth, and position the fence flush with the edge of the bearing. Make several light passes from right to left to rout slot.

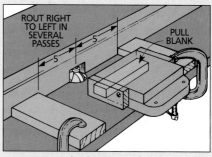

4 Use the other end of the jig to shape the front of the pull. First, screw the blank to the jig. Then cut off the "ears," leaving 1/16" to trim.

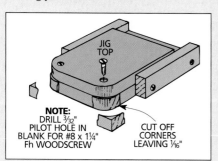

5 Now, with a flush trim bit in the router, trim the corners and front edge flush with the jig. Do this on all the pulls before going to Step 6.

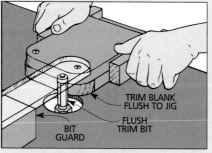

6 With a 1/2" roundover bit in the router table, raise the bit to full depth. Make several light passes to round over the front and ends of the pull.

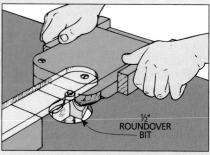

FILE DRAWER

From the front, the optional file drawer looks like two regular drawers. To achieve this, it's built differently.

FALSE FRONT. The first difference is that the file drawer has a false front. It's made of two regular drawer fronts (U) plus a spacer (AA) *(Fig. 11)*.

NARROWER DRAWER. The file drawer is also narrower than the other drawers for two reasons. First, the file drawer holds hanging file folders that hang on the top edge of the drawer without any hardware *(Fig. 10a)*. Also, the narrower drawer allows clearance for the full-extension slides it rides on.

MAKING THE DRAWER. First, build a dovetailed box to fit the large drawer opening *(Fig. 10)*. I used $1/2$" poplar for the front, back, and sides (Y, Z), and $1/4$" plywood for the bottom (BB).

Note: Before assembling the box, cut $1/4$"-deep rabbets on the top edges of the drawer sides for the hanging file folders *(Fig. 10a)*.

Next, cut a $3/8$"-thick spacer (AA) $7/8$" wide and glue this between two drawer fronts (U) *(Fig. 11)*. Then attach the false front to the drawer, and install the drawer in the pedestal with the extension slides. (See page 126 for sources of full-extension slides.)

FITTING DRAWERS

Once the file drawer is installed, you'll probably need to work on the "fit" of the other drawers. Don't expect them to fit properly the first time. In order for the drawers to slide easily — and also look good — they have to fit side to side, top to bottom, and front to back *(Fig. 12)*.

SIDE TO SIDE. First, check the gap between each drawer side and the guide (Q). You want just enough gap on each side to allow the drawer to move in and out without binding *(Fig. 13)*.

If there's no gap, or if the gap is too narrow, the guides need to be removed and planed to fit. If you do plane the guides, plane each guide an equal amount. Then screw them back into the pedestal and test the fit again.

TOP TO BOTTOM. Now check the distance above each drawer front when the drawer is in the closed position. It will probably be about $1/8$". To create a uniform $1/16$" gap above and below the drawer front, I stuck self-adhesive nylon glide strips to the top of the runners *(Fig. 12)*. The strips do two things: they even out the gap, and they make the drawers slide easily.

FRONT TO BACK. When the drawer is closed, the drawer front should stick out $3/8$" from the face frame *(Fig. 13)*. This means you can see the entire molded edge of the drawer front, but the dovetails aren't visible. To prevent the drawer from sliding in further, I glued a small stop block (R) onto the runner behind the drawer *(Fig. 14)*.

To make it easier to position the drawer while securing the stop block, see the Shop Tip at right.

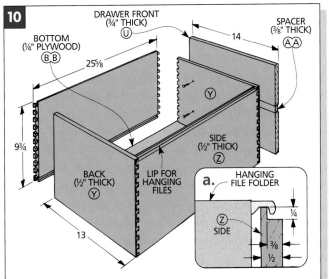

10
BOTTOM ($1/4$" PLYWOOD) (BB)
DRAWER FRONT ($3/4$" THICK) (U)
25⅝
14
SPACER ($3/8$" THICK) (AA)
Y
9¾
SIDE ($1/2$" THICK) (Z)
BACK ($1/2$" THICK) (Y)
LIP FOR HANGING FILES
13

a. HANGING FILE FOLDER
Z SIDE
$1/4$
$3/8$
$1/2$

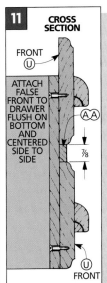

11 **CROSS SECTION**
FRONT (U)
ATTACH FALSE FRONT TO DRAWER FLUSH ON BOTTOM AND CENTERED SIDE TO SIDE
(AA)
$7/8$
(U) FRONT

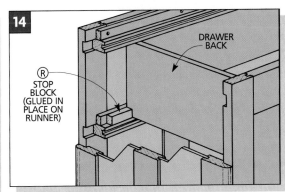

SHOP TIP
Drawer Gauge

To help position the drawers from front to back in the pedestals, I made a simple gauge. The gauge is a piece of $3/4$"-thick scrap cut to an "L" shape. The "foot" of the gauge extends $3/8$" beyond the "body."

To use the gauge, hold the foot against the face frame. When properly positioned, the drawer front should touch the body of the gauge.

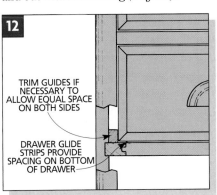

12
TRIM GUIDES IF NECESSARY TO ALLOW EQUAL SPACE ON BOTH SIDES
DRAWER GLIDE STRIPS PROVIDE SPACING ON BOTTOM OF DRAWER

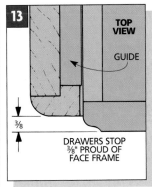

13
TOP VIEW
GUIDE
$3/8$
DRAWERS STOP $3/8$" PROUD OF FACE FRAME

14
DRAWER BACK
(R)
STOP BLOCK (GLUED IN PLACE ON RUNNER)

One of the traditional features of a desk like this is a writing surface or slide that pulls out from the top of each pedestal.

SLIDES. To build the slides, first glue up stock for two panels (S). Then, trim them to rough length (26^1/$_4$") and ^{1}/$_8$" narrower than the opening in the pedestal *(Fig. 15)*. Now, cut a tongue along the front edge *(Fig. 16)*.

HANDLES. Next cut a pair of handle (T) blanks to finished length and width *(Fig. 15a)*. Then cut a groove along the inside edge of each handle to accept the tongue on the panel *(Fig. 16)*.

To rout a stopped finger slot on the bottom side of each handle *(Figs. 15a and 16)*, I used a ^{1}/$_2$" core box bit and stop blocks clamped to the router table.

Then, taper the front corners of each handle, and glue the handles onto the panels *(Fig. 15)*.

POSITIONING THE SLIDES. Each slide gets cut to length so that when it's slid into the pedestal, the handle extends ^{3}/$_4$" past the front stiles *(Fig. 17)*.

ARCHED SUPPORTS

Finally, the pedestals can be joined. This is done by a pair of arched supports between the pedestals.

Note: If you add the optional vanity panel (refer to page 72) or the computer keyboard tray (page 74), you need only one support. If you add both options, you don't need the arched supports.

CUTTING THE ARCH. Begin making the arched support(s) (CC) by first cutting ^{3}/$_4$" stock to finished width and length *(Fig. 18)*. To lay out the curve of the arch, first mark the high point of the curve (1" up from the bottom edge) centered across the back of the workpiece. Then drive a finishing nail into each of the bottom corners, about ^{1}/$_8$" above the bottom edge.

Next, spring a flexible wood strip (like a yard stick) between the two nails until it reaches the high point of the curve. Now, draw this curve on the workpiece and cut it to shape.

Finally, round over the bottom edge with a ^{1}/$_2$" roundover bit *(Fig. 18a)*.

SUPPORT BLOCKS. To attach the support to the pedestals, blocks (DD) are added to the back face *(Fig. 18)*. Bore a ^{5}/$_{16}$"-diameter hole through each block to accept a carriage bolt *(Fig. 18a)*. Then glue the blocks to the support.

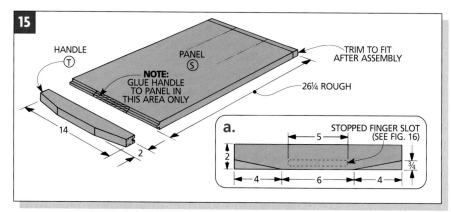

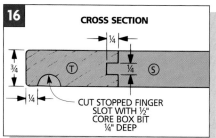
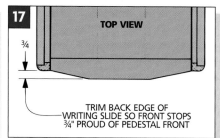

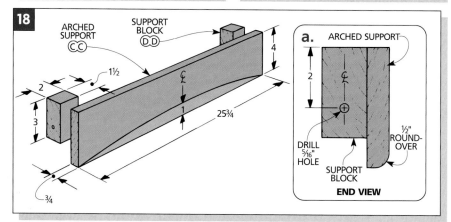

JOINING THE PEDESTALS

Before installing the arched supports, you'll need to drill holes in each pedestal for the carriage bolts *(Fig. 19)*. To locate these holes, I clamped the pedestals together with the supports in place.

Note: Each support should be flush with the top edge of the pedestal. But the supports should be set in 1" from the outside of the pedestal *(Fig. 19a)*.

Now, using the holes in the blocks as a guide, drill ^{5}/$_{16}$"-diameter holes into the pedestals *(Fig. 19a)*. Once they're drilled, fasten the pedestals and supports together with carriage bolts.

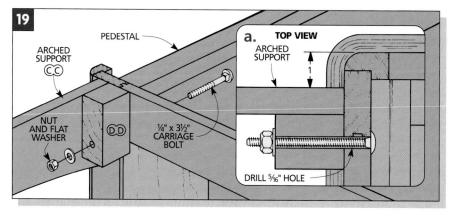

The final part to build is the top. It's a large frame and panel assembly — but here, the panels and frame are 1" thick.

FRAME. Start by cutting the frame pieces (EE, FF, GG) to size *(Fig. 20)*.

Next, cut ½"-wide by ½"-deep offset grooves on the inside edges of the front and back pieces (EE) and the ends (FF) (see Details in *Fig. 20*). Then cut grooves on both edges of the dividers (GG). Finally, cut matching tenons on the ends of the end pieces (FF) and dividers (GG).

BASE PANELS. Though the top panels are made of a piece of ¼" plywood on top of a piece of ¾" particleboard, I found it easiest to build the frame around the particleboard, and then add the plywood (and inlay strips) after the frame was assembled (refer to *Fig. 23*). So cut the particleboard base panels (HH, II) to size *(Fig. 21)*.

TONGUES. Next, cut tongues on all four edges of the panels to fit the grooves in the frame *(Fig. 20)*.

Note: The tongues are offset on the thickness of the particleboard so the ¼" plywood will be flush with the top of the frame (refer to *Fig. 23a*).

After the frame pieces and panels are cut, you can assemble the top *(Fig. 21)*.

ROUT OGEE. Once the glue has dried, the next step is to rout Roman ogee profiles on the outside edges of the top *(Figs. 22 and 22a)*.

INLAY STRIPS AND PANELS. Now the recess on top of the base panels can be filled with ¼" oak plywood surrounded by inlay strips (I used walnut) *(Fig. 23)*.

Start by cutting the inlay strips (LL) ¼" thick and ⅛" wide. Then miter them to fit snugly into the recesses.

After gluing the inlay strips in place, the inlay panels (JJ, KK) can be cut to fit inside the strips. (Note the grain direction.) Fitting these is tricky. Start by cutting the panels slightly oversize. Then sneak up on the exact fit. Finally, glue the panels in place.

ATTACH TOP. Once the top was finished, I attached it to the pedestals with figure-8 desktop fasteners *(Fig. 24)*.

To mount the fasteners, first drill shallow mortises on top of the pedestals and support blocks (DD) with a Forstner bit *(Fig. 24)*. Then screw in the fasteners. Now, center the top on the pedestals, and screw through the fasteners into the top *(Fig. 24a)*. ■

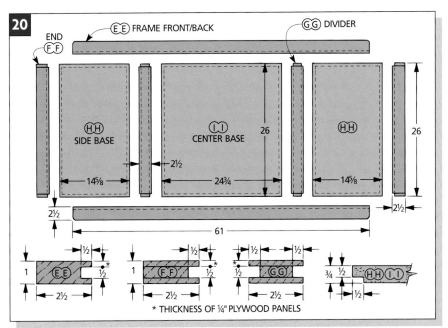

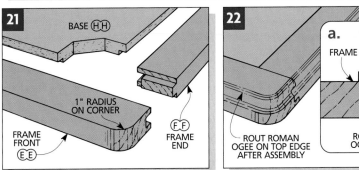

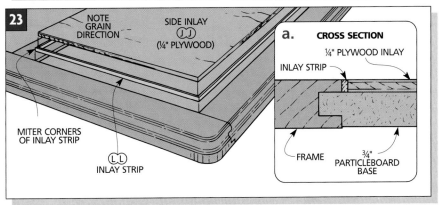

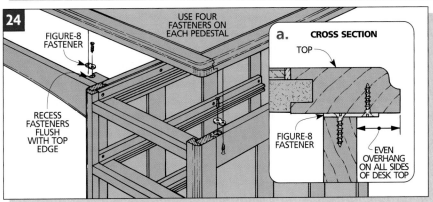

DESIGNER'S NOTEBOOK

Adding a vanity panel between the pedestals lends the desk a more formal appearance. It's built with the same techniques as the side and back panels, and features coped joints along the bottom.

CONSTRUCTION NOTES:

■ The vanity panel is made the same way as the pedestal sides, with a couple differences *(Fig. 1)*. First, the lower rail (OO) is wider. And there's a notch on each stile (MM) so the panel fits between the pedestal bases *(Fig. 1a)*.

■ A kickboard on each side of the panel

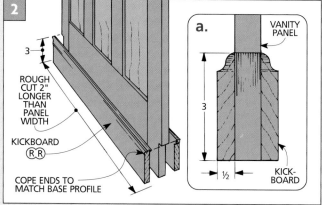

VANITY PANEL

MATERIALS LIST

NEW PARTS

MM	Stiles (2)	³/₄ x 2¹/₂ - 29¹/₈
NN	Upper Rail (1)	³/₄ x 2¹/₂ - 21¹/₄
OO	Lower Rail (1)	³/₄ x 5¹/₂ - 21¹/₄
PP	Muntins (2)	³/₄ x 2¹/₂ - 21⁵/₈
QQ	Panels (3)	¹/₄ ply - 5³/₄ x 21⁵/₈
RR	Kickboards (2)	¹/₂ x 3 - 26 rough

Note: Only need one of part CC, two of part DD.

HARDWARE SUPPLIES
(4) ¹/₄" x 1¹/₄" machine screws
(4) ¹/₄" washers
(4) ¹/₄" threaded inserts

hides the notches *(Fig. 2)*. For each kickboard (RR), cut a blank 2" longer than the width of the vanity panel *(Fig. 2)*.

■ Next, cope the ends to match the shape of the pedestal kickboards. (For more on doing this, see the Technique article on the opposite page.)

■ Now glue the kickboards to the panel.

■ Machine screws and threaded inserts

secure the panel between the pedestals *(Fig. 3a)*. To do this, first drill holes through the pedestals for the screws.

■ Next, temporarily clamp the vanity panel in place between the pedestals. Then, using the holes as a guide, mark the locations for the threaded inserts on the edges of the vanity panel.

■ Finally, install the threaded inserts.

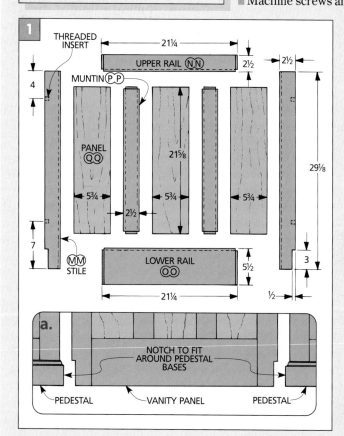

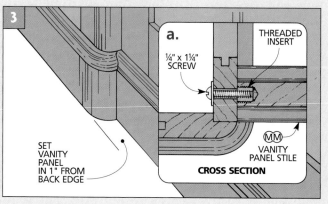

When I was installing the vanity panel on the Oak Desk, I ran into a situation often faced by house trim carpenters — joining two pieces of molding at an inside corner. The trick is getting a good, tight fit.

MITERS. Can't you just join the two pieces with a traditional miter joint? On the desk I couldn't do this, since the kickboard on the pedestal runs through and beyond the vanity panel. But even on a typical inside corner on house baseboards there are a couple of problems with using a miter joint.

First, it's almost impossible to find a way to nail or clamp the two mitered pieces together tightly. And, even if you could fit them together tight, there's a good chance a gap would develop in the corner as the wood shrinks and swells.

Since you'll be looking down into the corner, any gap will be noticeable. And, if the corner isn't perfectly square (and often it's not), it's difficult to get a tight-fitting miter joint.

COPED JOINT. The solution is a coped joint. On this type of joint, one of the mating pieces is cut (coped) to match the shape of the other. The other piece has a square end that's hidden behind the coped piece. Yet from above, it still appears that both are mitered.

The first step in making a coped corner is to attach the square-end piece. This is "Molding B" in *Fig. 1* at right. (On the Oak Desk, this piece, the kickboard, is a little different than on a typical inside corner since it doesn't have a square end. It runs around the pedestal. But the procedure is the same.)

CUT MITER. From this point, all of the remaining work is done only on

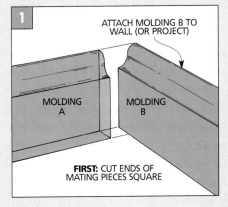

FIRST: CUT ENDS OF MATING PIECES SQUARE

ATTACH MOLDING B TO WALL (OR PROJECT)

MOLDING A

MOLDING B

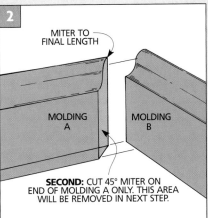

MITER TO FINAL LENGTH

MOLDING A

MOLDING B

SECOND: CUT 45° MITER ON END OF MOLDING A ONLY. THIS AREA WILL BE REMOVED IN NEXT STEP.

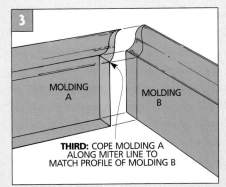

MOLDING A

MOLDING B

THIRD: COPE MOLDING A ALONG MITER LINE TO MATCH PROFILE OF MOLDING B

"Molding A" (on the desk, that's the vanity panel kickboard).

First, mark the location of the miters near the ends of the molding (*Step 1* below). To make these marks on the vanity panel kickboard, I placed the two pedestals on my workbench overhanging the bench top.

Next, use a table saw or miter saw to make a 45° miter cut just barely outside the pencil marks (*Step 1 and Fig. 2*).

BEGIN COPING. Now the actual coping can begin. For this I use a coping saw with a new blade. (You could also use a band saw with a narrow blade, or a scroll saw.) The first section to cope is the straight section (*Step 2*).

Note: It's easiest to see the cutting line if the workpiece is positioned so there's a shadow cast on the miter.

When you reach the molded edge, stop. Then make a second cut, this time cutting in from the end of the piece to remove the waste block (*Step 2*).

Next is the tricky part — coping the molded edge. The secret is to take your time and cut with smooth, even strokes (*Step 3*). But don't expect a perfect fit with the mating piece when you're done coping. You'll still have some touch-up before you get a tight fit.

SAND TO FIT. After both ends of the molding have been coped, test-fit the coped molding (A) with its mating piece (B) (*Fig. 3*).

To get a perfect fit — a tight joint line — you will probably need to sand carefully across the coped ends (*Step 4*). Wrapping a dowel with sandpaper will help you sand curved surfaces evenly. Just keep working at it a little bit at a time until the pieces fit together.

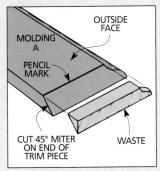

OUTSIDE FACE

MOLDING A

PENCIL MARK

CUT 45° MITER ON END OF TRIM PIECE

WASTE

1 First mark the distance between the pedestal bases on the ends of the kickboard. Now miter the ends.

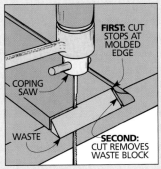

FIRST: CUT STOPS AT MOLDED EDGE

COPING SAW

WASTE

SECOND: CUT REMOVES WASTE BLOCK

2 Make a straight cut along the miter line and stop at molded edge. Remove waste piece before coping the tip.

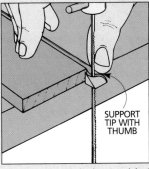

SUPPORT TIP WITH THUMB

3 Cut around the molded edge, supporting the tip with your finger to keep a point on tip of the molding.

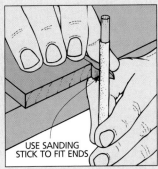

USE SANDING STICK TO FIT ENDS

4 Now test the fit. Use a sanding stick to smooth the end so it fits tightly along the entire joint.

DESIGNER'S NOTEBOOK

The look of yesterday can work with the technology of today by adding this slide-out keyboard tray. When it's not in use, the keyboard is cleverly hidden out of sight behind a drop-down wrist rest.

CONSTRUCTION NOTES:

■ Begin by cutting the tray sides (SS) to rough length (24") and finished width (3") *(Fig. 1)*. (The sides are cut to finished length after the tray is assembled.)

■ Next, lay out and cut the taper on each tray side *(Fig. 1)*.

■ Now cut a $2^1/2$"-long notch off the front end of each tray side to leave a $3/4$"-thick "arm." This provides room for the tray front (added later) to fold down and serve as a wrist rest (refer to *Fig. 4a*).

■ The tray front (TT) is the same width as the tray sides (3"). To determine its length, measure between the pedestals and subtract $1/8$".

■ Once the tray front is cut to length, rout a $1/2$" roundover along its bottom edge *(Fig. 1)*. Also ease the top edges with sandpaper. (Don't ease the bottom inside edge or the ends.)

■ The tray back (UU) fits between the tray sides (SS) *(Fig. 1)*. The length of the back equals the length of the tray front (TT) less the combined thickness of the tray sides (SS). (Mine was $24^1/8$" long.) The tray back is narrower ($2^3/8$") than the tray sides to allow room for the keyboard cable to pass over it.

■ The tray front (TT) hides the keyboard when the tray is pushed back into the desk. But when the tray is pulled out so the keyboard can be used, the front drops down to serve as a wrist rest.

To accomplish this, the tray front is hinged to the front rail (VV) (refer to *Fig. 4a*). The front rail also joins the tray sides. Unlike the tray sides and back, the front rail lies flat *(Fig. 3)*.

■ Cut the front rail to a width of 2". Its length is the same as the tray back

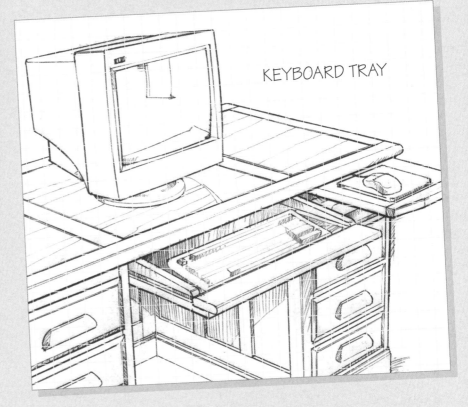

KEYBOARD TRAY

MATERIALS LIST

NEW PARTS

SS	Tray Sides (2)	$3/4$ x 3 - 24
TT	Tray Front (1)	$3/4$ x 3 - $25^5/8$
UU	Tray Back (1)	$3/4$ x $2^3/8$ - $24^1/8$
VV	Front Rail (1)	$3/4$ x 2 - $24^5/8$
WW	Tray Bottom (1)	$1/4$ ply - $24^5/8$ x 16
XX	Tray Guides (2)	$7/16$ x $3/4$ - 24

Note: If building vanity panel, do not need parts CC, DD. If not building vanity panel, need only one part CC, two part DD.

HARDWARE SUPPLIES

(2) No. 8 x $1^1/4$" Fh woodscrews
(6) No. 8 x 1" Fh woodscrews
(1) Piano hinge, 24" long w/ screws

1 SIDE VIEW

LEFT TRAY SIDE (SS)

17⅞
12
2½
1¼
3
1
24
¾

TRAY BACK (UU)
24⅛
2⅜
17½
1½"-WIDE PIANO HINGE
3
TRAY BOTTOM (WW)
#8 x 1¼" Fh WOODSCREW
TRAY SIDE (SS)
CUT ALL DRAWER PARTS EXCEPT BOTTOM FROM ¾" STOCK
FRONT RAIL (VV)
24⅝
½" ROUND-OVER
25⅝
TRAY FRONT (TT)

(UU), plus $\frac{1}{2}$" to allow for a $\frac{1}{4}$"-long tongue on each end *(Fig. 3)*.

■ Before the tray pieces can be assembled, a number of cuts need to be made. First, a $\frac{3}{4}$"-wide groove in each side (SS) allows the tray to slide on guides fastened to the desk (refer to *Fig. 6*). These grooves are positioned $1\frac{1}{2}$" from the top edge of the tray side *(Fig. 2)*.

■ A groove is also cut along the inside face of each tray side and the tray back (UU) to hold the tray bottom *(Fig. 2)*.

■ While you're set up, cut a matching groove along the inside edge of the front rail (VV) *(Fig. 3a)*.

■ Next, a tongue needs to be cut on each end of the front rail to fit the grooves in the tray sides. Position this tongue so that the bottom of the rail is flush with the bottoms of the tray sides *(Fig. 4a)*.

■ Now cut a rabbet on the top face of the front rail to accept the piano hinge that the tray front will pivot on *(Fig. 4a)*.

■ Finally, I routed a 1"-wide finger pull centered on the bottom face of the front rail *(Fig. 3a)*. To do this, I made two passes with a $\frac{1}{2}$" core box bit, then cleaned up between the cuts with a $\frac{1}{2}$" straight bit.

■ Once all these cuts are made, the tray back (UU) can be screwed between the sides (SS). The back should be positioned $17\frac{1}{2}$" from the front of the drawer side *(Fig. 1)*.

■ Once the back and sides are fastened together, you can measure for the tray bottom (WW). To do this, clamp the front rail in place so it's flush with the front edge of the tray *(Fig. 4)*. Add $\frac{1}{2}$" to each of the tray's inside measurements to account for the $\frac{1}{4}$"-deep grooves. Cut a tray bottom to these dimensions from $\frac{1}{4}$" plywood.

■ Glue the bottom into the assembly, then glue the front rail in place.

■ Now fasten one leaf of the piano hinge to the front rail (VV) and the other to the tray front (TT) *(Fig. 4)*. The tray front should be flush with the bottom and outside edges of the tray sides *(Figs. 4a and 5)*.

■ Before applying a finish to the tray, lightly sand any sharp edges.

■ Now cut two tray guides (XX) to fit the grooves in the tray sides.

Note: The width of the guides should be just a hair less than the width of the grooves so the tray slides in and out smoothly *(Fig. 6a)*.

■ To complete the keyboard tray, fasten a tray guide to each pedestal of the desk *(Fig. 6)*. To determine their positions,

measure from the top edge of the tray side to the top of the groove and add $\frac{1}{16}$".

■ To properly position the tray with its front edge set back 1" from the front edge of the desk *(Fig. 5)*, trim the back ends of the tray sides.

■ Finally, screw figure-8 fasteners to each pedestal *(Figs. 5 and 6)*.

Note: When mounting the top, make sure the pedestals are parallel so the drawer doesn't bind.

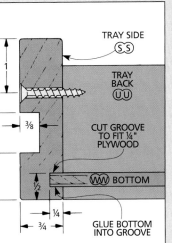

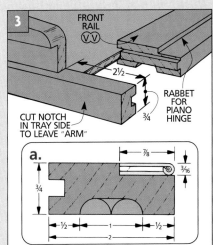

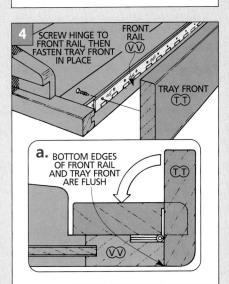

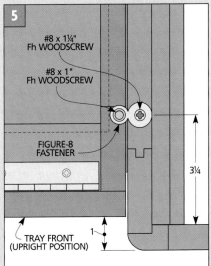

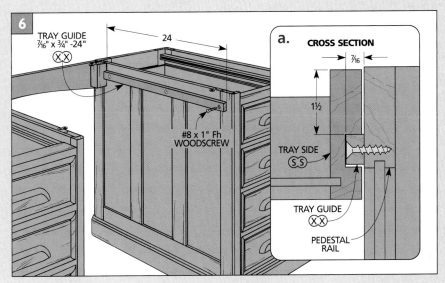

Roll-Top Desk

A tambour door is only part of what makes this desk special. It also features a simple, classic shape and straightforward construction. An optional organizer behind the roll-top holds papers and accessories.

Sometimes the more obvious things tend to hide the important ones. Take this Roll-Top Desk. Your eye is automatically drawn to the tambour door. There's just something about a door that opens and closes without swinging on a hinge. But you really need to look past the door to see more of what makes this desk special.

For one thing, take a look at the decorative cutout on the bottom edge of the front rail. It provides visual appeal, but at the same time, it allows for clearance when sitting down to write at the desk. And the tapered legs give the desk a light, graceful appearance.

Another example is the desk hardware. Or more accurately, the lack of it. The only hardware you need for this whole desk is a few woodscrews.

JOINERY. In keeping with the desk's traditional appearance, mortise and tenon joints are used to secure the rails between the legs. This joint is cut easily using a drill press and table saw.

TAMBOUR. When it comes to the tambour door, it's easier to make than you might think. Step-by-step instructions for doing so start on page 87.

ORGANIZER. An optional desk organizer with pigeonholes and drawers is hidden behind the door. Normally, an organizer is built as an integral part of the desk. But this one is designed as a separate, removable assembly. (Details for building the organizer are in the Designer's Notebook on page 84.)

WOOD. I built this project from solid cherry. It looks great, and has a fairly tight grain. This provides a nice writing surface, although using a desk blotter will help protect the wood from being damaged by pen and pencil points.

FINISH. When finishing a project that has a lot of crevices like the tambour on the Roll-Top Desk, I like to use an oil finish. On this project I used a tung oil and urethane combination.

EXPLODED VIEW

OVERALL DIMENSIONS:
43W x 24D x 40¾H

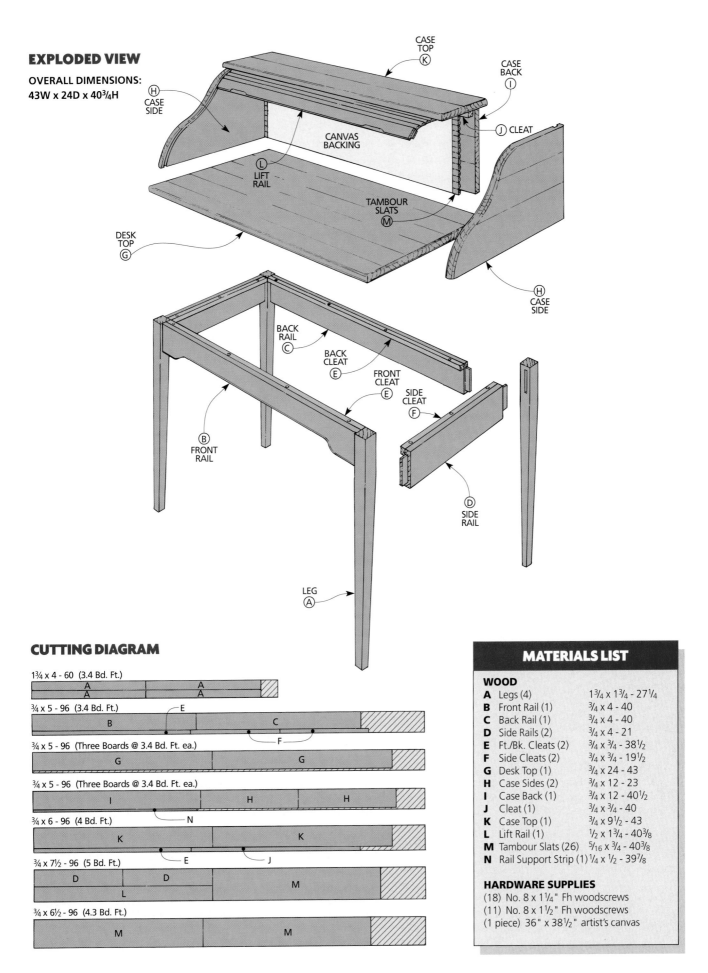

CASE
TOP
Ⓚ

CASE
BACK
Ⓘ

Ⓗ
CASE
SIDE

Ⓙ CLEAT

CANVAS
BACKING

Ⓛ
LIFT
RAIL

TAMBOUR
SLATS
Ⓜ

DESK
TOP
Ⓖ

Ⓗ
CASE
SIDE

BACK
RAIL
Ⓒ

BACK
CLEAT
Ⓔ

FRONT
CLEAT
Ⓔ

SIDE
CLEAT
Ⓕ

Ⓑ
FRONT
RAIL

Ⓓ
SIDE
RAIL

LEG
Ⓐ

CUTTING DIAGRAM

1¾ x 4 - 60 (3.4 Bd. Ft.)

| A | A |
| A | A |

¾ x 5 - 96 (3.4 Bd. Ft.)

E

| B | C |

F

¾ x 5 - 96 (Three Boards @ 3.4 Bd. Ft. ea.)

| G | G |

¾ x 5 - 96 (Three Boards @ 3.4 Bd. Ft. ea.)

| I | H | H |

N

¾ x 6 - 96 (4 Bd. Ft.)

| K | K |

E   J

¾ x 7½ - 96 (5 Bd. Ft.)

| D | D | M |
| L | | |

¾ x 6½ - 96 (4.3 Bd. Ft.)

| M | M |

MATERIALS LIST

WOOD

A	Legs (4)	1¾ x 1¾ - 27¼
B	Front Rail (1)	¾ x 4 - 40
C	Back Rail (1)	¾ x 4 - 40
D	Side Rails (2)	¾ x 4 - 21
E	Ft./Bk. Cleats (2)	¾ x ¾ - 38½
F	Side Cleats (2)	¾ x ¾ - 19½
G	Desk Top (1)	¾ x 24 - 43
H	Case Sides (2)	¾ x 12 - 23
I	Case Back (1)	¾ x 12 - 40½
J	Cleat (1)	¾ x ¾ - 40
K	Case Top (1)	¾ x 9½ - 43
L	Lift Rail (1)	½ x 1¾ - 40⅜
M	Tambour Slats (26)	5/16 x ¾ - 40⅜
N	Rail Support Strip (1)	¼ x ½ - 39⅞

HARDWARE SUPPLIES

(18) No. 8 x 1¼" Fh woodscrews
(11) No. 8 x 1½" Fh woodscrews
(1 piece) 36" x 38½" artist's canvas

The base for the Roll-Top Desk is built like a simple table. There are four legs and a top joined by rails. I started work on the base by making the legs.

LEGS. These legs (A) start out as $1\frac{3}{4}$"-square pieces of 8/4 stock cut to a finished length of $27\frac{1}{4}$" *(Fig. 1)*. Near one end, I marked the location for a pair of $\frac{1}{4}$"-wide mortises to hold the tenons cut later on the rails. These mortises are drilled on adjacent faces *(Fig. 1a)*. But they aren't centered on the leg. Instead, they're positioned $\frac{1}{2}$" from the outside edges *(Fig. 2a)*.

To cut the mortises, I used a $\frac{1}{4}$" Forstner bit and drilled overlapping holes $\frac{13}{16}$" deep to remove most of the waste *(Fig. 2)*. This depth provides a little extra clearance for the $\frac{3}{4}$"-long tenons on the ends of the rails. Since the bit cuts a clean, flat-bottomed hole, it only takes a few minutes to square up the ends and clean up the sides of each mortise with a chisel.

TAPERS. Now to make the legs look more graceful, I cut tapers on all four sides *(Fig. 3)*. (See page 86 for more on making and using the taper jig.)

RAILS. After tapering the legs, set them aside until the rails are completed. The rails that hold the legs together are identical in width (4"). But their lengths are different. The front rail (B) and back rail (C) are 40" long, while the side rails (D) are only 21" long *(Fig. 1)*.

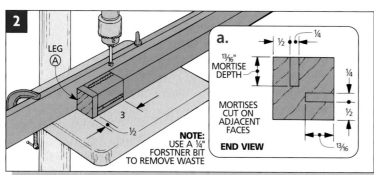

Next, I cut a $\frac{3}{4}$"-long tenon on each end of each rail *(Fig. 4a)*. This tenon is centered on the thickness, but there's really no trick to cutting a centered tenon on the table saw. Just flip the rail over between passes to remove stock from both sides. But to make sure the tenon fits snug in the mortise, you'll want to sneak up on the final thickness.

To complete each tenon on the rails, all that's left is to create shoulders on the top and bottom so the tenon matches the length of the mortise in the leg. To do that, stand the workpiece up on edge, and remove $\frac{1}{2}$" of the tenon from each edge *(Fig. 4a)*.

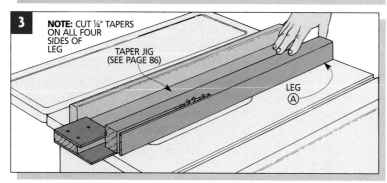

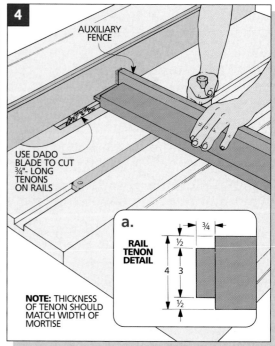

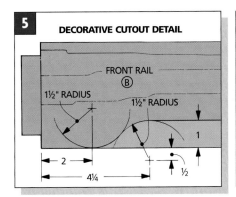

5 DECORATIVE CUTOUT DETAIL

FRONT RAIL Ⓑ

1½" RADIUS
1½" RADIUS
2
4¼
1
½

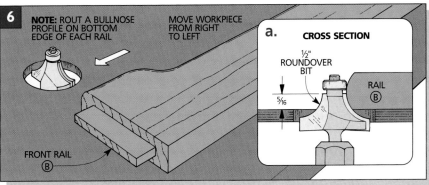

6 NOTE: ROUT A BULLNOSE PROFILE ON BOTTOM EDGE OF EACH RAIL

MOVE WORKPIECE FROM RIGHT TO LEFT

FRONT RAIL Ⓑ

a. CROSS SECTION

½" ROUNDOVER BIT

RAIL Ⓑ

5/16

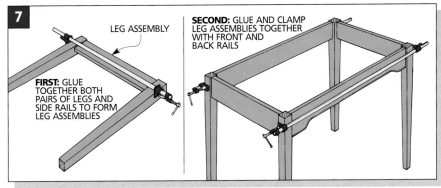

7

LEG ASSEMBLY

SECOND: GLUE AND CLAMP LEG ASSEMBLIES TOGETHER WITH FRONT AND BACK RAILS

FIRST: GLUE TOGETHER BOTH PAIRS OF LEGS AND SIDE RAILS TO FORM LEG ASSEMBLIES

DECORATIVE CUTOUT. Up to this point the front and back rails are identical. But to provide extra clearance for sitting at the desk, I cut a decorative shape in the front rail *(Fig. 5)*. To do this, simply lay out the curves at each end of the rail and connect them with a straight line. Then remove most of the waste with a band saw, and complete the profile by sanding to the line.

BULLNOSE PROFILE. The legs and rails could now be assembled, but I wanted to break the sharp corners on the rails and create a smooth edge. So I routed a bullnose profile on the bottom edges of all the rails *(Fig. 6)*. To do this, I used a ½" roundover bit raised 5/16" above the router table *(Fig. 6a)*.

With the bullnose complete, the base can now be glued together. To make this easier, I glued the legs and side rails first *(Fig. 7)*. Then I clamped the front and back rails between the side assemblies.

CLEATS. Next, I worked on making the cleats that hold the desk top in position. These are ¾"-square pieces of stock with oversized shank holes drilled in them *(Fig. 8a)*. (This allows the top to expand and contract with changes in humidity.) The front and back cleats (E) are the same length (38½"), while the side cleats (F) are shorter (19½").

These cleats are simply glued to the desk rails. But to make sure the desk

top is pulled down tight against the tops of the rails, the cleats aren't flush with the top edges *(Fig. 8a)*. Instead, they're glued on just a little bit below the edges to create a small clearance gap.

DESK TOP

Next, I edge-glued six ¾"-thick boards to create a solid wood blank for the desk top (G) *(Fig. 9)*. After the glue dried, I planed and sanded the top until it was flat and smooth.

Then after cutting the top to finished size (24" x 43"), rout bullnose profiles on all four edges. Here again this required a ½" roundover bit, but since the top is too big to rout easily on my router table, this time I used a handheld router. Rout the ends first, so that any chipout will be cleaned up when you rout the sides.

Finally, it's a good idea to attach the table top to the base for the time being *(Fig. 9)*. It will help strengthen the base as you move it around in the shop. You can go ahead and drill the holes, but don't put in all the screws just yet. Later, you'll have to remove the desk top before the roll-top case and tambour door can be installed.

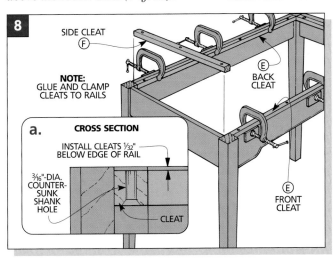

8

SIDE CLEAT Ⓕ

NOTE: GLUE AND CLAMP CLEATS TO RAILS

BACK CLEAT Ⓔ

a. CROSS SECTION

INSTALL CLEATS 1/32" BELOW EDGE OF RAIL

3/16"-DIA. COUNTER-SUNK SHANK HOLE

CLEAT

FRONT CLEAT Ⓔ

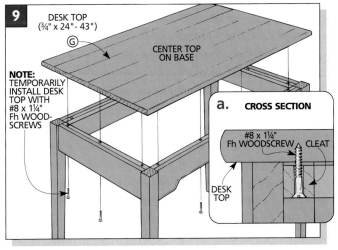

9

DESK TOP (¾" x 24"- 43") Ⓖ

CENTER TOP ON BASE

NOTE: TEMPORARILY INSTALL DESK TOP WITH #8 x 1¼" Fh WOODSCREWS

a. CROSS SECTION

#8 x 1¼" Fh WOODSCREW

CLEAT

DESK TOP

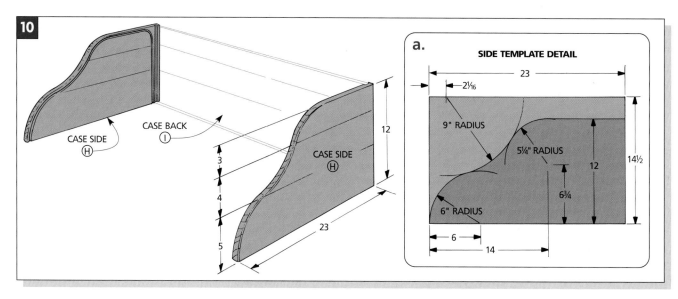

10

CASE SIDE (H)

CASE BACK (I)

CASE SIDE (H)

12

3

4

5

23

a.

SIDE TEMPLATE DETAIL

23

2¹⁄₁₆

9" RADIUS

5¼" RADIUS

6" RADIUS

12

6¾

14½

6

14

ROLL-TOP CASE

After completing the base, I turned my attention to building the roll-top case. It consists of two case sides (H) held together by a back panel (I) *(Fig. 10)*.

BLANKS. I started by working on the sides. They're glued-up blanks that are cut oversize (mine were 12½" x 24").

SIDE TEMPLATE. Once the glue dries, the "S-shape" for the sides can be drawn on the blanks. An easy way to do this is by making a template *(Fig. 10a)*. Draw the shape on a piece of ¼" hardboard, cut it out, and sand the edges smooth.

Now the template can be used to transfer the profile to each blank. Just trace around it and cut out the case sides (H). To make sure these pieces

were identical, I stuck them together with double-sided carpet tape and sanded them smooth.

GROOVE TEMPLATE. Once the side pieces are sanded, the next step is to rout identical grooves on the inside face of each piece. This ¼"-deep groove follows the shape of the case side and provides a channel for the tambour door to slide in. To allow the door to slide smoothly, the grooves have to be positioned exactly the same on both pieces.

So I used a template again, this time to guide my router. But I didn't make a new template. I just downsized the old one. This smaller template is used with a ⅝"-dia. guide bushing in the router (see the Shop Tip below).

How much smaller is the template?

To determine this, add up the distance from the edge of the workpiece to the groove (⅜"), the groove width (⅜"), and the distance from the edge of the router bit to the outer edge of the guide bushing (⅛"). This adds up to ⅞".

Now use a compass set at ⅞" and trace the template along the front edge and across the top *(Figs. 11 and 11a)*. But the back edge is a little unusual.

Here you need a 1½" radius so the door can slide around the corner. And for clearance between the door and case back, the distance changes to 1¾" *(Fig. 11a)*. Once the lines are drawn, cut the template to its new size and sand the edges smooth.

Now, using double-sided carpet tape, stick the template to a case side with the

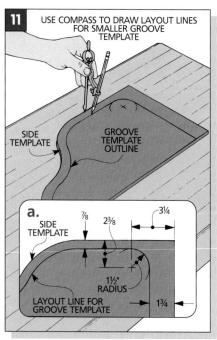

11 USE COMPASS TO DRAW LAYOUT LINES FOR SMALLER GROOVE TEMPLATE

SIDE TEMPLATE

GROOVE TEMPLATE OUTLINE

a.

SIDE TEMPLATE

⅞

2⅜

3¼

1½" RADIUS

1¾

LAYOUT LINE FOR GROOVE TEMPLATE

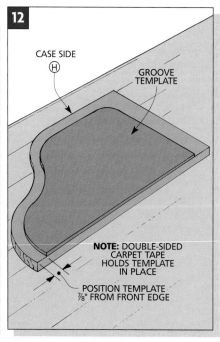

12

CASE SIDE (H)

GROOVE TEMPLATE

NOTE: DOUBLE-SIDED CARPET TAPE HOLDS TEMPLATE IN PLACE

POSITION TEMPLATE ⅞" FROM FRONT EDGE

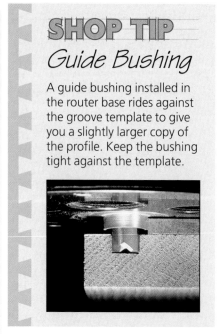

SHOP TIP

Guide Bushing

A guide bushing installed in the router base rides against the groove template to give you a slightly larger copy of the profile. Keep the bushing tight against the template.

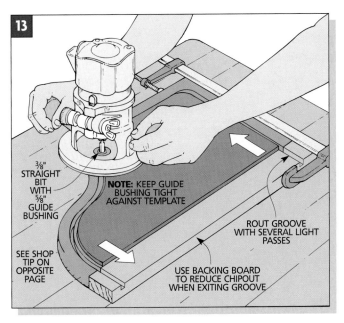

13

³⁄₈" STRAIGHT BIT WITH ⁵⁄₈" GUIDE BUSHING

NOTE: KEEP GUIDE BUSHING TIGHT AGAINST TEMPLATE

ROUT GROOVE WITH SEVERAL LIGHT PASSES

SEE SHOP TIP ON OPPOSITE PAGE

USE BACKING BOARD TO REDUCE CHIPOUT WHEN EXITING GROOVE

bottom edges flush and the front edge of the template set back ⁷⁄₈" (*Fig. 12*).

ROUTING GROOVE. Before routing the groove, I clamped a backing board to the workpiece where the bit exits the groove (*Fig. 13*). This keeps the edge of the board from chipping out.

Now you can rout the groove. I made two passes to reach the full (¹⁄₄") depth. You could do it in one pass, but it's easier to keep the bushing tight against the template by making lighter cuts.

Note: Be sure to position the groove on the *inside* face of each case side.

PROFILE. Next I moved to the router table to rout the bullnose profiles on all the edges except the top (*Fig. 14*). I didn't want a radius here so the case top would sit nice and flat. To do that, just measure out about 9" from the back edge and make a mark where you want to stop the profile.

BACK DADO. To complete each side

piece, a dado is cut along the back edge to hold the case back (I) (*Fig. 15*). This ¹⁄₄"-deep dado is cut to match the thickness of the back panel.

CASE BACK. With the dado cut, the case back (I) is added next to join the sides. This glued-up panel matches the height of the sides (12") and is glued in the dadoes (*Fig. 16*).

But before the glue dries, it's important to check that the sides are perpendicular to the back. If not, the tambour door may "rack" in the opening.

CLEAT. One more thing to add to the case is a cleat (J) for securing the top (*Fig. 16*). It fits between the sides and is glued and clamped to the back, just below the top edge (*Fig. 16b*).

CASE TOP. All that's left to complete the case is building the case top (K). Like the side pieces, it's also a solid wood panel with bullnose profiles routed on the edges.

The case top is then screwed to the cleat (*Fig. 16b*). But the front edge is glued in place in just a couple spots (*Fig. 16a*). If you glued the whole edge, the top couldn't expand or contract.

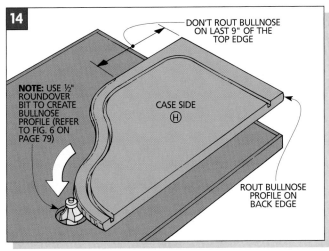

14

DON'T ROUT BULLNOSE ON LAST 9" OF THE TOP EDGE

NOTE: USE ¹⁄₂" ROUNDOVER BIT TO CREATE BULLNOSE PROFILE (REFER TO FIG. 6 ON PAGE 79)

CASE SIDE (H)

ROUT BULLNOSE PROFILE ON BACK EDGE

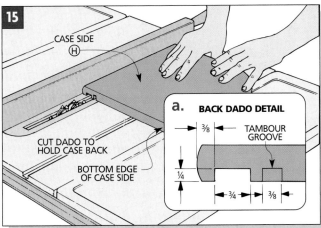

15

CASE SIDE (H)

CUT DADO TO HOLD CASE BACK

BOTTOM EDGE OF CASE SIDE

a. **BACK DADO DETAIL**

³⁄₈"

TAMBOUR GROOVE

¹⁄₄

³⁄₄   ³⁄₈

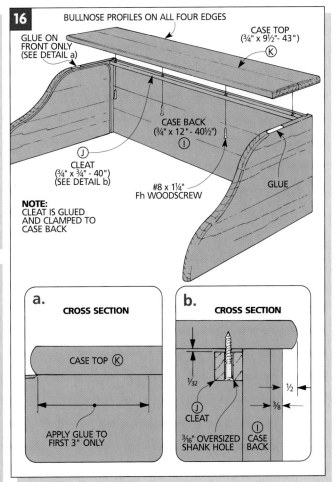

16

BULLNOSE PROFILES ON ALL FOUR EDGES

GLUE ON FRONT ONLY (SEE DETAIL a)

CASE TOP (³⁄₄" x 9¹⁄₂"- 43") (K)

CASE BACK (³⁄₄" x 12"- 40¹⁄₂") (I)

(J) CLEAT (³⁄₄" x ³⁄₄" - 40") (SEE DETAIL b)

#8 x 1¹⁄₄" Fh WOODSCREW

GLUE

NOTE: CLEAT IS GLUED AND CLAMPED TO CASE BACK

a. **CROSS SECTION**

CASE TOP (K)

APPLY GLUE TO FIRST 3" ONLY

b. **CROSS SECTION**

¹⁄₃₂

¹⁄₂

³⁄₈

(J) CLEAT

³⁄₁₆" OVERSIZED SHANK HOLE

(I) CASE BACK

After putting the case together, the next step is building the tambour door that fits inside. Tambour doors are basically all the same. There's a lift rail to grasp when you open and close the door, slats that make up the body, and a fabric "hinge" on the backside that holds everything together *(Fig. 17)*. (For more details on making tambours, see the Technique article on pages 87-89.)

CUT BLANK. Begin work on the door by making the lift rail (L). I started with an extra-wide (3") blank of $\frac{1}{2}$"-thick stock. (You'll see the reason for the extra width in a minute.) Though it's extra wide, cut the blank to finished length. To determine the length, measure the distance between the bottoms of the grooves in the case sides and subtract $\frac{1}{8}$" for clearance. (My rail ended up $40\frac{3}{8}$" long.)

CUTOUTS. Next, a pair of cutouts are routed in the front face of the lift rail that will become hand grips *(Fig. 17)*.

To do this, first draw a couple of stop lines across the front face to mark the location for each cutout *(Fig. 18)*. Then use a handheld router and a $\frac{1}{2}$" cove bit to create each recess *(Fig. 18a)*. (Here's why you need an extra-wide workpiece. The extra width helps to keep the router steady during the cut.)

Note: This is a fairly deep cut, so I didn't make it in one pass. I set the router for the finished depth, but didn't push the router bearing all the way to the workpiece on the first pass.

BEVEL. Next, I ripped a 7° bevel along the bottom edge of the lift rail so it would sit flush on the desk top when the door was closed *(Fig. 17a)*. (The lift rail

leans backwards slightly when the door is mounted in the case.) Once the bevel is cut, rip the opposite edge of the lift rail to bring it to final width ($1\frac{3}{4}$").

RABBET AND ROUNDOVER. Now to complete the lift rail there are two more steps. First, the ends need to be thinner so they'll slide in the grooves in the case

sides *(Fig. 17b)*. I did this by setting up a dado blade in the table saw to cut a rabbet on each end of the rail to create a $\frac{1}{4}$" x $\frac{1}{4}$" tongue *(Figs. 19 and 19a)*.

And finally, I used a $\frac{3}{8}$" roundover bit to rout the top outside edge of the lift rail so that it would match the finished profile of the slats *(Fig. 17a)*.

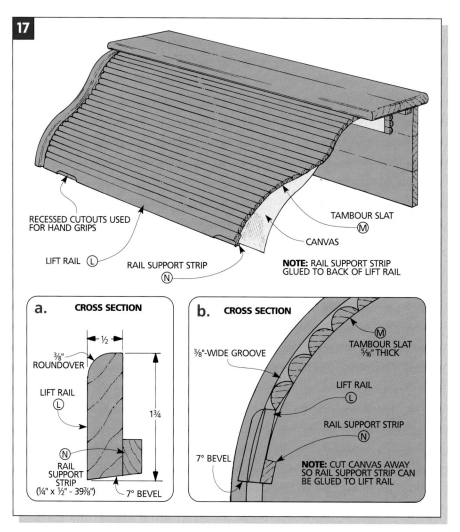

17

RECESSED CUTOUTS USED FOR HAND GRIPS

TAMBOUR SLAT Ⓜ

CANVAS

LIFT RAIL Ⓛ

RAIL SUPPORT STRIP Ⓝ

NOTE: RAIL SUPPORT STRIP GLUED TO BACK OF LIFT RAIL

a. CROSS SECTION

$\frac{1}{2}$

$\frac{3}{8}$" ROUNDOVER

LIFT RAIL Ⓛ

$1\frac{3}{4}$

Ⓝ RAIL SUPPORT STRIP ($\frac{1}{4}$" x $\frac{1}{2}$" - $39\frac{7}{8}$")

7° BEVEL

b. CROSS SECTION

TAMBOUR SLAT Ⓜ $\frac{5}{16}$" THICK

$\frac{3}{8}$"-WIDE GROOVE

LIFT RAIL Ⓛ

RAIL SUPPORT STRIP Ⓝ

7° BEVEL

NOTE: CUT CANVAS AWAY SO RAIL SUPPORT STRIP CAN BE GLUED TO LIFT RAIL

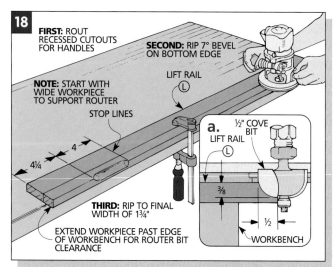

18

FIRST: ROUT RECESSED CUTOUTS FOR HANDLES

SECOND: RIP 7° BEVEL ON BOTTOM EDGE

LIFT RAIL Ⓛ

NOTE: START WITH WIDE WORKPIECE TO SUPPORT ROUTER

STOP LINES

4

$4\frac{1}{4}$

a. $\frac{1}{2}$" COVE BIT

LIFT RAIL Ⓛ

$\frac{3}{8}$

$\frac{1}{2}$

WORKBENCH

THIRD: RIP TO FINAL WIDTH OF $1\frac{3}{4}$"

EXTEND WORKPIECE PAST EDGE OF WORKBENCH FOR ROUTER BIT CLEARANCE

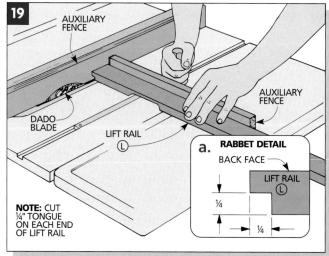

19

AUXILIARY FENCE

AUXILIARY FENCE

DADO BLADE

LIFT RAIL Ⓛ

NOTE: CUT $\frac{1}{4}$" TONGUE ON EACH END OF LIFT RAIL

a. RABBET DETAIL

BACK FACE

LIFT RAIL Ⓛ

$\frac{1}{4}$

$\frac{1}{4}$

SLATS

With the lift rail complete, I concentrated on the tambour slats (M). For the roll-top desk, 26 slats the same length as the lift rail are needed. But I made a few extra so I wouldn't come up short if any twisted out of shape.

Making the slats is a two-step process. First, I used a roundover bit to create a rounded profile on the edge of the workpiece (*Fig. 20a*). Then using a carrier board, it's quick and easy to rip a thin slat off the edge (*Fig. 21* and refer to *Fig. 5* on page 88).

The important thing is that all the slats end up $5/16$" thick. Then the door will slide freely in the $3/8$" groove.

GLUE-UP. Once you have your slats cut, both the lift rail and slats can be glued to a canvas backing (see page 89).

DRY ASSEMBLY. After the slats are glued to the canvas, it's a good time to check the fit of the door. If it doesn't slide freely in the grooves, refer to the troubleshooting tips on page 89.

Also, since I planned on adding the desk organizer later (refer to the Designer's Notebook on page 84), I checked the height of the opening (mine was 10").

RAIL SUPPORT STRIP. To complete the door, a rail support strip (N) is glued to the back of the lift rail flush with the bottom edge (refer to *Fig. 17a*). This

strip gives you something to grip to close the tambour door. Like the lift rail, there's a 7° angle ripped on one edge and the support strip is sized to fit easily between the case sides (39$7/8$").

Note: Cut away a strip of canvas to get a wood-to-wood joint between the lift rail and the strip.

FINAL ASSEMBLY

Once the tambour door is complete, the desk can be assembled. The first step is to install the case on the desk top. This means locating and drilling mounting

holes through the desk top and into the case sides and back.

SCREW HOLE LOCATION. To locate the holes, I centered the case on the desk top. Then to mark its position, place tape around the outside edges of the case (*Fig. 22*). When the case is removed, just measure in from the edge of the tape $3/8$" and drill the oversized shank holes.

Now, to complete the desk, install the door in the case, then screw the case to the desk top (*Fig. 22a*). Finally, set the desk top on the base and screw it in place (*Fig. 23*). ∎

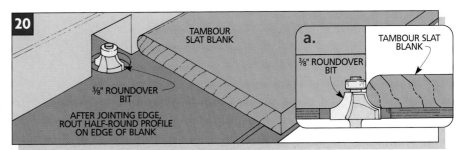

20

TAMBOUR SLAT BLANK

$3/8$" ROUNDOVER BIT

AFTER JOINTING EDGE, ROUT HALF-ROUND PROFILE ON EDGE OF BLANK

a. TAMBOUR SLAT BLANK

$3/8$" ROUNDOVER BIT

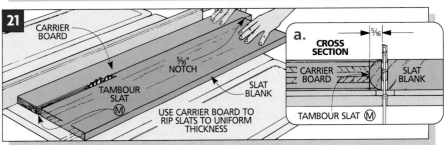

21

CARRIER BOARD

$5/16$" NOTCH

TAMBOUR SLAT Ⓜ

SLAT BLANK

USE CARRIER BOARD TO RIP SLATS TO UNIFORM THICKNESS

a. CROSS SECTION

$5/16$"

CARRIER BOARD

SLAT BLANK

TAMBOUR SLAT Ⓜ

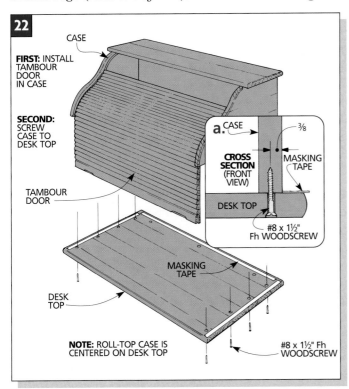

22

CASE

FIRST: INSTALL TAMBOUR DOOR IN CASE

SECOND: SCREW CASE TO DESK TOP

TAMBOUR DOOR

a. CASE

CROSS SECTION (FRONT VIEW)

$3/8$

MASKING TAPE

DESK TOP

#8 x 1½" Fh WOODSCREW

DESK TOP

MASKING TAPE

NOTE: ROLL-TOP CASE IS CENTERED ON DESK TOP

#8 x 1½" Fh WOODSCREW

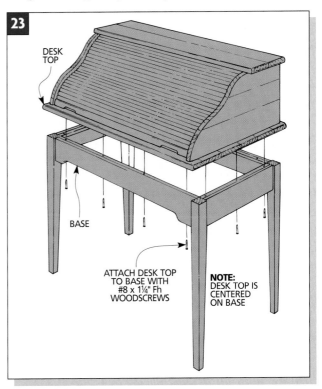

23

DESK TOP

BASE

ATTACH DESK TOP TO BASE WITH #8 x 1¼" Fh WOODSCREWS

NOTE: DESK TOP IS CENTERED ON BASE

DESIGNER'S NOTEBOOK

Sized to fit into the Roll-Top Desk, this organizer can be built with or without drawers. Besides providing storage, it also hides the back side of the tambour when the door is rolled up into the desk.

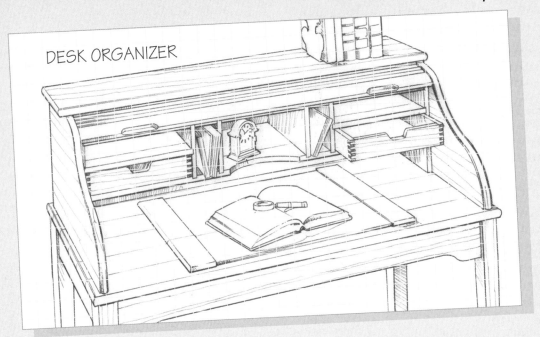

DESK ORGANIZER

CONSTRUCTION NOTES:

■ To build the Desk Organizer, I started with the top (O) and shelf (P) *(Fig. 1)*. They're made from $1/2$" stock edge-glued into 10"-wide panels (rough size).
■ When the top and shelf panels are dry and planed flat, they can be cut to the same length ($39\frac{1}{2}$" or a hair less). But their widths are different. The top is wider ($9\frac{1}{2}$") than the shelf (9") because

it holds a back panel added later.
■ To hold the back, I cut a $1/4$"-deep groove along the back edge of the top panel (O) *(Fig. 1b)*. This groove is cut to width to match the thickness of the $1/4$" plywood used for the back panel.
■ The shelf and top are connected by four dividers. These fit in $1/2$"-wide dadoes cut $1/4$" deep *(Fig. 1)*. To make

sure the dadoes align, clamp the shelf and top together and use a hand-held router and a straightedge guide.

But you don't want to rout all the way across *both* pieces. So stop the dado when the router bit reaches the groove in the top (O). Then chisel out the waste to square up the end of the dado.
■ After routing the dadoes, cut an arc in the front edge of the shelf, centered on the length of the shelf. To do this, you'll need to locate the arc's centerpoint in a piece of scrap *(Fig. 1a)*.
■ Next, the four vertical dividers (Q) can be cut to size *(Fig. 1)*.
■ The two outside dividers also hold

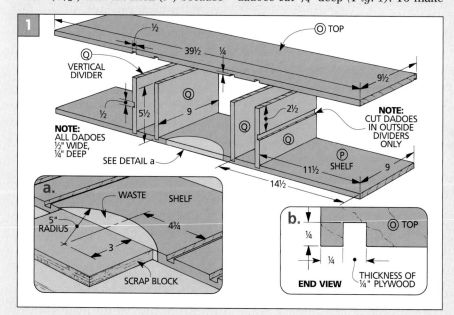

MATERIALS LIST	
NEW PARTS	
O Top (1)	$1/2$ x $9\frac{1}{2}$ - $39\frac{1}{2}$
P Shelf (1)	$1/2$ x 9 - $39\frac{1}{2}$
Q Vert. Dividers (4)	$1/2$ x 9 - $5\frac{1}{2}$
R Sides (2)	$1/2$ x $9\frac{1}{2}$ - 10
S Horiz. Dividers (2)	$1/2$ x 9 - $11\frac{3}{4}$
T Back Molding (1)	$1/2$ x $3/4$ - $39\frac{1}{2}$
U Back (1)	$1/4$ ply - $9\frac{1}{4}$ x $39\frac{1}{2}$
V Drwr. Frt./Bk. (4)	$1/2$ x $2\frac{1}{4}$ - $11\frac{3}{16}$
W Drawer Sides (4)	$1/2$ x $2\frac{1}{4}$ - 9
X Drwr. Bottoms (2)	$1/4$ ply - $8\frac{1}{2}$ x $10\frac{11}{16}$

horizontal dividers added later (refer to *Fig. 2*). Rout a $1/4$"-deep dado centered on the height of each of these two vertical dividers (*Fig. 1*).

■ When the dadoes are routed, the top, shelf, and vertical dividers can all be glued together (*Fig. 1*). Check that the assembly is square.

■ The next step is to add the sides (R) (*Fig. 2*). Begin by ripping two $1/2$"-thick panels to match the width of the top ($9^1/2$"). The length of each side panel should be just less than the desk's tambour opening. (I cut my sides 10" tall.)

■ Next, rout three $1/4$"-deep x $1/2$"-wide dadoes in each side (*Fig. 2a*). The first dado holds the top panel and is located $1/4$" down from the top edge. The other two align with the shelf (B) and the dado cut on the vertical divider (Q).

■ To hold the back (added later), each side also needs a $1/2$"-wide rabbet along its back inside edge (*Fig. 2b*). This rabbet is stopped as it hits the top dado in the side panel.

■ Finally, to soften the top end of each side panel, I used a $1/2$" roundover bit raised $5/16$" above the router table to rout a bullnose profile (*Fig. 2b*).

■ With the side panels complete, it's time to cut the horizontal dividers (S). The width of these pieces is the same as the shelf (P) (9"). To determine their length, dry-assemble the case (*Fig. 2*). Then cut the horizontal dividers to length to fit between the dadoes in the sides (R) and the vertical dividers (Q). When they've been cut to size, these pieces and the side panels can be glued and clamped to the ends of the case.

■ Before adding the plywood back, a back molding (T) is cut to fit between the rabbets in the sides (R) (*Fig. 2c*). Then I notched the front corners so the $3/4$"-wide molding would fit flush with the back edge of each side.

■ Next I cut a $1/4$"-deep groove in the molding. This groove is sized to hold the $1/4$"-thick plywood back (*Fig. 2c*).

■ Now that the molding is complete, you can cut the back (U) to size from $1/4$"-thick plywood (*Fig. 2*).

■ Once the back is cut to size, glue it to the back molding and then glue this assembly to the back of the organizer.

■ The case is complete, but I decided to add two drawers to fit in the organizer. (You could build four drawers if you want a drawer in each opening.)

■ Start by cutting the drawer fronts (V), backs (V), and sides (W) to size from $1/2$"-thick stock (*Fig. 3*). Allow for a $1/32$"

gap at each side. But for now, the height of each drawer should match its opening. The drawers will be trimmed for clearance after they're assembled.

■ The drawer is constructed with $1/4$" box joints at each corner (*Fig. 3*). The $1/4$" plywood bottom (X) is held in a groove that's cut in each piece. Align this groove with a slot in the drawer side (W). This way it will be hidden by a pin on the drawer front.

■ Before assembling the drawers, I laid out and cut an opening for a handle on each front piece (*Fig. 4*).

■ Next, cut a drawer bottom to fit and assemble the drawers. Then trim the top and bottom edges very slightly to create a $1/32$" gap above the drawer.

■ After each drawer is assembled, the grooves for the drawer bottom will be exposed on the sides. I cut small wood plugs and inserted them into the square holes to hide the grooves (*Fig. 3*).

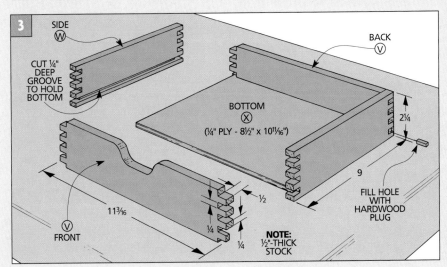

2

a. BULLNOSE TOP EDGE · $1/4$ · 3 · $5^3/4$ · **END VIEW** · **NOTE:** ALL DADOES $1/2$" WIDE · $1/4$

b. $1/4$ · **BACK VIEW** · $1/2$"-WIDE RABBET

NOTE: SIDE LENGTH DETERMINES HEIGHT OF ORGANIZER. CUT TO FIT DESK OPENING, IF NECESSARY.

$9^1/2$ · BACK (U) · BACK MOLDING (T) · 10 · (R) SIDE

(S) HORIZONTAL DIVIDER · 9 · $11^3/4$

c. CUT $1/4$" x $1/4$" GROOVE FOR BACK (U) · $1/4$ · $1/2$ · (T) · $1/2$ · $1/4$

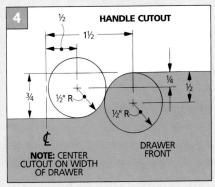

3

SIDE (W) · CUT $1/4$" DEEP GROOVE TO HOLD BOTTOM

BACK (V)

BOTTOM (X) ($1/4$" PLY - $8^1/2$" x $10^{11}/16$") · $2^1/4$ · 9 · FILL HOLE WITH HARDWOOD PLUG

(V) FRONT · $11^3/16$ · $1/2$ · $1/4$ · $1/4$ · **NOTE:** $1/2$"-THICK STOCK

4 · $1/2$ · **HANDLE CUTOUT** · $1^1/2$ · $1/4$ · $3/4$ · $1/2$" R · $1/2$" R · $1/2$ · ₵ · **NOTE:** CENTER CUTOUT ON WIDTH OF DRAWER · DRAWER FRONT

SHOP JIG . . . . *Taper Jig*

Tapering all four sides of a leg requires a jig that's "adjustable." That's because after two faces of the leg are tapered, there aren't any more straight faces to place against the rip fence or on the table of the table saw.

To cut the tapers on the legs of the roll-top desk, I made a special jig with a piece of 3/4" plywood and a stop block *(Fig. 1)*. These pieces are screwed to a 1/4" hardboard sled that carries the leg and the jig past the saw blade.

STOP BLOCK. The stop block is the key to the jig. It's just a piece of 1/4" hardboard (or plywood) with two notches in it *(Fig. 1a)*. These notches offset the leg on the jig and set the angle of the taper.

One of the nice things about using this jig is that you don't have to worry about any angles. Just determine how much stock needs to be cut from each side of the leg (1/4" for the legs on the Roll-Top Desk). This is how far the first notch needs to be offset from the edge

of the plywood *(Fig. 1a)*. Then the second notch is offset the same distance (1/4") from the first.

The stop block also needs to be positioned on the length of the plywood *(Fig. 1b)*. This position determines the length of the taper. (The tapers on the desk legs are 22 1/4" long. Refer to *Fig. 1* on page 78).

Note: I attached the stop block to the front of the jig. This means you push the workpiece, not just the jig. I find it safer to use this way.

USING THE JIG. To use the taper jig, first lock down the rip fence so the distance from the fence to the blade is equal to the width of the plywood on the jig plus the width of the leg. (It's okay if you trim off a little bit of the sled on the very first pass.)

Now simply place the leg in the first notch and then make two passes, rotating the leg 90° between passes *(Fig. 2)*.

Note: For safety, I stuck the leg to the sled with double-sided carpet tape before making a pass.

To taper the last two faces, place the leg in the other notch (the one closest to the blade), and make two more passes, rotating the leg 90° between passes.

Once the tapers are cut, some light sanding on each face should take care of any blade marks.

1

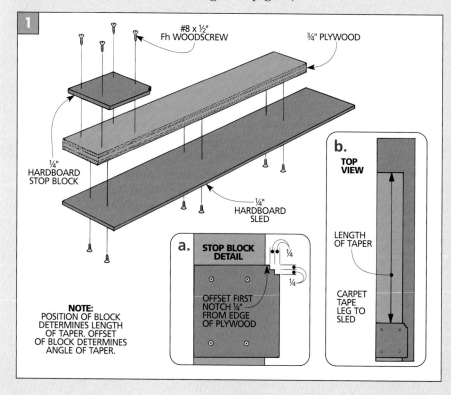

#8 x 1/2"
Fh WOODSCREW

3/4" PLYWOOD

1/4" HARDBOARD STOP BLOCK

1/4" HARDBOARD SLED

NOTE: POSITION OF BLOCK DETERMINES LENGTH OF TAPER. OFFSET OF BLOCK DETERMINES ANGLE OF TAPER.

a. **STOP BLOCK DETAIL**

1/4
1/4

OFFSET FIRST NOTCH 1/4" FROM EDGE OF PLYWOOD

b. **TOP VIEW**

LENGTH OF TAPER

CARPET TAPE LEG TO SLED

2

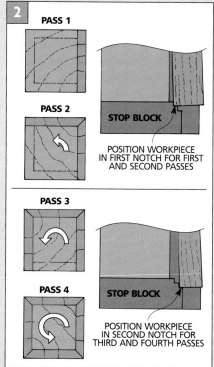

PASS 1

PASS 2

STOP BLOCK

POSITION WORKPIECE IN FIRST NOTCH FOR FIRST AND SECOND PASSES

PASS 3

PASS 4

STOP BLOCK

POSITION WORKPIECE IN SECOND NOTCH FOR THIRD AND FOURTH PASSES

TECHNIQUE .... *Building Tambours*

Some people think that tambour doors are a mystery. After all, there must be some trick to getting all those pieces to work together as a smoothly sliding door.

But once you understand the design, you'll see there's really no trick at all. You make a tambour flexible by gluing a bunch of thin slats to a piece of fabric. Then cut a groove for the pieces to follow so the door can slide out of sight inside its own cabinet. That's it. Nothing so mysterious about it after all.

TAMBOUR ANATOMY

All tambour or roll-top doors consist of the same three parts *(Fig. 1)*. There's usually a thick, heavier piece at the

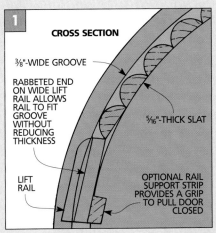

1

CROSS SECTION

³/₈"-WIDE GROOVE

RABBETED END ON WIDE LIFT RAIL ALLOWS RAIL TO FIT GROOVE WITHOUT REDUCING THICKNESS

⁵/₁₆"-THICK SLAT

LIFT RAIL

OPTIONAL RAIL SUPPORT STRIP PROVIDES A GRIP TO PULL DOOR CLOSED

front (a lift rail), followed by a series of thinner pieces (tambour slats), all held together with a piece of fabric.

CANVAS. I use canvas when building tambour doors. This allows the door to flex as it slides through the groove.

But it takes more than a piece of canvas to allow a door to flex in more than one direction (as it has to for the S-shaped tambour used in the Roll-Top Desk). The real "secret" is the style (or profile) of the tambour lift rail and slats.

SLAT PROFILE. The key to creating this flex is building in enough clearance between the slats. This can be accomplished easily by changing the slat profile. I wanted the door on the Roll-Top Desk to move through some pretty tight curves. By rounding over the slats, they can flex or move back and forth as the door moves through the curved groove *(Figs. 2 and 2a)*. The greater the clearance between the slats,

the tighter the curve the door can follow.

SLAT WIDTH. But there are a couple of other things that come into play. One is the width of the slat *(Fig. 3)*. A wider slat makes a sturdier door. But a wide slat can't slide through a tight curve. That's why you typically don't find slats wider than 1".

There is one exception to this: the lift rail at the front of the door. Here a wide piece is needed to take all the wear and tear as the door is pushed open and pulled closed.

To get a wide piece like this to work in a groove, simply reduce the thickness on each end by cutting a rabbet to create a tongue *(Fig. 1)*.

THICKNESS. When you reduce the thickness of a lift rail or slat, you can make it wider and still have it slide smoothly. This is because you've created more clearance around it. Of course you can go too far and make them too thin. Then on a wide door the slats could start to sag and even fall out of the grooves.

CLEARANCE. Finally, there's one other consideration for making tambour doors slide smoothly. You need to allow for clearance between the slat and the groove. The tambour door in the Roll-Top Desk used ⁵/₁₆"-thick slats in a ³/₈" groove *(Fig. 1)*. This provided just enough clearance so the tambour door would slide smoothly without rattling.

2 **CROSS SECTION**

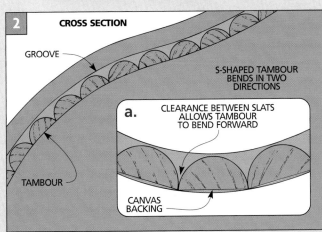

GROOVE

S-SHAPED TAMBOUR BENDS IN TWO DIRECTIONS

a. CLEARANCE BETWEEN SLATS ALLOWS TAMBOUR TO BEND FORWARD

TAMBOUR

CANVAS BACKING

3 **CROSS SECTION**

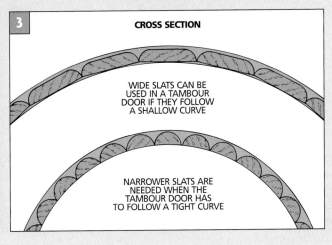

WIDE SLATS CAN BE USED IN A TAMBOUR DOOR IF THEY FOLLOW A SHALLOW CURVE

NARROWER SLATS ARE NEEDED WHEN THE TAMBOUR DOOR HAS TO FOLLOW A TIGHT CURVE

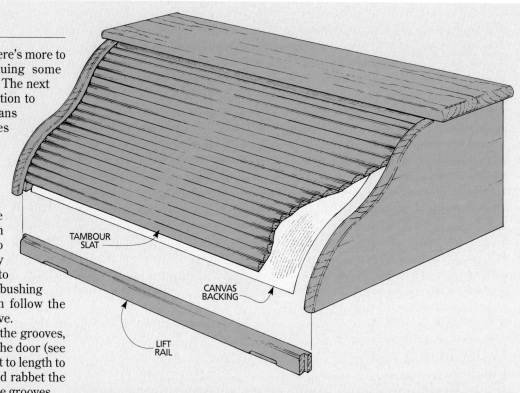

Okay, so now you know there's more to a tambour door than gluing some sticks to a piece of canvas. The next step is to put this information to use. For me this means starting on the case sides that hold the door.

TAMBOUR CASE. The first step is to cut the grooves in the sides that guide the door.

Since the grooves are mirror images of each other, the easiest way to keep them aligned is by making a template (refer to page 80). This way a guide bushing in a hand-held router can follow the template and rout the groove.

LIFT RAIL. After routing the grooves, the lift rail can be built for the door (see drawing at right). Just cut it to length to fit between the grooves and rabbet the ends so it slides easily in the grooves.

SLATS. Next I turn my attention to the tambour slats. The safest and most accurate way to make these is to start with a wide piece of stock and cut several slats off it like strips of bacon.

To do this, first rout the profile on one edge *(Figs. 4 and 4a)*. Then switch to the table saw to rip a slat from the edge of the board.

Here I use a carrier board with a notch cut at one end that matches the thickness of the slat *(Figs. 5 and 5a)*. As the slat is cut from the blank, the carrier pushes it safely past the blade.

TAMBOUR SLAT

CANVAS BACKING

LIFT RAIL

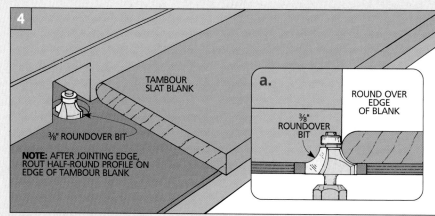

4

TAMBOUR SLAT BLANK

⅜" ROUNDOVER BIT

NOTE: AFTER JOINTING EDGE, ROUT HALF-ROUND PROFILE ON EDGE OF TAMBOUR BLANK

a.

ROUND OVER EDGE OF BLANK

⅜" ROUNDOVER BIT

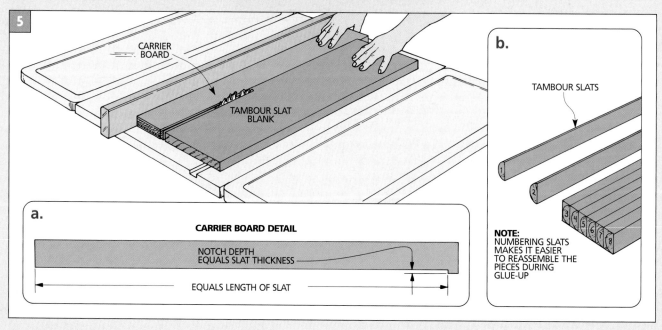

5

CARRIER BOARD

TAMBOUR SLAT BLANK

a.

CARRIER BOARD DETAIL

NOTCH DEPTH EQUALS SLAT THICKNESS

EQUALS LENGTH OF SLAT

b.

TAMBOUR SLATS

NOTE: NUMBERING SLATS MAKES IT EASIER TO REASSEMBLE THE PIECES DURING GLUE-UP

I also like to number the slats as they're cut *(Fig. 5b)*. That way they can be reassembled for the best color and appearance. And while you're set up, make some extras. It seems there are always a few slats that will twist or bow.

GLUE-UP

To hold all of the slats and the lift rail together, they're glued to a piece of canvas. Trim the canvas so it's narrower than the slats. This keeps the canvas out of the grooves. But allow some extra length to help you keep the fabric taut as you mount slats.

I use a couple of coats of contact adhesive to glue the slats to the canvas. A small roller spreads the adhesive quickly. This is easy on a big piece of canvas. But it can be tedious on the narrow slats. So I temporarily assemble a few slats by taping the ends *(Fig. 6)*.

Taping the slats together serves two purposes. First, it gives you a large surface to work on. And once you remove it, the ends are free of glue so the slats will slide freely in the grooves.

ASSEMBLY JIG. Now the challenge is

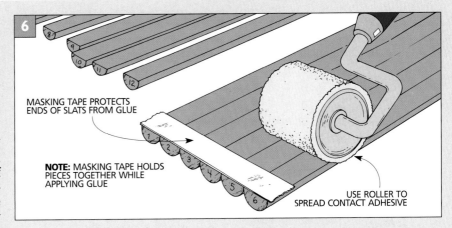

MASKING TAPE PROTECTS ENDS OF SLATS FROM GLUE

NOTE: MASKING TAPE HOLDS PIECES TOGETHER WHILE APPLYING GLUE

USE ROLLER TO SPREAD CONTACT ADHESIVE

getting the slats and lift rail installed on the canvas so they're square to each other. Here's where an assembly jig helps *(Figs. 7, 8* and the photo on page 87)*. This jig is just a couple of pieces of scrap screwed to a piece of plywood at a right angle to one another. These guide boards keep the door pieces straight at the sides and parallel to each other.

I stretch out the canvas first (adhesive side up) so it's flat and tight. Just screw a guide board at one end to hold the canvas in place, stretch it out, and secure the other end with a piece of

scrap. Then using a framing square, install the other guide board square to the first one.

Now the lift rail and slats can be installed on the canvas. Just remember, when they make contact, you won't be able to move them. It's also a good idea to check periodically that the slats are running true *(Fig. 8)*.

After the slats are all in place, tap them with a mallet to remove any air gaps under the slats. Finally, to complete the door, trim off the excess canvas at the ends.

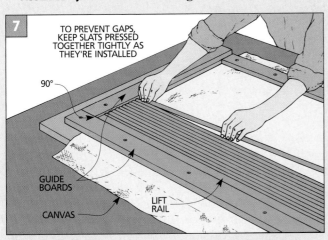

TO PREVENT GAPS, KEEP SLATS PRESSED TOGETHER TIGHTLY AS THEY'RE INSTALLED

90°

GUIDE BOARDS

CANVAS

LIFT RAIL

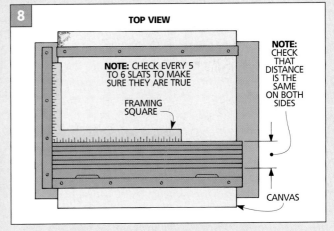

TOP VIEW

NOTE: CHECK EVERY 5 TO 6 SLATS TO MAKE SURE THEY ARE TRUE

FRAMING SQUARE

NOTE: CHECK THAT DISTANCE IS THE SAME ON BOTH SIDES

CANVAS

TROUBLESHOOTING TAMBOUR MOVEMENT

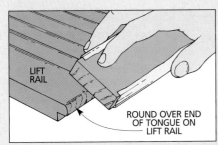

LIFT RAIL

ROUND OVER END OF TONGUE ON LIFT RAIL

LIFT RAIL. *When a tambour won't slide freely, check the lift rail. Sharp corners can hang up in the groove. Use a sanding block to round the corners.*

FILE OR SAND ENDS OF SLATS TO SMOOTH ROUGH SPOTS

SLATS. *The slats can also get hung up. Here again, round over the ends. But because the groove is shallow, keep the radius small so it's not exposed.*

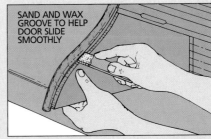

SAND AND WAX GROOVE TO HELP DOOR SLIDE SMOOTHLY

SAND AND WAX. *It's always a good idea to sand the groove lightly to remove any chatter marks left by the router. Then apply paste wax so door will slide freely.*

CHAIRS

Chairs can be intimidating for a woodworker. They feature some fairly uncommon techniques that can stretch your abilities. But it's a rewarding experience to stand back and admire a well-designed, well-built chair like the ones offered here.

Starting with a contemporary ladder-back oak chair, you'll have a chance to use templates to cut curved parts and to work with upholstery. A set of these chairs matches the dining table in this book. You can also choose a more formal style made of mahogany, walnut, or cherry.

For a little relaxation in the living room, try the traditional oak rocking chair. Finished to look like an antique, this inviting chair should last for generations.

If you'd like a longer, bench-style seat instead of a one-person chair, we're featuring a classic bench in the Shaker style, but built using modern tools and techniques. And to give you one more option, a few simple changes can turn the bench into a striking-looking chair.

Ladder-Back Chair

The curved shape of the back of this chair provides support and comfort. The curved slats and legs are easy when you use a template with a band saw and table-mounted router.

Building chairs: just the thought of it brings out a certain uneasiness in many woodworkers. Okay, I'll admit this chair isn't the easiest project I've ever built. But it isn't the most difficult either.

At first, the curved back leg and back slats may seem a little intimidating. But they're fairly easy to cut by using a template to rough out the shape on a band saw. Then you can use the same template to smooth them on a router table.

JOINERY. I found the process of building the chairs to be more time-consuming than it was difficult. It took me about 100 hours to complete a set of six chairs. There are 22 mortise and tenon joints on each chair.

It may appear as though you have to cut angled tenons on the back slats (see the Exploded View on the opposite page). That's not the case. All of the tenons are cut straight, on square stock. Then, after the tenons are cut, the stock is cut on a curve with the band saw.

DESIGN. The thing I like most about this chair is sitting in it. The curved back fits a body's shape nicely. And it's a comfortable angle — straight enough for eating, yet comfortable for sitting.

WOOD. The chairs are simple and contemporary. Using oak enhances the contemporary feel (and they'll match the Dining Table on page 38).

However, using mahogany or walnut gives the chairs a more formal, traditional appearance. (For a similar, but more formal chair, see the Designer's Notebook beginning on page 100.)

UPHOLSTERY. Woodworking is not the only challenge when building a chair. You also have to upholster the seat (see page 99 to do this without bunching at the corners).

FINISH. To provide a durable finish, I applied two coats of satin polyurethane to each chair, sanding lightly between coats with 220-grit sandpaper.

MATERIALS LIST

WOOD

A	Back Legs (2)	$1\frac{1}{16}$ x 4 - 39 rough
B	Front Legs (2)	$1\frac{3}{8}$ x $1\frac{3}{8}$ - $17\frac{3}{8}$
C	Seat Side Rails (2)	$\frac{5}{8}$ x 2 - $14\frac{1}{2}$
D	Lwr. Side Rails (2)	$\frac{5}{8}$ x 1 - $14\frac{1}{2}$
E	Back Seat Rail (1)	$\frac{5}{8}$ x 2 - $16\frac{1}{2}$
F	Front Seat Rail (1)	$\frac{5}{8}$ x 2 - $15\frac{15}{16}$
G	Back Slats (5)	$1\frac{1}{2}$ x $1\frac{3}{4}$ - $16\frac{1}{2}$

H	Back Cleat (1)	$\frac{3}{4}$ x 1 - 15
I	Seat (1)	$\frac{3}{4}$ ply - $15\frac{1}{4}$ x $15\frac{1}{4}$

HARDWARE SUPPLIES

(4) No. 8 x $1\frac{1}{2}$" Fh woodscrews
(1) 2" x $17\frac{1}{4}$" x $17\frac{1}{4}$" foam
(1 piece) 24" x 24" fabric
(20) $\frac{3}{8}$" staples

CUTTING DIAGRAM

$1\frac{1}{16}$ x $6\frac{1}{4}$ - 39 (2.1 Bd. Ft.)

$1\frac{3}{4}$ x $5\frac{1}{2}$ - 50 (3.8 Bd. Ft.)

$\frac{3}{4}$ x $2\frac{1}{4}$ - 33 (.5 Bd. Ft.)

ALSO NEED 24" x 24" PIECE
OF $\frac{3}{4}$" PLYWOOD FOR SEAT

EXPLODED VIEW

OVERALL DIMENSIONS:
$17\frac{3}{16}$W x $18\frac{3}{4}$D x 38H

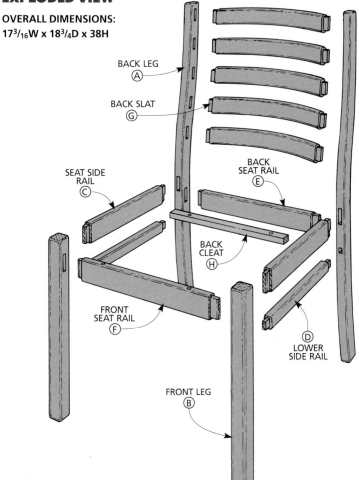

BACK LEG
Ⓐ

BACK SLAT
Ⓖ

SEAT SIDE
RAIL
Ⓒ

BACK
SEAT RAIL
Ⓔ

BACK
CLEAT
Ⓗ

FRONT
SEAT RAIL
Ⓕ

LOWER
SIDE RAIL
Ⓓ

FRONT LEG
Ⓑ

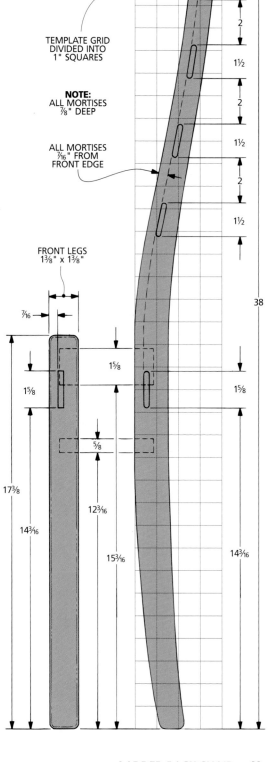

TEMPLATE GRID
DIVIDED INTO
1" SQUARES

NOTE:
ALL MORTISES
$\frac{7}{8}$" DEEP

ALL MORTISES
$\frac{7}{16}$" FROM
FRONT EDGE

FRONT LEGS
$1\frac{3}{8}$" x $1\frac{3}{8}$"

BACK LEGS

I began work on the chairs by making a back leg template. The template is used as a guide to cut both back legs to the same shape, and to lay out the mortises.

TEMPLATE. To make the template, I laid out the shape of the leg on a 4" x 38" piece of $1/4$" hardboard. (Follow the grid drawing on page 93.)

Also lay out the mortises for the back slats and back seat rail *(Fig. 1).*

After the mortises were laid out, I cut the template a little oversize on the band saw *(Fig. 2).* Then I carefully filed and sanded down to the line.

MORTISES. Since the template is used as a guide for the mortises, I drilled out the mortises on the template. To keep the mortises a consistent distance from the front edge of the template, I used a special jig *(Fig. 3).*

To make this jig, drill a $3/8$" hole in a piece of plywood and insert a short length of $3/8$"-dia. dowel. Then mark a reference line on the plywood straight out from the center of the dowel.

Now position the plywood on the drill press table so the dowel is $7/16$" behind the bit and the center of the bit is aligned with the reference line *(Fig. 3a).* Once everything is in place, clamp the plywood to the drill press table.

Now the mortises can be roughed out on the drill press. As each hole is drilled, keep the front edge of the template against the dowel stop pin, and the back edge 90° to the reference line on the plywood base *(Figs. 3 and 3a).*

CUT OUT LEG. When the template is completed, you can begin work on the back legs (A). I was able to get two back legs out of one $1^1/16$"-thick blank that measured $6^1/4$" by 39" (see the Cutting Diagram on page 93).

Start by fastening the template to the blank with double-sided carpet tape.

Then roughly cut out the first leg about $1/4$" oversize *(Fig. 4).*

Next, I cut out the leg exactly $1/16$" oversize by using a guide block on the band saw. Then it's cut to final size with a flush trim bit on a router table. (For a detailed explanation of these steps, see the article on page 98.)

MARK MORTISES. Before removing the template, draw through the mortises in the template to mark the mortises on the leg *(Fig. 5).*

MIRRORED SET. To make one chair, you need a mirrored set of back legs. Since both legs are the same shape, you can use the same template — but the mortises have to be cut into opposite faces. To do this, I stuck the template on the back side of the blank. Then cut out the second leg following the same procedure as the first leg.

MORTISES. After both legs are cut out and the mortises outlined, you can drill them out using the same stop jig and procedure used on the template. The only difference is these mortises are $7/8$" deep *(Fig. 6).*

These mortises will be slightly curved because they follow the curve of the leg (sort of a cooked hot dog shape). To get the tenon to fit, use a chisel to square the front edge of the

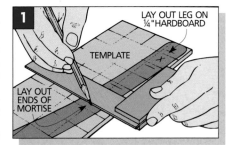

1

LAY OUT LEG ON $1/4$" HARDBOARD

TEMPLATE

LAY OUT ENDS OF MORTISE

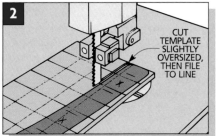

2

CUT TEMPLATE SLIGHTLY OVERSIZED, THEN FILE TO LINE

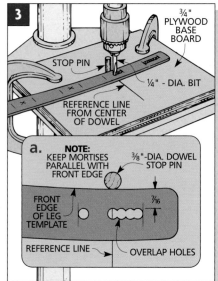

3

$3/4$" PLYWOOD BASE BOARD

STOP PIN

$1/4$" - DIA. BIT

REFERENCE LINE FROM CENTER OF DOWEL

a. NOTE: KEEP MORTISES PARALLEL WITH FRONT EDGE

$3/8$"-DIA. DOWEL STOP PIN

FRONT EDGE OF LEG TEMPLATE

$7/16$

REFERENCE LINE

OVERLAP HOLES

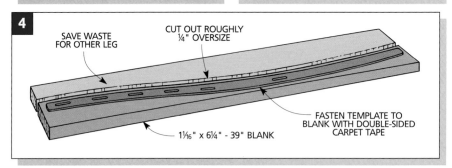

4

SAVE WASTE FOR OTHER LEG

CUT OUT ROUGHLY $1/4$" OVERSIZE

FASTEN TEMPLATE TO BLANK WITH DOUBLE-SIDED CARPET TAPE

$1^1/16$" x $6^1/4$" - 39" BLANK

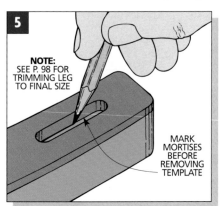

5

NOTE: SEE P. 98 FOR TRIMMING LEG TO FINAL SIZE

MARK MORTISES BEFORE REMOVING TEMPLATE

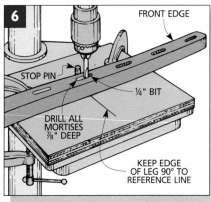

6

FRONT EDGE

STOP PIN

$1/4$" BIT

DRILL ALL MORTISES $7/8$" DEEP

KEEP EDGE OF LEG 90° TO REFERENCE LINE

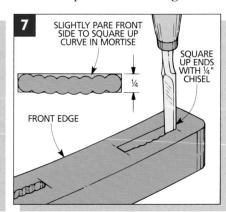

7

SLIGHTLY PARE FRONT SIDE TO SQUARE UP CURVE IN MORTISE

$1/4$

SQUARE UP ENDS WITH $1/4$" CHISEL

FRONT EDGE

mortise to a straight line. Also square up the ends of the mortise *(Fig. 7)*.

After drilling out five mortises for the slats and one for the back rail, you can begin laying out the mortises on the front edge of each back leg. These mortises will hold the seat side rail (C) and lower side rail (D).

MORTISE LAYOUT. The trick is to lay out the mortises so they will be at the exact same locations on both of the legs. Begin by laying one leg down on its side at the end of a bench *(Fig. 8)*. Then lay down a framing square so one arm of the square is flush with the end of the bench (and the bottom of the leg) and the other arm rests against the flat section on the front of the leg.

Now measure up $12^3/_{16}$" and $15^3/_{16}$" from the end of the framing square to mark the bottoms of the mortises. The lower mortise is $5/_8$" long and the upper one $1^5/_8$" long.

DRILL OUT MORTISES. To drill out these mortises, start by clamping a straight piece of 2x4 to the drill press table as a fence *(Fig. 9)*. Position the fence so the $1/_4$" bit is centered on the thickness of the leg.

Since the back of the leg is curved, there isn't a long enough flat spot on it to allow the leg to sit down flat on the drill press table. I solved this problem by putting a 5"-long scrap block under

the mortise locations to raise the leg up off the drill press table *(Fig. 9)*. (Stick the block to the leg with double-sided carpet tape.)

Now, drill $7/_8$"-deep mortises, moving the spacer block along with the leg as you drill. Complete the mortises by squaring up the ends with a chisel.

ROUND OVER EDGES. When all the mortises are cut in the back leg, the only step left is to round over the leg's edges and ends with a $1/_4$" roundover bit set $3/_{16}$" high in the router table *(Fig. 10)*.

FRONT LEGS

At this point, the back legs are complete. Now you can begin work on the front legs (B). It's critical that the mortises in the front legs align with those in the back legs.

CUT OUT LEGS. Start making the front legs by cutting out two blocks $1^3/_8$" square by $17^3/_8$" long.

MORTISE LAYOUT. Once the blocks are cut to size, lay out two $1/_4$"-wide mortises on the back face of each leg to join to the side rails (C, D) *(Fig. 11)*. These mortises are located the same distances ($12^3/_{16}$" and $15^3/_{16}$") from the bottom end of the front leg (B) as the two mortises on the back leg (A).

Note that the mortises are not centered on the thickness, but are $7/_{16}$" from

the outside edge of each leg. (Here's where you have to start thinking of the two front legs as a mirrored set.)

After the mortises are laid out on the back face of each leg, lay out a $1^5/_8$"-long mortise on the inside face of each leg to join to the front seat rail *(Fig. 11)*. Locate these mortises $14^3/_{16}$" up from the bottom ends of the legs, $7/_{16}$" from the outside edge (refer to page 93). And be sure they face each other. (Again, you want to end up with a mirrored set of legs.)

CUT MORTISES. Now you can drill out all the $7/_8$"-deep mortises on the drill press. (As before, clamp a fence to the top of the drill press table.)

When you drill out the mortises on adjacent sides, the bottoms will break through very slightly into each other *(Fig. 11)*. That's okay, the tenons will be cut back later where they meet.

ROUND EDGES. After squaring up the mortises with a chisel, I rounded over the edges and ends of the front legs on the router table. First, round over the two edges nearest the mortises with a $1/_4$" roundover bit set $3/_{16}$" high *(Steps 1 and 2 in Fig. 12)*.

Then raise the bit to rout full $1/_4$" roundovers on the inside edge *(Step 3)* and both top and bottom ends. Finally, switch to a $1/_2$" roundover bit and rout the outside edge *(Step 4)*.

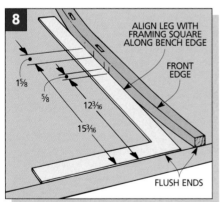

8 ALIGN LEG WITH FRAMING SQUARE ALONG BENCH EDGE
FRONT EDGE
$1^5/_8$
$5/_8$
$12^3/_{16}$
$15^3/_{16}$
FLUSH ENDS

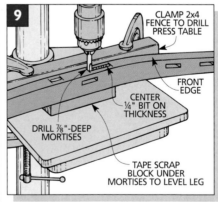

9 CLAMP 2x4 FENCE TO DRILL PRESS TABLE
FRONT EDGE
CENTER $1/_4$" BIT ON THICKNESS
DRILL $7/_8$"-DEEP MORTISES
TAPE SCRAP BLOCK UNDER MORTISES TO LEVEL LEG

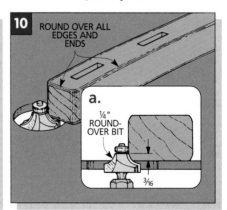

10 ROUND OVER ALL EDGES AND ENDS
a.
$1/_4$" ROUND-OVER BIT
$3/_{16}$

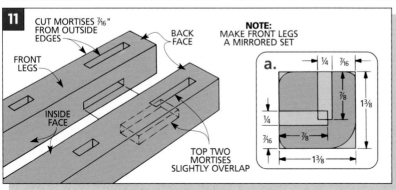

11 CUT MORTISES $7/_{16}$" FROM OUTSIDE EDGES
BACK FACE
FRONT LEGS
INSIDE FACE
TOP TWO MORTISES SLIGHTLY OVERLAP
NOTE: MAKE FRONT LEGS A MIRRORED SET
a.
$1/_4$ | $7/_{16}$
$7/_8$
$1^3/_8$
$1/_4$
$7/_{16}$
$7/_8$
$1^3/_8$

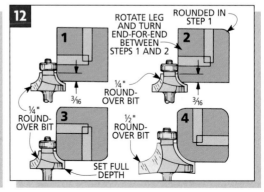

12 ROTATE LEG AND TURN END-FOR-END BETWEEN STEPS 1 AND 2
ROUNDED IN STEP 1
1
2
$1/_4$" ROUND-OVER BIT
$3/_{16}$
$3/_{16}$
$1/_4$" ROUND-OVER BIT
3
$1/_4$" ROUND-OVER BIT
$1/_2$" ROUND-OVER BIT
4
SET FULL DEPTH

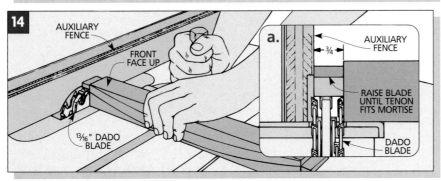

13 BACK SLAT (CUT FIVE PIECES) G — CUT DEEP RABBET ON BACK FACE

15

16½

CUT ⅛" RABBETS ON FRONT FACE, TOP, AND BOTTOM

¼   ⅛   ¾

1¾   1½

1½

END VIEW   FRONT VIEW

After the legs are complete, you can begin working on the back slats (G).

CUT TO SIZE. Start by cutting five blanks of 1¾"-thick stock to a width of 1½" and length of 16½" *(Fig. 13)*.

CUT TENONS. It's easiest to cut the ¾"-long offset tenons on the ends of the back slats *before* cutting the slats to shape. To do this, first raise a ¹³⁄₁₆" dado blade ⅛" high and cut rabbets on the ends of the blank.

Note: I "buried" the dado blade ¹⁄₁₆" into an auxiliary fence *(Fig. 14a)*.

Cut rabbets on the front face and top and bottom (not the back) of the blank.

To complete the offset tenon, I cut a deeper rabbet into the back face of the block. Since it's a heavy cut, make it in a series of passes sneaking up on the finished height *(Fig. 14)*. Check the fit of the tenon in one of the mortises cut in the back legs as you work.

MAKE A TEMPLATE. After all the tenons are cut to fit the mortises, you can cut the back slats to shape. I started by making a curved template out of a 3" x 15" blank of ¼" hardboard (see the Shop Tip below).

CUT ARC ON BLANK. After the arc on the template has been filed smooth, attach the template to the top of the slat blank with double-sided carpet tape. Be sure to face the arc on the template to the front of the blank. (That's the face nearest the tenon that's offset by ⅛".)

Now, cut out the curved front face of the slat ¹⁄₁₆" from the template *(Fig. 15)*. (Use the same technique used to cut out the back legs.) Then mark the front of the template on the blank and remove the template.

To remove the last ¹⁄₁₆", I used a rasp and a drum sander *(Fig. 16)*.

14 AUXILIARY FENCE
FRONT FACE UP
¹³⁄₁₆" DADO BLADE

a. AUXILIARY FENCE
¾
RAISE BLADE UNTIL TENON FITS MORTISE
DADO BLADE

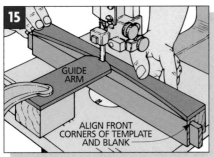

15 GUIDE ARM
ALIGN FRONT CORNERS OF TEMPLATE AND BLANK

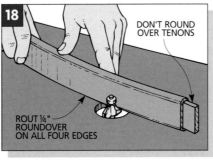

16 FILE FRONT FACE UP TO LINE WITH RASP AND DRUM SANDER

17 SET POINTED BLOCK ⁹⁄₁₆" FROM BLADE

18 DON'T ROUND OVER TENONS
ROUT ¼" ROUNDOVER ON ALL FOUR EDGES

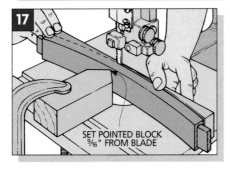

SHOP TIP . . . . *Drawing An Arc*

To make the curved hardboard template for the back slats, I needed a simple way to draw an arc accurately (it's a 36"-radius arc).

To strike this radius, I made a trammel from a strip of hardboard (see drawing at right).

BACK SLAT TEMPLATE
CENTERLINE
FASTEN TEMPLATE TO BENCH WITH CARPET TAPE
15
¼" HARDBOARD TRAMMEL
36
1½
90°
SQUARE TEMPLATE TO CENTERLINE
LOCATE PIVOT NAIL STRAIGHT DOWN FROM CENTER OF TEMPLATE

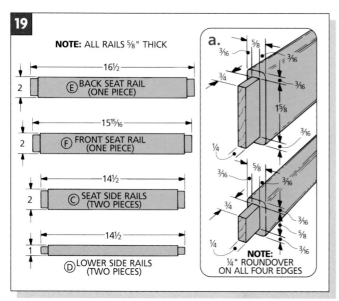

NOTE: ALL RAILS ⅝" THICK

19

16½"

2 | (E) BACK SEAT RAIL (ONE PIECE)

15¹⁵⁄₁₆"

2 | (F) FRONT SEAT RAIL (ONE PIECE)

14½"

2 | (C) SEAT SIDE RAILS (TWO PIECES)

14½"

1 | (D) LOWER SIDE RAILS (TWO PIECES)

a.
3/16 5/8 3/16
3/4 3/16
1⁵⁄₈
3/16
1/4 5/8
3/16 3/16
3/4
1/4 5/8 3/16
3/16
NOTE: ¼" ROUNDOVER ON ALL FOUR EDGES

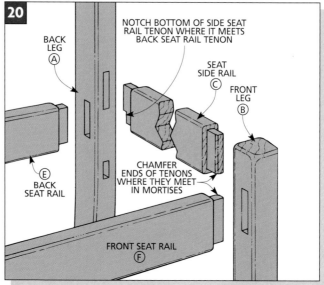

20

NOTCH BOTTOM OF SIDE SEAT RAIL TENON WHERE IT MEETS BACK SEAT RAIL TENON

BACK LEG (A)

SEAT SIDE RAIL (C)

FRONT LEG (B)

BACK SEAT RAIL (E)

CHAMFER ENDS OF TENONS WHERE THEY MEET IN MORTISES

FRONT SEAT RAIL (F)

CUT BACK FACE. To form the back face, make a guide block with a pointed end and clamp the guide so the point is ⁹⁄₁₆" away from the blade *(Fig. 17)*. Cut the back slat to shape by running it between the pointed block and the blade, and file (or plane) the back edge smooth so it ends up about ½" thick.

ROUND OVER EDGES. The last step is to round over the four edges with a ¼" roundover bit *(Fig. 18)*.

SEAT RAILS

Next, you can make the seat rails and side rails. I started by resawing enough wood for the four seat rails and two lower side rails to ⅝" thick.

CUT TO SIZE. Now, cut all of the seat rails 2" wide and the lower side rails 1" wide *(Fig. 19)*. As for length, the seat side rails (C) and the lower side rails (D) are both cut 14½" long.

The back seat rail (E) is cut the same length as the back slats (16½"). Since the front legs are thicker than the back legs, the front seat rail (F) is ⁹⁄₁₆" shorter (15¹⁵⁄₁₆").

CUT TENONS. After all of the pieces are cut to length, cut ¾"-long tenons centered on the ends of all the rails *(Fig. 19a)*. Cut the tenons to thickness and width to fit the mortises in the legs.

ROUND OVER EDGES. Next, round over all four edges of each rail (but not the tenons) with a ¼" roundover bit on the router table (refer to *Fig. 18*).

NOTCH AND CHAMFER. There are a couple more things that have to be done before assembly. When the rails are mounted into the legs, the tenons of the

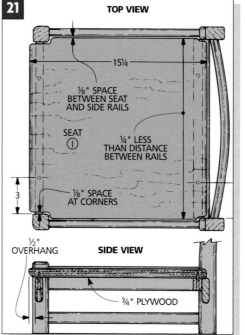

21

TOP VIEW

15¼"

⅛" SPACE BETWEEN SEAT AND SIDE RAILS

SEAT (I)

¼" LESS THAN DISTANCE BETWEEN RAILS

3

⅛" SPACE AT CORNERS

½" OVERHANG

SIDE VIEW

¾" PLYWOOD

seat side rails (C) will run into the back and front seat rails (E, F) *(Fig. 20)*.

To solve this problem at the back, I notched the bottoms of the tenons on the seat side rails. Since the overlap at the front is slight, you only need to chamfer the tenons of the side and front seat rails.

ASSEMBLY & SEAT

I started assembling the chair by gluing and clamping each side independently. Connect the front and back legs with the side rails, checking for square.

After these units are dry, glue the front/back rails and the slats between the side units to complete the chair.

22

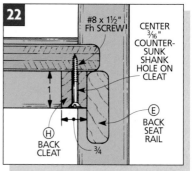

#8 x 1½" Fh SCREW

CENTER ³⁄₁₆" COUNTER-SUNK SHANK HOLE ON CLEAT

1

(H) BACK CLEAT

¾"

(E) BACK SEAT RAIL

23

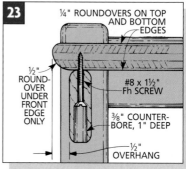

¼" ROUNDOVERS ON TOP AND BOTTOM EDGES

½" ROUND-OVER UNDER FRONT EDGE ONLY

#8 x 1½" Fh SCREW

⅜" COUNTER-BORE, 1" DEEP

½" OVERHANG

Note: I used the flattest surface in my shop (the table saw) for assembly.

CLEAT. The seat is mounted to a back cleat (H) that's glued to the front of the back seat rail (E) *(Fig. 22)*. To attach the seat, drill screw holes through the back cleat and the front seat rail (F).

SEAT. The last piece to make is the ¾" plywood seat (I) *(Fig. 21)*. It's cut to overhang ½" on the front, but leave ⅛" space between the sides and corners of the seat for the upholstery.

Before upholstering the seat, rout ¼" roundovers on the top and bottom edges and a ½" roundover under the front edge *(Fig. 23)*. After finishing the chair, screw the upholstered seat in place. ■

The trick to making uniform curved-back legs for the chairs is to use a template. The template makes cutting out the pieces a simple two-step operation on a band saw and router table — a process that produces all the pieces you want with the exact same shape.

TEMPLATE. You can use either $1/4"$ hardboard or plywood to make the template. The important thing is that the edge of the material doesn't have any knots or voids in it.

LAY OUT PATTERN. Start by laying out the pattern of the chair leg right on the template material (see grid drawing on page 93). Or you can cut a full-size pattern out of paper and glue it to the hardboard or plywood. Then cut out the shape (slightly oversize), and file up to the line.

Note: Any gouges on the edge of the template will show up later on the finished pieces, so it's important to take the time to work the edges smooth.

It's not critical your template is exactly the same as the pattern. If the curve is slightly different, that's okay. All your legs will be identical — they will match your template.

CUTTING TO SHAPE. After the template is made, attach it to the leg blank with double-sided carpet tape. Then,

roughly saw the leg out of the blank so it's about $1/4"$ larger than the template.

Next, cut the shape again, but this time carefully so it's $1/16"$ oversize. (Since the next step is to rout the leg to exact size, there's less chipout when only routing off $1/16"$.) Although you can make this cut freehand, I clamped a "guide arm" to the band saw to make a more precise cut *(Fig. 1).*

The arm is made from a piece of $1/4"$ hardboard glued to the top of a $1\frac{1}{8}"$-thick block. The arm is mounted to the

block so it's raised up high enough to rub against the template, not the rough edge of the workpiece.

The trick to this arm is to round the end, and then cut a notch for your blade to fit in. (I cut a $3/8"$ notch for the $1/4"$ band saw blade I used.) Now clamp the guide arm to the table so the blade is $1/16"$ from the outside edge of the curved end *(Fig. 1a).*

To cut out the leg, push the blank so the template rubs against the guide arm *(Fig. 2).* As you're cutting, move the tail end of the blank right or left to keep the template parallel to the blade.

ROUTING TO FINAL SHAPE. Now you can rout off the last $1/16"$ with a flush trim bit on the router table.

With the template still taped to the workpiece, raise the bit up until the bearing rides on the template *(Step 1 in Fig. 4).* Then to cut the leg the exact shape of the template, rout in a clockwise direction around the bit *(Fig. 3).*

Note: Since the bit I used only has a 1"-long cutting edge and the leg is $1\frac{1}{16}"$ thick, I had to lower the bit to make a second cut *(Step 2 in Fig. 4).* Also, you have to use a $1/4"$-shank flush trim bit when routing a piece this thick. The shank of a $1/2"$-shank bit would rub against the workpiece on the first cut.

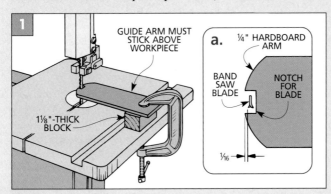

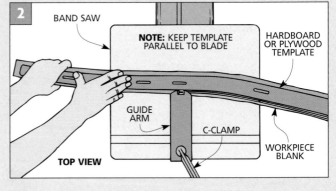

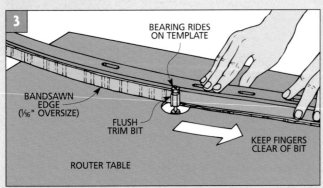

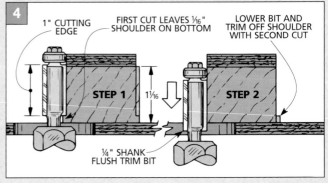

The simple truth is, I know very little about fabric and foam. So when it came time to upholster the ladder-back chairs, I went to a local upholstery supplier for information and materials. As usual, there was more to learn than I thought there would be.

The foam I used on the chairs is not foam rubber. Foam rubber is latex rubber, which is made from the sap of the rubber tree. The foam I used on the chairs is polyurethane foam, which is a synthetic product.

There are three different densities of polyurethane foam: low, medium, and high. The difference among them is the higher the density, the less likely you are to "bottom out" when you sit on it and the longer it will last.

The fabric I used on the seats of the chairs also has some special features. First, the back of the fabric has a special surface coating on it. This surface coating will help keep the weave of the fabric from becoming distorted when it's stretched tight.

Second, I wanted a fabric that would stand up well to everyday use but would look appropriate in a dining room. The fabric I used is a nylon/polyester blend. The thread size is fairly large and the weave of the fabric is rather loose, which gives the seat a soft texture and allows the air to escape from the foam when you sit down.

To get professional quality results, I suggest you go to an upholstery shop or a fabric store and ask for materials that are intended specifically for upholstery.

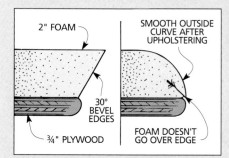

1 Before upholstering plywood, round over edges with a ¼" roundover and front bottom edge with a ½" roundover. Then file point off bottom front corner.

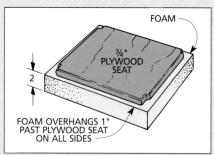

2 Cut 2"-thick foam 2" wider and longer than the plywood seat. This leaves a 1" overhang on each side. You can cut the foam easily on the band saw.

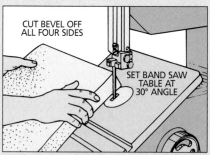

3 Next, tilt the band saw table to 30° and bevel each edge of the foam. Start the bevel right on the extreme outside edge of the foam.

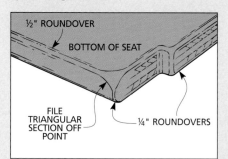

4 Foam is placed on top of the seat with the bevel facing down. Undercutting the foam allows it to be pulled down to a smooth outside curve.

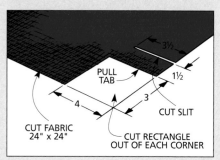

5 Cut a piece of fabric to a 24" x 24" square. To keep the fabric from bunching up in the corner, cut a rectangle from each corner, then slit a pull tab.

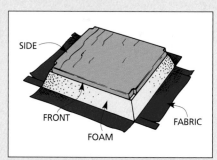

6 Center the foam and the plywood on the back side of the fabric. Align sides of the plywood seat with the sides of the fabric that have the 3½" slits.

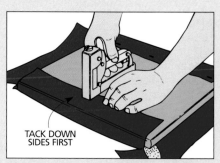

7 Beginning with the sides, push down on plywood and pull fabric up and over the plywood. Use a staple gun to tack the fabric in place every 2" or 3".

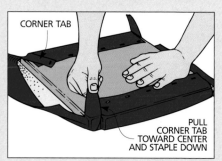

8 Now pull corner tabs in toward the center of the plywood. Lap corner tabs over the stapled-down fabric, so the fold is in the notch. Staple tab down.

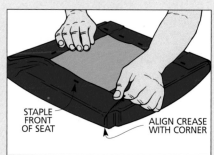

9 With the tabs stapled down, stretch the remaining fabric around the front and back of the plywood. Staple down the fabric to form a crease at the corner.

DESIGNER'S NOTEBOOK

Built from mahogany, this Formal Dining Chair could be used with a desk or as part of a formal dining set. But even though its look is different, it's built using the same techniques as the Ladder-Back Chair.

CONSTRUCTION NOTES:

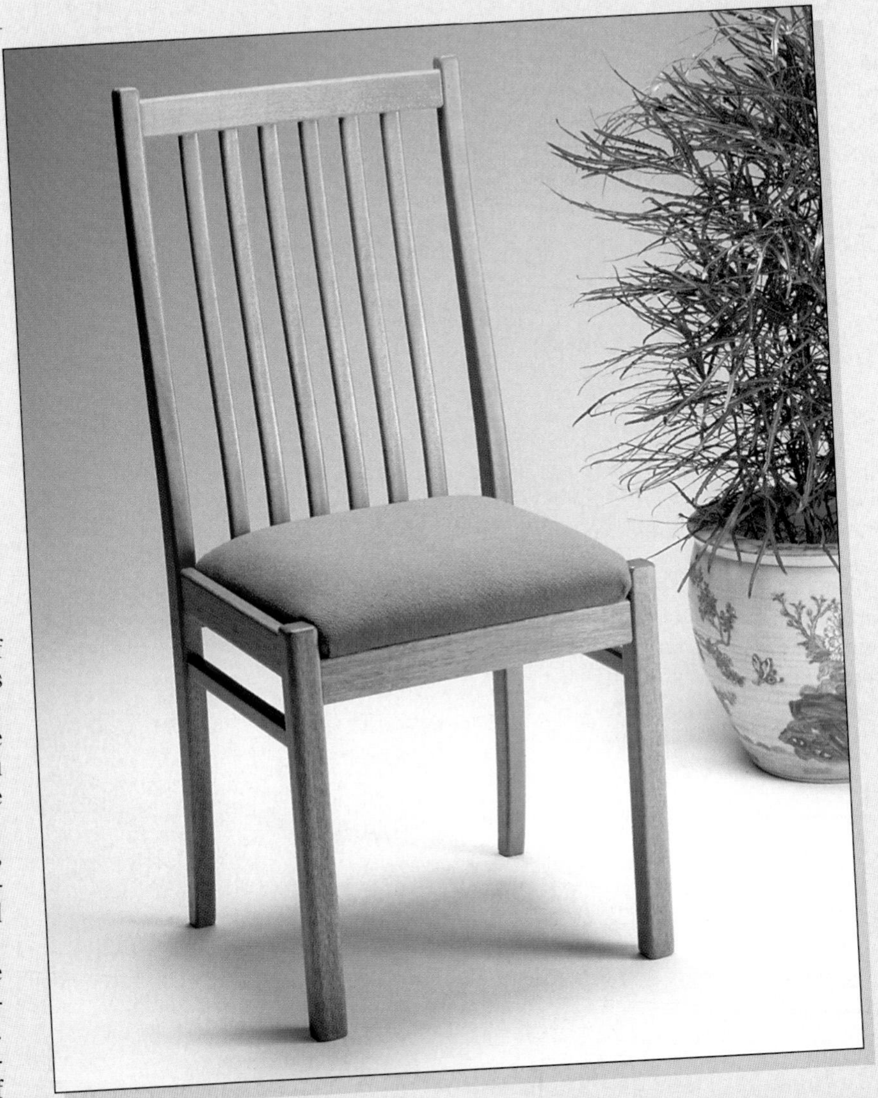

■ Making a slight change to the design of the chair changes its whole "look." What I did was use vertical back slats instead of the horizontal "ladder-back" slats. At the same time, I made the slats narrower, and therefore a little more elegant.

■ A more formal design called for a more formal wood. So this time I built the chairs from Honduras mahogany. It has a light reddish color when first cut, but over time it takes on a beautiful deep reddish-brown patina. It is a medium-textured wood with fairly straight, consistent grain. Straight-grained walnut or cherry would also be a good choice for this formal chair.

■ The steps to building this chair are almost identical to the ladder-back chair — until it's time to work on the back slats. I started by following all of the same steps for making the legs as on the Ladder-Back Chair (pages 94-95) with one exception. Since the slats are vertical rather than horizontal, you don't need four of the mortises (the middle four) on the back legs *(Fig. 1)*.

■ The top and bottom mortises, though, are still needed in exactly the same locations to hold the back top rail (G) and the back seat rail (E) in place.

■ All six back slats (H) are cut out of one blank of $1^{1}/_{16}$"-thick stock that measures $6^{1}/_{4}$" wide by $20^{3}/_{4}$" long *(Fig. 2)*. The trick is following the correct cutting sequence to get all six slats out of the blank so each slat ends up the exact same thickness and shape.

■ Since the six slats follow the same contour as the back legs, you can use the back leg template to set up the first cut on the slat blank.

■ Start by attaching the template along one edge of the blank with double-sided carpet tape so the top end of the template sticks out $1^{7}/_{8}$" beyond the end of the blank *(Fig. 2)*.

■ Next, I clamped the guide arm to the band saw to make the initial cut $^{1}/_{16}$" away from the template *(Fig. 3)*. (This is the same guide arm used to cut out the back legs. See page 98.)

■ Once the oversized cut was made along the front edge of the template, I switched to the router table to clean up the bandsawn edge. This is done with a flush trim bit mounted so the pilot bearing rides along the edge of the template *(Fig. 4* and page 98).

■ Now that you have established the front contour of the first slat, the trick is cutting the back face to the same shape so the slat will be a uniform thickness. To do this, make a guide block with a pointed end *(Fig. 5)*. Clamp this guide block to the band saw table so it's $^{9}/_{16}$" away from the blade. Now, you can cut the back edge of the slat by pushing the front (routed) edge against the guide block. The slat will end up a uniform $^{9}/_{16}$" thickness.

MATERIALS LIST

CHANGED PARTS

E	Back Seat Rail (1)	$^{3}/_{4}$ x 2 - $16^{1}/_{2}$
G	Back Top Rail (1)	$1^{1}/_{2}$ x $1^{3}/_{4}$ - $16^{1}/_{2}$
I	Seat (1)	$^{3}/_{4}$ ply - $14^{7}/_{8}$ x $15^{1}/_{4}$

NEW PARTS

J	Vert. Back Slats (6)	$^{1}/_{2}$ x $1^{1}/_{16}$ - $20^{3}/_{4}$

HARDWARE SUPPLIES

(1) 2" x $16^{7}/_{8}$" x $17^{1}/_{4}$" foam

■ To get another slat out of the blank, just repeat these steps. First, reattach the template so it's inside the cut edge of the blank and trim it flush on the router table *(Fig. 4)*.

■ Then remove the template and cut off another $^9/_{16}$"-thick slat *(Fig. 5)*. Continue this process until all six slats have been cut from the blank.

■ At this point, the slats should be fairly uniform in thickness, but the back faces will be rough from the band saw cuts. I smoothed the back faces with a sanding drum on the drill press *(Fig. 6)*.

■ To do this, clamp the guide block (with the pointed end) to the drill press table $^1/_2$" away from the outside of the sanding drum. Then feed the slats at a steady rate between the drum and the guide block.

■ The goal here is not only to remove the band saw marks, but also to be sure the slats are sanded to a uniform $^1/_2$" thickness (especially at the ends). Later, the ends fit into $^1/_2$" mortises. If the slats are too thick, they won't fit in, and if they're too thin, the fit will be loose and sloppy.

■ After all the slats have been sanded smooth, round over all four of their edges with a $^1/_4$" roundover bit on the router table *(Fig. 7)*.

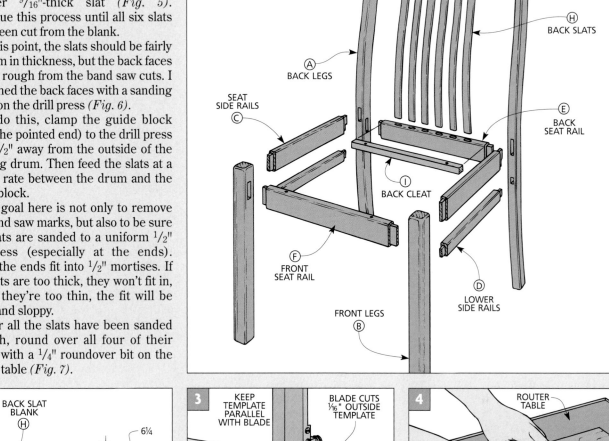

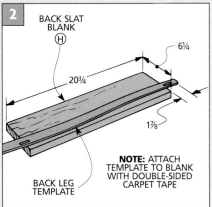

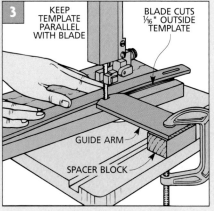

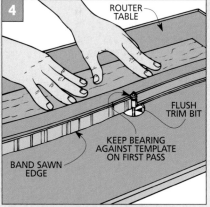

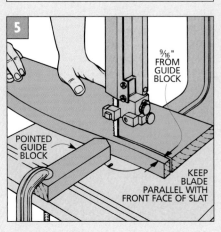

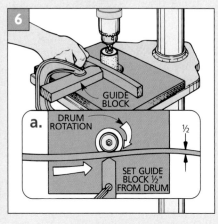

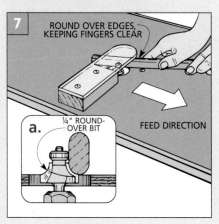

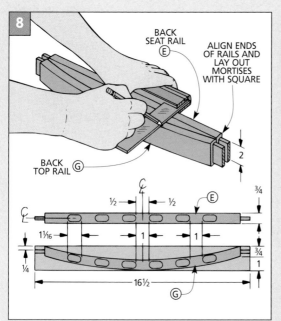

8

BACK SEAT RAIL (E)

ALIGN ENDS OF RAILS AND LAY OUT MORTISES WITH SQUARE

BACK TOP RAIL (G)

2

C

½ | ½

(E)

¾

1¹/₁₆

1 | 1

¾

¼

1

16½

(G)

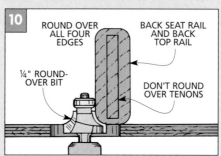

9

½" DRILL BIT

STOP PIN

DRILL MORTISES ⁷/₁₆" DEEP, CENTERED ON THICKNESS

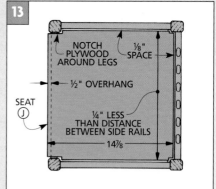

10

ROUND OVER ALL FOUR EDGES

BACK SEAT RAIL AND BACK TOP RAIL

¼" ROUND-OVER BIT

DON'T ROUND OVER TENONS

11

SHAPE ENDS OF BACK SLATS FOR GOOD FIT IN MORTISES

NOTE: DO NOT SQUARE UP ENDS OF MORTISES

■ The back slats are held between a top rail and a seat rail.

■ Start by cutting the back seat rail (E) from ³/₄" stock, 2" wide and 16¹/₂" long (*Fig. 8*). Then cut ³/₄"-long centered tenons on the ends of the rail.

■ The basic procedure for cutting the curved back top rail (G) is the same as the procedure used on the back slats on the Ladder-Back Chair (refer to page 96), but the back top rail for this chair is thicker. This means there are two changes to the procedure.

■ First, set the tenon back a little farther (¹/₄") from the front face (*Fig. 8*). Second, when cutting out the piece on the band saw, set the pointed block ¹³/₁₆" from the band saw blade. After filing, this will make the back top rail about ³/₄" thick.

■ After these two rails are cut, lay out 1¹/₁₆"-long mortises (with 1" between them) for the vertical slats. To do this, align the two rails and use a square to mark the mortises across from each other (*Fig. 8*).

■ Now drill out ⁷/₁₆"-deep mortises with a ¹/₂" bit on the drill press. Since the seat rail (E) is straight, clamp a straight-edge to the drill press table to keep the mortises centered on the workpiece. But on the curved top rail (G) you will have to run the workpiece against a stop pin (*Fig. 9*).

■ After the mortises are drilled (don't square them up), round over the edges of both rails with a ¹/₄" roundover bit (*Fig. 10*). Then fit the slats into the mortises. If they're too tight, you may have to shave the ends slightly (*Fig. 11*).

■ When all the back slats fit into the mortises, the chair can be assembled.

■ Start by gluing a front leg, side rails, and back leg to form a side unit. After assembling the other side unit, set both units aside to dry.

■ Next, dry-assemble the vertical back slats (H) into the back rails (G, E). The slats aren't glued in since there isn't anywhere they can go once the chair is assembled.

■ Now fit the back assembly and front seat rail (F) between the side units (*Fig. 12*). Then in order to keep the chair sitting flat, I placed the chair on top of my table saw.

■ After the chair is assembled, glue a back cleat (I) to the front face of the back seat rail (E) (*Fig. 14*). Position the cleat so it's located ¹/₄" down from the top edge of the back seat rail.

■ Since the plywood seat (J) on this formal chair has to fit inside the back slats, it's cut shorter (14⁷/₈") than on the ladder-back chair and rests on the cleat (*Figs. 13 and 14*).

■ After the chair is finished and the seat upholstered, the seat can be screwed down to the back cleat and front rail.

■ To finish the chairs, I hand-rubbed in four coats of tung oil and then buffed it to a soft shine with paste wax.

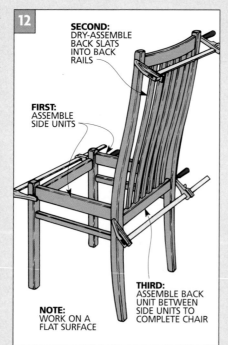

12

SECOND: DRY-ASSEMBLE BACK SLATS INTO BACK RAILS

FIRST: ASSEMBLE SIDE UNITS

THIRD: ASSEMBLE BACK UNIT BETWEEN SIDE UNITS TO COMPLETE CHAIR

NOTE: WORK ON A FLAT SURFACE

13

NOTCH PLYWOOD AROUND LEGS

¹/₈" SPACE

½" OVERHANG

SEAT (J)

¼" LESS THAN DISTANCE BETWEEN SIDE RAILS

14⁷/₈

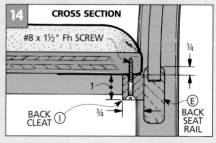

14

CROSS SECTION

#8 x 1½" Fh SCREW

¼

1

BACK CLEAT (I)

¾

(E) BACK SEAT RAIL

Rocking Chair

To rock smoothly, the curved rockers on this traditional oak chair have to be identical. The most efficient way to do this is to cut and sand one curved piece, then use it as a template to make the second.

urved parts. That's the one main aspect that makes building a rocking chair different from building an ordinary chair. And cutting curved parts efficiently and accurately can seem intimidating. But it doesn't have to be, as long as you follow a certain procedure.

EXACT DUPLICATES. The usual way of making curved pieces that are graceful and smooth is to start out with a grid pattern and then re-use that same grid pattern on all of the matching pieces of the project.

On this Rocking Chair, though, I did something a little different. Because there have to be exact duplicates of many of the curved parts, I didn't re-use the same patterns. It doesn't matter if the duplicate pieces aren't exactly like the original pattern. The only thing that matters is that they're exact duplicates of *each other*.

The secret to ensuring this is to concentrate on the first piece. After cutting it to rough shape, I sanded it until it had a consistently smooth curve. Then, to lay out the matching pieces, I used the first piece as the pattern, *not* the original grid pattern.

CUTTING ANGLED TENONS. There are also a couple pieces in this project that join with mortises and tenons at an angle. Now, cutting mortise and tenon joints that come together at right angles is one thing, but when they join at an angle, it makes it that much more challenging. To make cutting these pieces as easy as possible, I built a special jig for the router table. For more on this jig, see page 110.

WOOD AND FINISH. To give this Rocking Chair the authentic look of a Mission-style antique, I used quartersawn white oak throughout the project. Then I stained it with a special walnut stain, and finally applied two coats of polyurethane to protect the oak.

EXPLODED VIEW

OVERALL DIMENSIONS:
25W x 38D x 42H

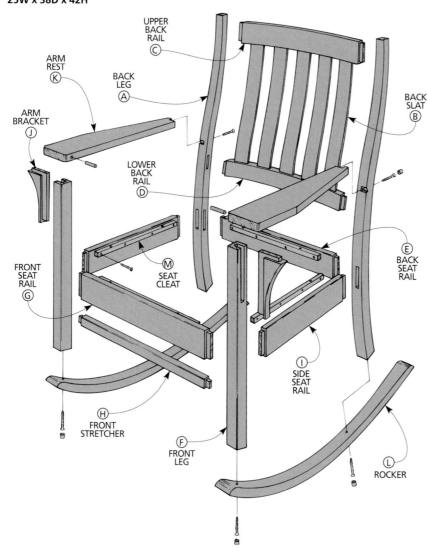

- UPPER BACK RAIL (C)
- ARM REST (K)
- BACK LEG (A)
- ARM BRACKET (J)
- BACK SLAT (B)
- LOWER BACK RAIL (D)
- FRONT SEAT RAIL (G)
- SEAT CLEAT (M)
- BACK SEAT RAIL (E)
- FRONT STRETCHER (H)
- SIDE SEAT RAIL (I)
- FRONT LEG (F)
- ROCKER (L)

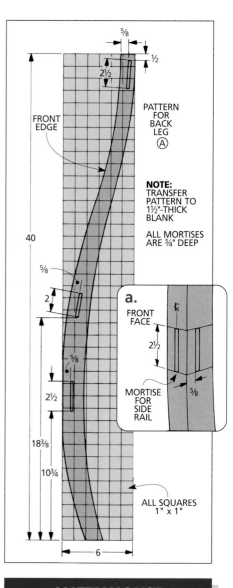

PATTERN FOR BACK LEG (A)

5/8
1/2
2 1/2

FRONT EDGE

NOTE:
TRANSFER PATTERN TO 1 1/2"-THICK BLANK

ALL MORTISES ARE 3/4" DEEP

40
5/8
2
5/8
2 1/2
18 3/8
10 3/4

ALL SQUARES 1" x 1"

6

a.
FRONT FACE
2 1/2
MORTISE FOR SIDE RAIL
5/8

CUTTING DIAGRAM

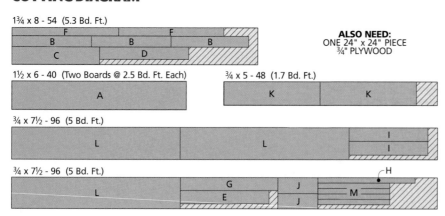

1 3/4 x 8 - 54 (5.3 Bd. Ft.)

F	F
B	B	B
C	D

ALSO NEED:
ONE 24" x 24" PIECE 3/4" PLYWOOD

1 1/2 x 6 - 40 (Two Boards @ 2.5 Bd. Ft. Each)

| A |

3/4 x 5 - 48 (1.7 Bd. Ft.)

| K | K |

3/4 x 7 1/2 - 96 (5 Bd. Ft.)

| L | L | I |
| | | I |

3/4 x 7 1/2 - 96 (5 Bd. Ft.)

| L | G | J | H |
| | E | J | M |

MATERIALS LIST

WOOD

A	Back Legs (2)	1 1/2 x 6 - 40 rough
B	Back Slats (5)	1 3/4 x 2 - 17 1/2
C	Upper Back Rail (1)	1 3/4 x 3 - 19 5/8
D	Lower Back Rail (1)	1 3/4 x 2 1/2 - 19 5/8
E	Back Seat Rail (1)	3/4 x 3 - 19 5/8
F	Front Legs (2)	1 1/2 x 1 1/2 - 23 1/2
G	Front Seat Rail (1)	3/4 x 3 - 21 1/4
H	Front Stretcher (1)	3/4 x 1 1/4 - 21 1/4
I	Side Seat Rails (2)	3/4 x 3 - 17
J	Arm Brackets (2)	3/4 x 2 15/16 - 8 9/16
K	Arm Rests (2)	3/4 x 4 1/2 - 21 1/4
L	Rockers (2)	2 1/4 x 7 1/2 - 38 rgh.
M	Seat Cleats (4)	3/4 x 3/4 - 15
N	Seat Panel (1)	3/4 ply - 17 x 22 rgh.

HARDWARE SUPPLIES

(24) No. 8 x 1 1/4" Fh woodscrews
(2) No. 8 x 1 1/2" Fh woodscrews
(4) No.12 x 2 1/2" Fh woodscrews
(6) Wood plugs (or short dowel rod)
(1 piece) 2"-thick foam, 17" x 22"
(1 piece) 25" x 30" fabric or leather

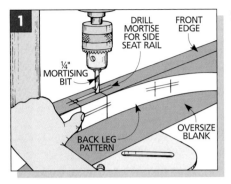

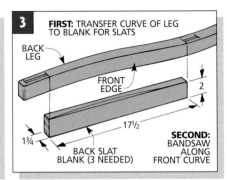

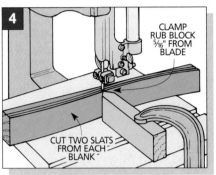

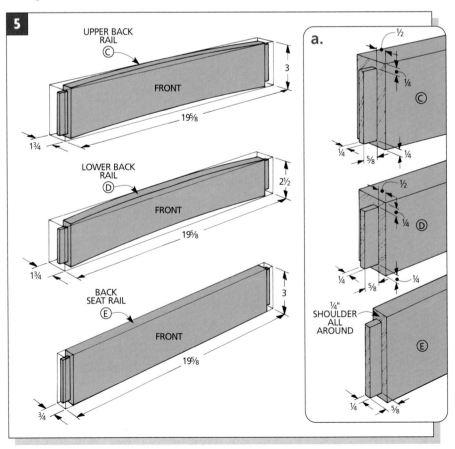

BACK LEGS

The chair has two main sub-assemblies (back/front). I started on the vertical parts of the back: the back legs and slats.

LEG BLANKS. Although curved, the back legs of this chair aren't delicate — they're made from $1^1/2$" stock.

First I cut two oversized blanks to rough dimensions (see pattern at left).

LAY OUT SHAPE. Now transfer the leg pattern to one of the blanks.

LAY OUT MORTISES. Before cutting the leg to shape, first lay out all the mortises. Then drill the mortise in the edge for the side seat rail *(Fig. 1)*.

LEGS. Cut the first back leg (A) in two stages. First, bandsaw the curve to within $1/16$" of the pencil lines. Then sand to the lines to smooth the curves.

Now transfer the shape of the first leg to the blank for the second. (I used the leg itself.) Transfer the mortise locations and drill the one for the side rail *(Fig. 1)*.

Bandsaw the second leg to rough shape and sand it to match the first.

DRILL MORTISES. When the back legs are sanded to the same shape, the three mortises are drilled on the sides *(Fig. 2)*.

BACK SLATS

The five back slats have the same curve as the upper part of the back legs.

LAY OUT SHAPE. Cut three oversized blanks from $1^3/4$" stock *(Fig. 3)*. (Two slats are cut from each, leaving one extra.)

Transfer the curve of the top of the back leg (*front* edge only) to this blank.

BANDSAW. Bandsaw within $1/16$" of the pencil mark, then sand the curve to the mark. To cut all five back slats (B) the same, I used a pointed rub block *(Fig. 4)*.

Clamp this block $5/16$" from the blade. Then push the workpiece through the saw with its curved front edge sliding across the point. This slices off a slat like a slab of bacon.

THICKNESS SAND. Now sand all the

slats to final thickness ($1/4$") and rout $1/8$" roundovers on all four edges.

BACK RAILS

The back legs are held together by three rails. The top two rails also hold the back slats. The bottom one supports the seat.

OVERSIZED BLANKS. I began by cutting each rail to finished dimensions. They're all the same length *(Fig. 5)*, but *not* all the same width or thickness.

The upper (C) and lower back rails (D) are $1^3/4$" thick so they can be cut to a curved shape. Since the back seat rail (E) is *not* curved, it's cut from $3/4$" stock.

CUT TENONS. It's easiest to cut the tenons on all the pieces before cutting the top two rails to their curved shape.

Note: The tenons on the upper and lower back rails (thicker pieces) are cut the same — *offset* on the thickness *(Fig. 5a)*. But on the back seat rail (E), they are *centered* on the thickness.

Now set aside the back seat rail (E) until the chair back is assembled.

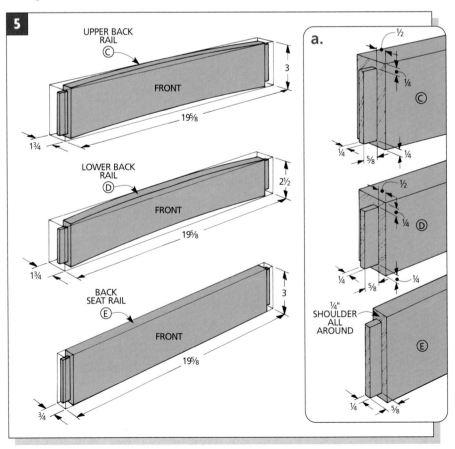

LAY OUT ARCS. Now that tenons have been cut on all three pieces, the upper and lower back rails (C, D) can be bandsawn to an arc. To lay out this arc, first cut a template (I used posterboard) with a 60"-radius arc (Shop Tip on page 96 and *Fig. 6*).

Now, place the template on the inside edge of the workpiece to draw the inside arc. Then you can move the template to the outside edge to draw the outside arc *(Fig. 7)*.

After the two rails are sawn to the curved shape, sand them to finished thickness ($^3/_4$") using a drum sander in the drill press.

DRILL MORTISES. To hold the back slats in place, a series of matching mortises is drilled in the upper back rail and lower back rail *(Fig. 8)*.

Note: The mortises are drilled on the facing edges of each piece — the lower edge of the upper rail, and the upper edge of the lower rail.

To keep all the mortises an equal distance from the edge of the curved rail, I used a platform with a simple guide pin on the drill press table (see the Shop Tip below).

ASSEMBLE CHAIR BACK. Now all the back parts are ready to be assembled. I started by assembling (but not gluing) the back slats between the upper and lower back rails.

Then assemble this unit (and the back seat rail) between the back legs. Glue all the tenons in the mortises, then clamp across each of the three rails.

FRONT ASSEMBLY

As the glue was drying on the back assembly, I began work on the chair front. This consists of two legs connected by a seat rail and a stretcher.

LEG BLANKS. The front legs are as solid as the curved back legs. That's because they're also $1^1/_2$" thick *(Fig. 9)*.

After cutting each front leg (F) to finished dimensions, mark the top inside edge of each leg. This will help orient the legs when laying out the mortises on the sides. (You have to make a "mirrored" set of legs.)

RAIL AND STRETCHER MORTISES. Each leg has four mortises *(Fig. 9)*. One mortise — on the inside — is for a tenon on the front seat rail. A second, shorter mortise below the first is for the front stretcher.

A third mortise is located on the

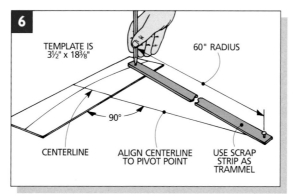

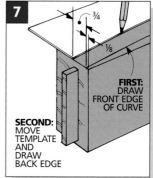

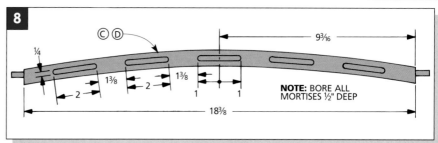

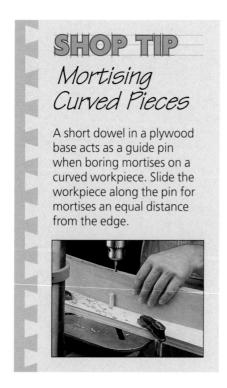

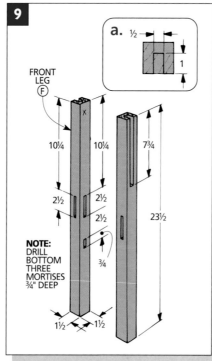

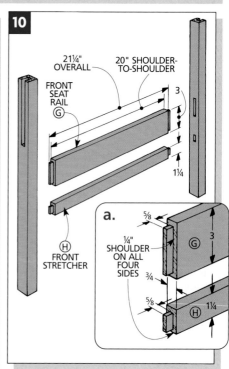

back of each leg (adjacent to the first two mortises). This is for a tenon on the side seat rail.

After these three mortises are laid out on the leg, bore them the same depth ($^3/_4$").

Note: I used a $^1/_4$" mortising bit in the drill press to bore all three mortises. Then I squared up the ends of each mortise with a chisel. (If you prefer, you could round over the ends of the tenons instead.)

ARM SUPPORT MORTISES. The last mortise on each leg is a long one that's open at the top end *(Fig. 9)*. This accepts a tenon on the arm bracket (J) (refer to *Fig. 12a*).

Note: I used a $^1/_2$" mortising bit and bored this open-ended mortise to a depth of 1" by making a long row of overlapping holes *(Fig. 9a)*.

RAIL AND STRETCHER. After the mortises are drilled, rip one piece of $^3/_4$"-thick stock to finished width for the front seat rail (G), and one for the front stretcher (H). Then cut both pieces to the same length ($21^1/_4$") *(Fig. 10)*.

CUT TENONS. Next, cut a tenon on both ends of the front seat rail and the front stretcher *(Fig. 10a)*. To do this, I used a dado blade in the table saw. Sneak up on the thickness until it fits the mortise snugly.

ASSEMBLY. After cutting the tenons, glue the rail and stretcher in the mortises between the front legs. Then set the assembly aside until the side rails are complete.

SIDE RAILS

The next step is to connect the front and back assemblies and create a chair.

RAIL BLANK. First cut two side rails (I) to finished width from $^3/_4$"-thick stock *(Fig. 11)*. Then, cut them to length with a 3° miter on each end *(Figs. 11 and 11a)*.

LAY OUT TENONS. To lay out the tenons, first make a mark $^5/_8$" from the long point of each end *(Fig. 11a)*. Then, draw a line at 3° to this mark for the shoulder of the tenon.

Now you need to draw two parallel lines to indicate the thickness of the tenon *(Fig. 11a)*. From the shoulder mark, extend these lines at a 3° angle to the end of the rail.

CUT TENONS. The angled tenon can be cut by hand with a tenon saw, then cleaned up with a chisel. Or, use the

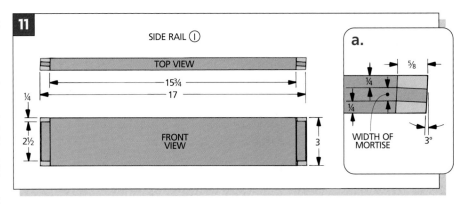

Angled Tenon Jig on the router table as shown on page 110.

ARM RESTS

When the back and front assemblies are connected, the project is almost a chair. But it wouldn't be a very comfortable chair without a pair of arm rests.

ARM BRACKETS. To support each arm rest at the front, I added an arm bracket. Each of these arm brackets (J) starts out as a rectangular blank of $^3/_4$"-thick stock *(Fig. 12)*.

TENONS. The next step is to cut a tenon along one side and one end of the blank *(Fig. 12a)*. (The tenons are more like tongues — they don't have very wide shoulders.)

I used a dado blade in the table saw to cut each tenon. First position the rip fence to the desired tenon length. Then make two passes over the dado blade, flipping the piece between passes. Sneak up on the height of the dado

blade until the tenon fits the mortise in the front leg *(Fig. 12a)*.

Then you can cut all four tenons to this thickness.

DECORATIVE ARC. Complete the arm brackets by cutting a decorative arc on the outside edge *(Fig. 12)*.

Next, trim back the tenon on the top outside corner and also the bottom inside corner of each bracket *(Figs. 12 and 12a)*. This creates a shoulder that hides the joint line between the tenon and the mortise.

ARM REST. When the arm brackets were complete, I began work on the two arm rests (K). First, cut the blanks to rectangular shape *(Fig. 13)*. Next, make an angled cut to remove the back outside corner of each blank.

ARM REST NOTCH. When each of these blanks has been cut to shape, cut a small notch in the back inside corner *(Fig. 13)*. This allows the arm rest to "wrap around" the back leg (refer to *Fig. 17* on page 108).

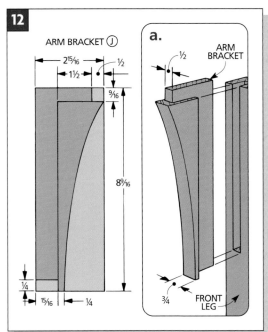

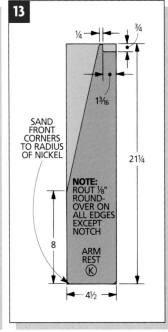

BACK LEG LEDGE. The back of the arm rest is supported by a small triangular "ledge" cut in the back leg *(Fig. 14b)*. To locate its position, rest the front of the arm rest on the front leg and support the back on a 10"-long temporary spacer *(Fig. 14)*. Draw a line around the arm rest *(Figs. 14 and 14a)*, then chisel between these lines to form the ledge.

FRONT MORTISE. Now glue the arm brackets in the mortises in the front legs (refer to *Fig. 12a*). Place the arm rest in the ledge and trace around the tenon at the top of the bracket *(Figs. 15 and 15a)* to show where to drill a mortise on the arm rest. Drill a $5/8$"-deep mortise to match the tenon's thickness ($1/2$").

PINS AND SCREWS. Now the arm rests are attached to the chair. To keep the tenon in place, I glued the joint and drove a dowel into the tenon through a hole in the arm rest *(Fig. 16)*.

Secure the back of the arm rest with a screw and plug it with a dowel *(Fig. 17)*.

ROCKERS

Next I started on the rockers. Both are cut from a blank that's made from three glued-up pieces of $3/4$" stock *(Fig. 18)*. This forms a $2^1/4$"-thick blank. (You could also start with thin, wide strips, then laminate them in a bending jig.)

TRANSFER PATTERN. When the glue is dry, transfer the grid pattern *(Fig. 20)* to the side of one blank *(Fig. 18)*.

SAW AND SAND. Bandsaw the rocker (L) within $1/16$" of the pattern line, and sand to the line to smooth the curves.

Use the first rocker as a pattern to make the second *(Fig. 19)* the same way.

Note: Both rockers must be shaped exactly the same. Otherwise, when the chair is assembled, it could "walk."

When I was sure they were identical, I prepared to attach them to the legs.

The legs are a couple inches longer than needed. This is so they can be cut to match the curve of the rocker.

MARK FRONT LEG. To find the point where the rockers attach, measure down from the side seat rail and mark where the front leg is cut off *(Fig. 21)*.

MARK BACK LEG. For accuracy on the back leg, first I made a mark on the edge to indicate the bottom edge of the side rail *(Fig. 21)*. Then I used a straightedge to measure $8^3/4$" down and made a second mark at this point on the inside.

Note: The procedure for measuring down from the side rail is not as critical as

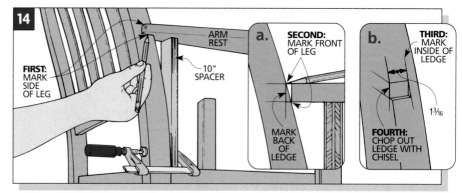

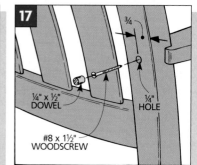

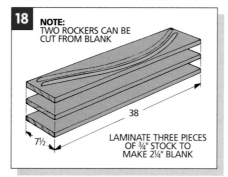

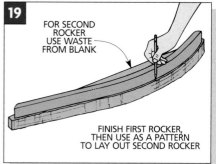

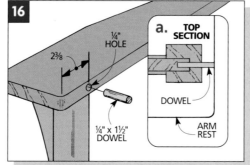

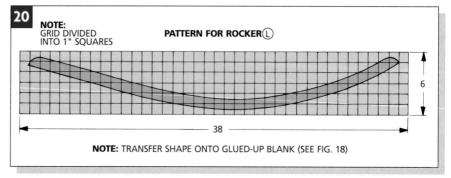

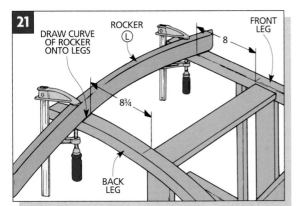

21
DRAW CURVE OF ROCKER ONTO LEGS
ROCKER L
FRONT LEG
8
8¾
BACK LEG

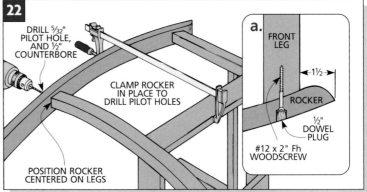

22
DRILL 5/32" PILOT HOLE, AND ½" COUNTERBORE
CLAMP ROCKER IN PLACE TO DRILL PILOT HOLES
POSITION ROCKER CENTERED ON LEGS

a.
FRONT LEG
1½
ROCKER
½" DOWEL PLUG
#12 x 2" Fh WOODSCREW

doing the *same* thing on *both* back legs.

POSITION ROCKERS. Place the rocker across the legs so its top aligns to the leg marks *(Fig. 21)*. It should overhang 1¹/₂" in front *(Fig. 22a)*. Draw a line across the legs using the rocker as a guide.

CUT OFF LEG BOTTOMS. Now cut off the legs at the line. For a clean, straight cut, use a block clamped to the leg as a guide. Then, sand the bottoms of the legs to fit the rockers (see Shop Tip below).

ATTACH ROCKERS. Fasten the rockers to the legs with woodscrews plugged with dowels *(Fig. 22a)*. A bar clamp between the top of the side rail and the bottom of the rocker holds the rocker in place for drilling a pilot hole for the screw and counterbore for the plug *(Fig. 22)*.

CHAIR SEAT

The plywood seat rests on cleats inside the chair opening and is upholstered with fabric-wrapped foam *(Fig. 23)*.

CLEATS. To make the cleats, start by ripping four strips of ³/₄" stock to finished width (³/₄"). Then cut all four seat cleats (M) to the same length (15"). Before installing them, drill six countersunk shank holes in each cleat (four for the screws into the rails, two for the

23
SEAT CLEAT M
FABRIC SEAT COVER
2"-THICK FOAM CUSHION
SEAT PANEL N
3/4" PLYWOOD

a.
SEAT PANEL N
1/16
1/8
1/16
CUT NOTCH TO FIT AROUND LEG
1/8
FRONT LEG

b.
FOAM CUSHION
FRONT SEAT RAIL
#8 x 1¼" Fh WOODSCREW
SEAT PANEL
FABRIC
SEAT CLEAT
½
3/4
3/4

screws into the platform) *(Fig. 23b and the Exploded View on page 104)*.

Then glue and screw the cleats to the inside of the seat opening. Center them left to right on the rails and position them ¹/₂" down from the rail tops *(Fig. 23b)*.

SEAT PANEL. Now the seat panel (N) is cut. Start with an oversized piece of ³/₄" plywood and cut a taper along each

side so it's ¹/₁₆" smaller in both dimensions than the opening *(Fig. 23a)*.

So the panel will fit around the legs, a notch is cut in each corner *(Fig. 23a)*.

FOAM AND FABRIC. Before screwing in the seat, I upholstered it with fabric and foam (refer to page 99). But you might prefer to stop now and just take it to a professional upholsterer. ∎

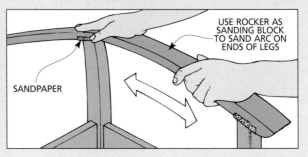

SHOP TIP . . . . *Fitting Legs to Rockers*

After cutting the legs, I turned the chair over and set the rockers on them.

The bottoms of the legs needed to be sanded to a slight arc to match the curve of the rockers.

To prevent over-sanding, I used the rockers like giant sanding blocks (so

the legs could be sanded to match them perfectly).

To do this, attach adhesive-backed sandpaper to each rocker where the legs will join it (see drawing).

Now place a rocker on its corresponding legs and gently sand the legs until they match the arc.

SANDPAPER
USE ROCKER AS SANDING BLOCK TO SAND ARC ON ENDS OF LEGS

SHOP JIG .... *Angled Tenon Jig*

When you want to use a mortise and tenon joint to join two pieces at an angle, you have a choice: cut an angled tenon or bore an angled mortise. I always choose the angled tenon.

The challenge is finding the best way to cut the tenons at an identical angle at both ends of the workpiece — with the least amount of fuss. So I built a jig for the router table.

For the Rocking Chair on page 103, the tenons on the side rails have to be cut at a 3° angle. The problem is the tenons at each end must be parallel, and so must the shoulders (see inset photo).

With this jig, angled tenons up to about 1" long can be cut with a straight bit. And by following a simple procedure, the shoulders and tenons are cut parallel and at the exact same angle.

The jig can also be used for other projects (it's adjustable for different angles).

ANY ANGLE. This jig holds the workpiece at any angle, up to approximately 45° from vertical. Then, as the jig is run along the front edge of the router table, a perfect angled tenon can be routed on the workpiece with just one pass in each direction. (See "Using the Jig" on the facing page.)

THICKNESS. Besides being able to cut tenons at different angles, another feature that makes this jig useful is that it can be used to cut tenons of about any thickness, on almost any size stock.

What makes this possible is a carriage bolt in a slot and a wing nut. These hold the two main parts of the jig together and allow the working end of the jig (the pivoting face) to be positioned at different distances from the bit.

MATERIALS. I made the jig from a couple short lengths of scrap hardwood plus a handful of hardware. A pair of butt hinges permits the jig to tilt, and a pivot arm made from hardboard securely holds the pivoting face at an angle while the tenon is being routed.

MAKING THE JIG

The Angled Tenon Jig consists of two main assemblies: a base assembly and a runner assembly. The base assembly has a base piece that lies flat on the router table, and also a pivot face that holds the standing workpiece at an angle *(Fig. 1)*.

The runner assembly is attached to the end of the base assembly. It consists of a runner that slides along the front of the router table to keep the base a fixed distance from the router bit.

Attached to the runner are a pair of guide blocks that hold the base perpendicular to the front edge of the table.

Note: To make the jig more comfortable to use, I rounded over the edges of the guide blocks *(Fig. 1)*. Also, I sanded a radius on each corner of the runner assembly pieces, and the outside corners of the base. Rout and sand these pieces before assembly.

ASSEMBLY. To assemble the parts, start by attaching the guide blocks to the runner. Install the screws from the

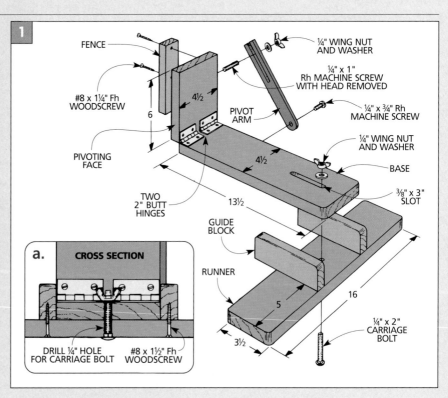

bottom of the runner, using the base as a spacer to keep the blocks the correct distance apart *(Fig. 2)*.

Then hinge the pivoting face to the inside end of the base *(Fig. 3)*. (I used 2"-long butt hinges.) Now, attach the base to the runner with a 2"-long carriage bolt through a hole in the runner and a slot in the base *(Figs. 1 and 2)*.

PIVOT ARM. To support the pivoting face at an angle, I cut a pivot arm from a piece of $1/4$"-thick hardboard *(Fig. 3)*.

The arm has a pivot hole in one end and an adjustment slot in the other end.

Cut (or sand) a radius on the lower end of the arm and attach it to the base and pivoting face with machine screws.

FENCE. Finally, cut and screw a short fence to the front of the pivoting face *(Fig. 4)*. This holds the workpiece to the jig as the tenon is being routed.

As long as the fence is attached at a 90° angle to the router table, the shoulders of the tenon will be square to the

end of the tenon.

Safety Note: Attach the fence to the pivoting face with the screws positioned at least 3" up from the bottom of the fence. This way, the router bit won't cut into the screws as the jig is being used.

On a tenon longer than $3/4$", the router bit can cut into the lower ends of the fence and pivoting face. That's all right because these can be replaced later if necessary — just remove them from the hinges on the inside.

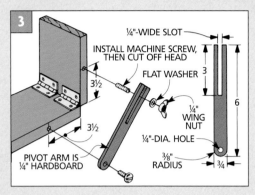

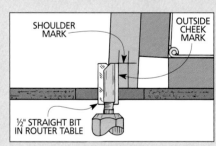

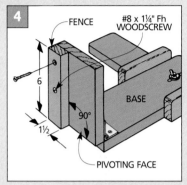

USING THE JIG

Most angled tenons can be cut in just two passes over a $1/2$" straight bit in the router table. The first pass cuts one cheek of the tenon. Then the tenon is completed in a second pass. Only the jig is moved between passes — the workpiece stays clamped on the front.

LAY OUT TENON. Before using the jig, first cut the ends of the workpiece at the correct angle. Then draw the outline of the tenon at the desired angle on the edge of the workpiece at each end.

The layout marks indicate the angle, length, and thickness of the tenon.

SET UP JIG. When the tenon is laid out on the piece, the jig and router bit need to be adjusted *(Steps 1 through 3 below)*.

Note: *Don't* raise the bit higher than 1" — it can cut into the hinge screws. And to avoid tear-out on the shoulder, stick a piece of masking tape to the face *(Step 2)*.

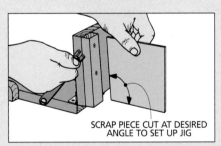

1 *Miter a piece of scrap to use as a guide for setting tenon angle. Then tighten the wing nut on the end of pivot arm.*

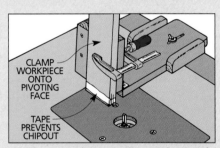

2 *Clamp workpiece to jig so edge is tight to upright fence. The end of the workpiece should be flat on the router table.*

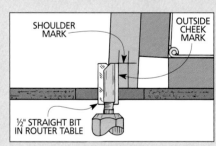

3 *Slide the body of the jig so bit aligns to the outside cheek mark. Raise the bit to align to the shoulder mark.*

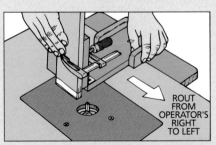

4 *Cut the outside of tenon by holding the runner tight to the front of the table and sliding the jig from right to left.*

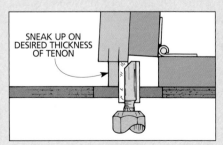

5 *To complete the tenon, adjust the jig so the bit aligns to the inside cheek mark. Do not change height of the bit.*

6 *To rout the inside cheek, you have to slide the jig in the opposite direction (from left to right) to avoid kickback.*

Shaker Bench

This bench isn't built the Shaker way, but it would take a Shaker craftsman to notice. Whether you build the long seat or a chair, you'll be able to use modern tools and jigs to get a classic look.

When building furniture, I'm always looking for better techniques. For this Shaker Bench, I started with the contoured seat. The Shakers would have shaped it by hand, using a scorp or inshave. But that's a lot of work, and unless you've already had some experience with these hand tools, it can be difficult to get a uniform shape. Instead, I used the table saw to rough-shape the profile.

SPINDLES AND LEGS. I also made the legs and spindles for this bench differently than the Shakers would have. The Shaker craftsman probably used a lathe, and no two of the pieces turned out exactly the same. That's part of the unique Shaker look.

But I wanted to save time, and also produce identical legs and spindles. So I made a couple of handy jigs to form these parts with a router and an electric drill. A bit unusual, maybe, but it produces a ready-to-use leg or spindle in a matter of minutes. The jigs are shown in the Technique article that begins on page 122.

DIFFERENT WOOD COLORS. There's something else about different ways of working. The Shakers knew their woods and how to make the best use of various types of wood. They used a strong wood (such as maple) for the legs. And a softer, easier to shape wood (such as pine) for the contoured seat.

Since I didn't have to hand-shape the seat, I didn't have to use a soft wood. But I still like the look of contrasting woods, so I used cherry for the seat and back rest, and hard maple for the spindles and legs.

CHAIR. A long bench can sometimes be a nice departure from simple chairs and sofas, depending on the style of the room it will be featured in. But if you prefer, simple plans for turning this bench into an eye-catching chair are included on page 121.

EXPLODED VIEW

OVERALL DIMENSIONS:
54W x 18¼D x 33H

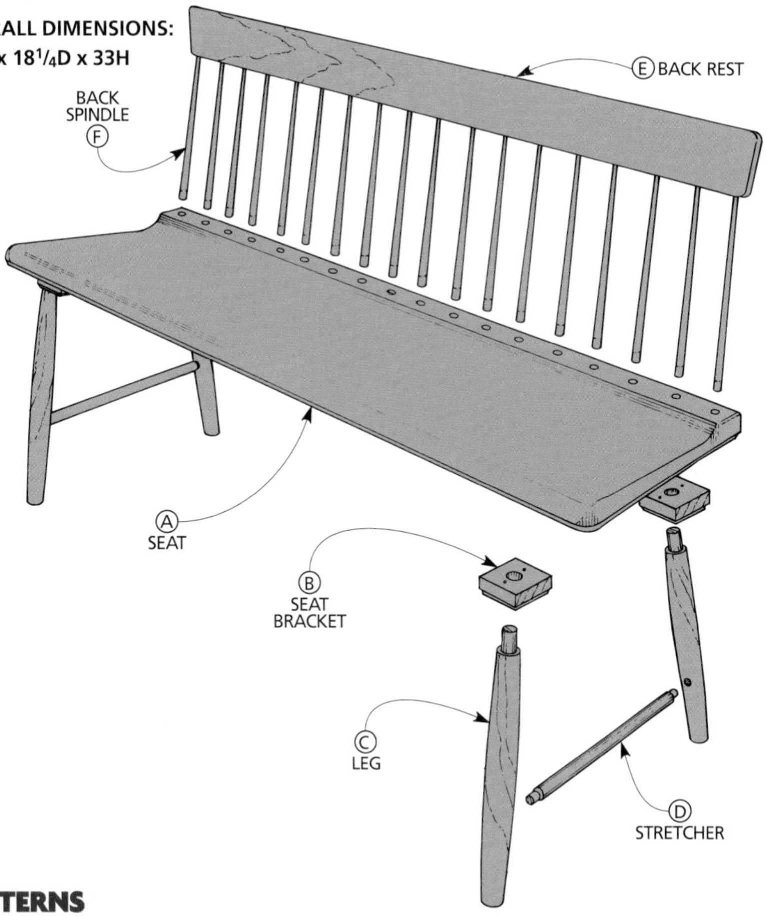
BACK SPINDLE
F
E BACK REST
A
SEAT
B
SEAT BRACKET
C
LEG
D
STRETCHER

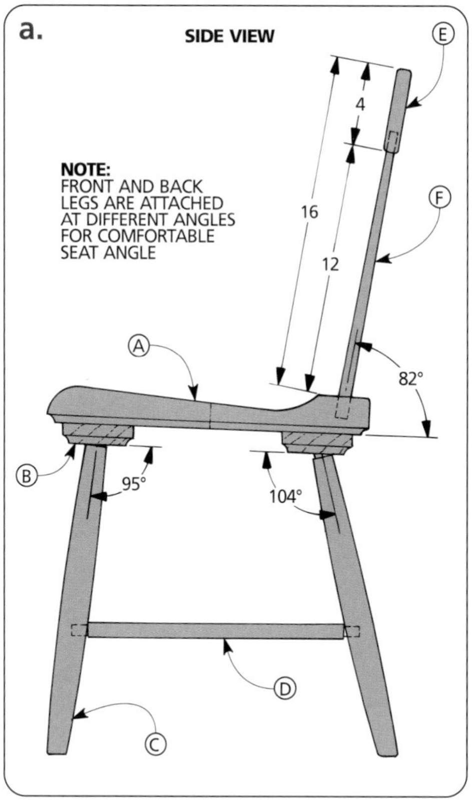
a.
SIDE VIEW
E
4
NOTE:
FRONT AND BACK LEGS ARE ATTACHED AT DIFFERENT ANGLES FOR COMFORTABLE SEAT ANGLE
F
16
12
A
82°
B
95°
104°
D
C

PATTERNS

NOTE:
SEAT PATTERN MUST BE ENLARGED TO 320% TO BRING UP TO FULL-SIZE

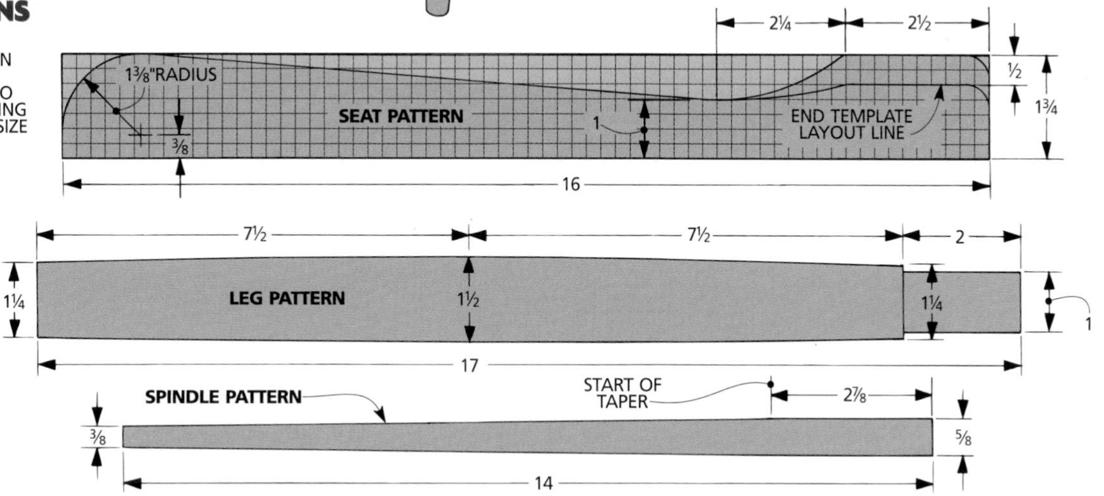
2¼
2½
1⅜"RADIUS
SEAT PATTERN
1
END TEMPLATE LAYOUT LINE
½
1¾
⅜
16
7½
7½
2
1¼
LEG PATTERN
1½
1¼
1
17
SPINDLE PATTERN
START OF TAPER
2⅞
⅜
⅝
14

MATERIALS LIST

WOOD

A	Seat (1)	1¾ x 16 - 54
B	Seat Brackets (4)	1 x 3½ - 2½
C	Legs (4)	1½ dowel x 17
D	Stretchers (2)	⅝ dowel x 18 rgh.
E	Back Rest (1)	¾ x 4 - 54
F	Back Spindles (18)	⅝ dowel x 18 rgh.

HARDWARE SUPPLIES

(8) No. 8 x 1½" Fh woodscrews

CUTTING DIAGRAM

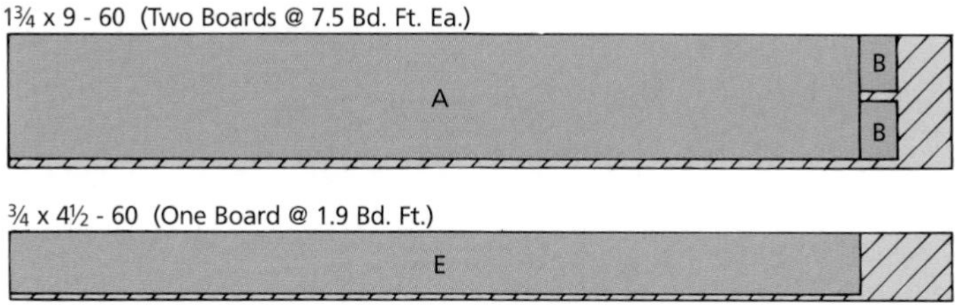
1¾ x 9 - 60 (Two Boards @ 7.5 Bd. Ft. Ea.)
A
B
B
¾ x 4½ - 60 (One Board @ 1.9 Bd. Ft.)
E

For Shakers, the seat for a bench like this would have been cut from a wide, thick slab of wood. But finding wood that size today is almost impossible. So I started with two narrower boards so I could shape the seat on a table saw.

First, I cut the two blanks to the same rough size from 1³/₄"-thick stock (*Fig. 1*). Then, to make it easier to handle, I started work on the blank for the back half of the seat (*Fig. 1a*).

SPINDLE HOLES. Before shaping the back half, I laid out a series of holes along the blank for the spindles. But I didn't mark the positions of these holes on the workpiece right away — I started with a template. (This template can be used again later for other operations.)

LAYOUT TEMPLATE. First, rip the template to match the flat area along the back of the seat (2¹/₂") (refer to *Fig. 1a*).

Note: The template is shorter than the seat blank — it's the finished length of the back of the seat (53") (*Fig. 2*).

Mark the positions of the spindle holes on the template and drill holes at each mark (*Fig. 2a*). (The holes should match the diameter of a scratch awl.)

Then place the template on the workpiece and use the scratch awl to mark the locations of the spindle holes.

ANGLED WEDGE. For comfort, the back spindles are installed at an angle. To drill holes for all the spindles at the same angle, I wanted to use the drill press. But its table doesn't tilt front-to-back.

Instead, I bevel-ripped a wedge to the desired angle (*Figs. 3 and 3a*). This wedge is used to support the workpiece as you drill the spindle holes on the drill press (*Fig. 4* and the Shop Tip below).

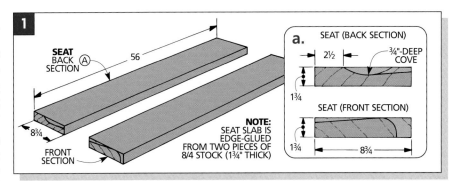

1

SEAT BACK SECTION Ⓐ

56

8¾

FRONT SECTION

a. SEAT (BACK SECTION)

2½ ¾"-DEEP COVE

1¾

SEAT (FRONT SECTION)

1¾ 8¾

NOTE: SEAT SLAB IS EDGE-GLUED FROM TWO PIECES OF 8/4 STOCK (1¾" THICK)

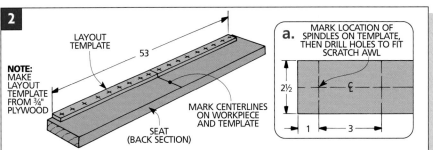

2

LAYOUT TEMPLATE

53

NOTE: MAKE LAYOUT TEMPLATE FROM ¾" PLYWOOD

MARK CENTERLINES ON WORKPIECE AND TEMPLATE

SEAT (BACK SECTION)

a. MARK LOCATION OF SPINDLES ON TEMPLATE, THEN DRILL HOLES TO FIT SCRATCH AWL

2½

1 3

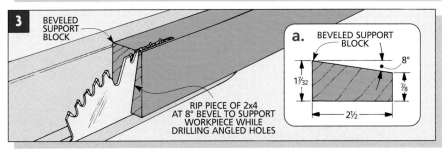

3

BEVELED SUPPORT BLOCK

RIP PIECE OF 2x4 AT 8° BEVEL TO SUPPORT WORKPIECE WHILE DRILLING ANGLED HOLES

a. BEVELED SUPPORT BLOCK

8°

1⁷/₃₂ ⅞

2½

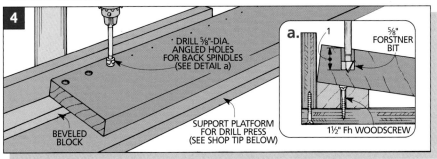

4

DRILL ⅝"-DIA. ANGLED HOLES FOR BACK SPINDLES (SEE DETAIL a)

BEVELED BLOCK

SUPPORT PLATFORM FOR DRILL PRESS (SEE SHOP TIP BELOW)

a. 1 ⅝" FORSTNER BIT

1½" Fh WOODSCREW

SHOP TIP . . . . *Drilling Holes In Long Stock*

To drill angled holes in a long workpiece (like the seat), I use a plywood support platform bolted to the drill press table (*Fig. 1*). Cut it 2" *longer* and *wider* than the seat, and attach a short fence and a beveled block. The angled holes can then be drilled with two hands (*Fig. 2*).

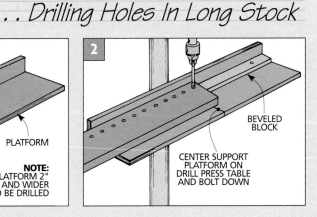

1 SUPPORT PLATFORM IS CUT FROM ¾"-THICK PLYWOOD

BACK FENCE

BOLT HOLES

PLATFORM

NOTE: CUT PLATFORM 2" LONGER AND WIDER THAN PIECE TO BE DRILLED

2

BEVELED BLOCK

CENTER SUPPORT PLATFORM ON DRILL PRESS TABLE AND BOLT DOWN

CUTTING THE COVE

I didn't make the template just for the spindles. I also used it to set up the table saw for cutting a cove on the seat blank.

To set up for the cove, adjust the blade height to the cove depth ($^3/_4$") *(Fig. 5)*.

Then place the template on the saw table on the outfeed side of the blade and adjust the miter gauge angle to 56° *(Fig. 5)*. This determines the width of the cove (for a 10"-dia. saw blade).

GUIDE FENCE. With the template front touching the blade's back tooth, clamp a long guide fence to the table *(Fig. 6)*.

SECOND GUIDE FENCE. Now lower the saw blade and clamp a second guide fence to the other side of the workpiece *(Fig. 7 and photo above right)*. Position this fence parallel to the first so the distance between them is equal to the width of the workpiece ($8^3/_4$").

COVE. While cutting the cove, the drilled side of the slab should be against the upper guide fence.

Note: Cut the cove in multiple passes. Start with the blade set $^1/_{16}$" high, and raise the blade only $^1/_{16}$" between passes. (Use a push stick to keep your hands clear of the blade as the end of the slab passes through.)

OUTFEED SUPPORT. The slab is long and awkward, so it needs additional

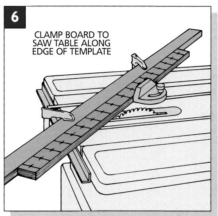

It's easier to cut a cove on a long workpiece with a pair of guides. And a platform (with a support leg) clamped between the guides keeps the piece from tipping down.

support as it leaves the table. If you don't have an outfeed table, clamp plywood between the guide fences to "lengthen" the table (see photo).

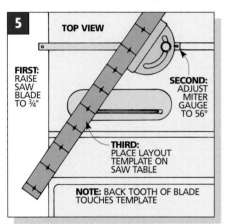

5 TOP VIEW

FIRST: RAISE SAW BLADE TO $^3/_4$"

SECOND: ADJUST MITER GAUGE TO 56°

THIRD: PLACE LAYOUT TEMPLATE ON SAW TABLE

NOTE: BACK TOOTH OF BLADE TOUCHES TEMPLATE

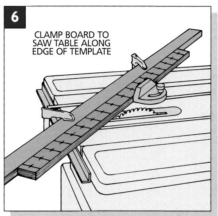

6 CLAMP BOARD TO SAW TABLE ALONG EDGE OF TEMPLATE

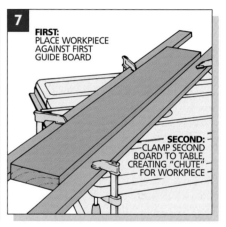

7 FIRST: PLACE WORKPIECE AGAINST FIRST GUIDE BOARD

SECOND: CLAMP SECOND BOARD TO TABLE, CREATING "CHUTE" FOR WORKPIECE

JOINING THE SEAT HALVES

With the cove cut on the back of the seat, the front can be shaped. This is actually an extension of the cove on the back.

But first the two sections of the seat (A) are edge-glued together *(Fig. 8)*.

TEMPLATE. The seat shape is shown in a scale drawing on page 113. But I didn't draw it directly on the workpiece. Instead, I enlarged the shape and made a template from the enlargement.

To do this, have the drawing on page 113 enlarged 320% at a copy shop, or redraw the shape full-size onto a piece of grid paper. Then transfer the shape to a piece of scrap plywood (at least $^1/_2$" thick). Finally, cut the template to rough shape and sand it smooth.

Now transfer the shape from the template to the ends of the seat *(Fig. 8)*.

SET UP TABLE SAW. Now the template can be used as a set-up gauge for cutting the shape on the front of the seat *(Fig. 9)*.

The actual shaping is done with a stacked dado blade in the table saw.

First, the blade is tilted to match the angle of the curve ($84^1/_2$°) (top drawing in *Fig. 10*). Then the fence is moved until the inside edge of the blade aligns to the desired area of cut. (Set up to start shaping where the cove shape "blends" into the flat shape.)

CUT AND MOVE. After each pass, use the template to adjust the position of the rip fence and height of the blade *(Fig. 9)*.

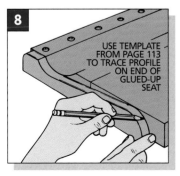

8 USE TEMPLATE FROM PAGE 113 TO TRACE PROFILE ON END OF GLUED-UP SEAT

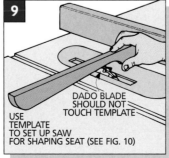

9 DADO BLADE SHOULD NOT TOUCH TEMPLATE

USE TEMPLATE TO SET UP SAW FOR SHAPING SEAT (SEE FIG. 10)

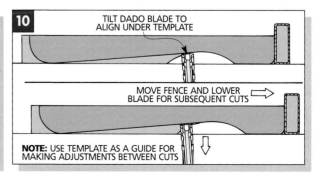

10 TILT DADO BLADE TO ALIGN UNDER TEMPLATE

MOVE FENCE AND LOWER BLADE FOR SUBSEQUENT CUTS

NOTE: USE TEMPLATE AS A GUIDE FOR MAKING ADJUSTMENTS BETWEEN CUTS

SMOOTHING THE SEAT

When the top of the blank is shaped, the seat should look a bit more inviting. But there's still a sharp corner at the front. Before cutting off this corner, rip the seat to finished width *(Fig. 11)*.

Then knock off the corner with a bevel cut on the table saw *(Fig. 11a)*.

PLANE AND SAND. The bench is beginning to look more sculpted. But there's still a series of ripples running the length of the blank where the dado cuts didn't quite align.

To smooth out the seat, I used a hand plane, just like the Shakers would have *(Fig. 12)*. (I used a low-angle block plane.) Plane the entire length of the seat, starting at the cove and working toward the front.

Note: For the most consistent shape while planing, use the pencil marks on the ends of the seat as a visual guide. The best way to tell when to quit planing is to use your hand — feel the surface of the seat to check for dips and ridges.

When all the bumps are gone, sand the surface of the seat smooth *(Fig. 13)*.

CUTTING OFF THE ENDS

After the top of the seat is smooth, the ends of the bench can be shaped. And like most Shaker designs, the simpler the better.

TEMPLATE. When it came time to lay out the shape on the ends of the seat, I had a certain look in mind. I noticed

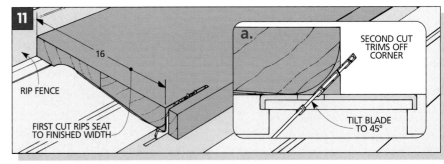

11

16

RIP FENCE

FIRST CUT RIPS SEAT TO FINISHED WIDTH

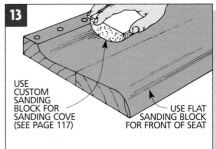

a.

SECOND CUT TRIMS OFF CORNER

TILT BLADE TO 45°

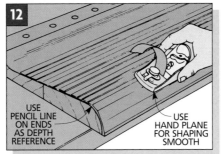

12

USE PENCIL LINE ON ENDS AS DEPTH REFERENCE

USE HAND PLANE FOR SHAPING SMOOTH

13

USE CUSTOM SANDING BLOCK FOR SANDING COVE (SEE PAGE 117)

USE FLAT SANDING BLOCK FOR FRONT OF SEAT

that the template I used for the top of the seat was just about right *(Fig. 14)*.

At first I thought I would cut the ends to match the shape of the template. But I didn't like the look of a big "bump" sticking out at the back of the seat. So I modified the shape of the template to "flatten" the area at the back *(Fig. 14a)*.

KERF AND JIG SAW. After drawing the shape of the modified template on the ends of the seat, they can be cut to shape. (This also cuts the blank to length).

The easiest way to shape the ends of the seat is to use the jig saw. But to keep the blade from bending when cutting such thick stock, first I made a series of

short relief cuts at right angles to the pencil line *(Fig. 15)*.

Then the short cuts are connected with a smooth cut that follows the line.

SAND SMOOTH. The blade of the jig saw will leave some "ripples" on the ends of the seat. To remove these and smooth the curves, I used a hand drill with a sanding drum *(Fig. 16)*.

Note: A drill guide (such as a Portalign) helps to keep the ends square to the faces.

ROUT COVE. There's one more decorative detail involved in shaping the seat. It's just a small cove that's routed all around the lower edge *(Fig. 17)*.

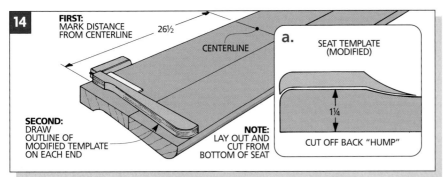

14

FIRST: MARK DISTANCE FROM CENTERLINE

26½

CENTERLINE

SECOND: DRAW OUTLINE OF MODIFIED TEMPLATE ON EACH END

NOTE: LAY OUT AND CUT FROM BOTTOM OF SEAT

a.

SEAT TEMPLATE (MODIFIED)

1¼

CUT OFF BACK "HUMP"

15

FIRST: MAKE RELIEF CUTS

SECOND: USE JIG SAW TO CUT JUST OUTSIDE PENCIL LINE

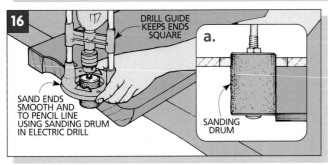

16

DRILL GUIDE KEEPS ENDS SQUARE

SAND ENDS SMOOTH AND TO PENCIL LINE USING SANDING DRUM IN ELECTRIC DRILL

a.

SANDING DRUM

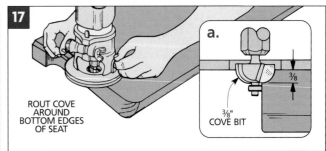

17

a.

ROUT COVE AROUND BOTTOM EDGES OF SEAT

⅜"

⅜" COVE BIT

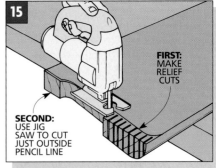

The best sanding block is one that matches the shape to be sanded. But where do you find one to match a large cove, like the seat of the Shaker Bench?

One solution is to make a custom sanding block from a 1½"-thick scrap of foam insulation board.

First, band saw or file the foam block to rough

shape (see left photo).

To smooth the shape, place adhesive-backed sandpaper across the cove and rub the block across it (see middle photo).

To use the block, remove the sandpaper from the workpiece. Then stick a new piece of sandpaper on the coved face of the block (see right photo).

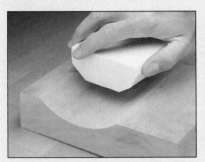

A piece of foam insulation board can be used to sand an irregular shape. First cut the block to rough shape.

Smooth the shape of the block by rubbing it across a piece of sandpaper stuck to the workpiece.

Now peel the sandpaper off the workpiece and stick a fresh piece on the block to sand the workpiece.

SEAT BRACKETS

Joining legs to the seat of a bench like this one can present some problems. There are two things to be concerned with — strength and comfort. But the solutions aren't complicated.

BRACKETS. There's a lot of stress on the legs of a bench. If they're not securely attached to the seat, the whole bench can wobble, or the legs can even snap off. So on this Shaker Bench, I added blocks to increase the strength of the leg joints.

The seat brackets (B) start out as a 1"-thick piece of stock (again I used cherry) *(Fig. 18)*. Then the brackets are cut to finished dimensions.

Note: It's a good idea to cut these rectangular brackets so that when they're attached later, the grain will run parallel to the grain on the seat (see photo at right).

ANGLED HOLES. The seat brackets add strength to the leg joints. And angled holes in the blocks allow the legs to be spread out under the seat. This adds some extra stability.

Note: By drilling a steeper angle for the back legs, the seat will tilt slightly to the back (refer to the Cross Section on page 113). This will make the bench more comfortable to sit on.

Drilling holes at an angle can be almost impossible if the table on your drill press doesn't tilt. However, you can end up with the same result by keeping the table flat and instead tilting the

A rectangular block strengthens each leg joint. First, an angled hole is drilled on the drill press. This guides an electric drill that completes the mortise for the leg.

workpiece (refer to *Fig. 19*).

For the holes in the seat brackets, I did this by resting the brackets on blocks that were beveled to the desired angle *(Fig. 19a)*.

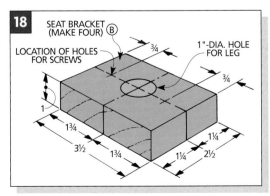

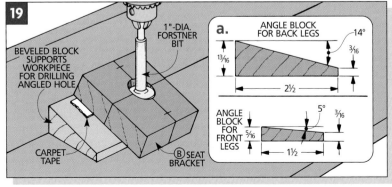

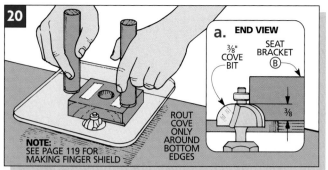

20

NOTE:
SEE PAGE 119 FOR
MAKING FINGER SHIELD

a. **END VIEW**

³⁄₈"
COVE
BIT

SEAT
BRACKET
B

ROUT
COVE
ONLY
AROUND
BOTTOM
EDGES

³⁄₈

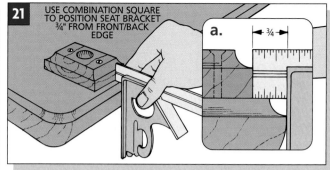

21

USE COMBINATION SQUARE
TO POSITION SEAT BRACKET
³⁄₄" FROM FRONT/BACK
EDGE

a. ³⁄₄

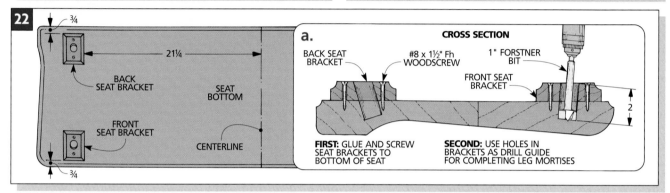

22

³⁄₄

BACK
SEAT BRACKET

21¼

SEAT
BOTTOM

FRONT
SEAT BRACKET

CENTERLINE

³⁄₄

a. **CROSS SECTION**

BACK SEAT
BRACKET

#8 x 1½" Fh
WOODSCREW

1" FORSTNER
BIT

FRONT SEAT
BRACKET

2

FIRST: GLUE AND SCREW
SEAT BRACKETS TO
BOTTOM OF SEAT

SECOND: USE HOLES IN
BRACKETS AS DRILL GUIDE
FOR COMPLETING LEG MORTISES

ROUT COVES. After the angled holes have been drilled in the seat brackets, a cove can be routed around the bottom edges. This matches the cove routed earlier on the seat, but I routed these coves on the router table *(Fig. 20)*.

ATTACH TO SEAT. Now the seat brackets can be screwed to the seat. They're positioned an equal distance from the centerline of the seat *(Fig. 22)* and ³⁄₄" from the edges *(Fig. 21)*.

After the brackets are glued and screwed to the bottom of the seat, use the angled holes as a guide for drilling the mortises into the seat *(Fig. 22a)*.

LEGS & STRETCHERS

To make legs for a bench, the Shakers would use a lathe. But I wanted all the legs to be identical, so I made them from dowels using a shop-made jig (see the Technique article starting on page 122).

Note: I also cut flutes on the tenon ends *(Fig. 23* and Shop Tip at right).

STRETCHERS. After the legs (C) are shaped, they can be dry-assembled into the seat *(Fig. 23)*. This is to test the fit of the tenons, and also to measure for the stretchers (D). The stretchers are cut from a ⁵⁄₈"-dia. dowel rod *(Fig. 24)*.

I used the router table with a core box bit to rout a round tenon on the ends of each stretcher *(Fig. 24a)*. (This is similar to the procedure shown for the table saw on page 123.)

CUT OFF BOTTOMS. Before assembling the stretchers and legs, I cut the bottom off each leg so the bench would sit flat on the floor. To do this, place the bench on a large, flat surface. (I used a door on the floor.)

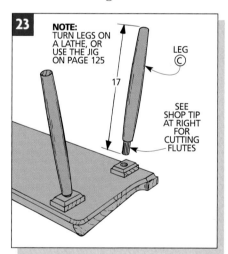

23

NOTE:
TURN LEGS ON
A LATHE, OR
USE THE JIG
ON PAGE 125

LEG
C

17

SEE
SHOP TIP
AT RIGHT
FOR
CUTTING
FLUTES

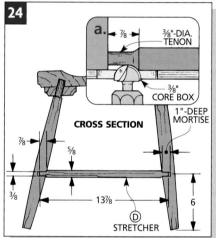

24

a. ⁷⁄₈

³⁄₈"-DIA.
TENON

³⁄₈"
CORE BOX

1"-DEEP
MORTISE

CROSS SECTION

⁷⁄₈

⁵⁄₈

³⁄₈

13⁷⁄₈

6

D
STRETCHER

SHOP TIP .... *Fluting Tenons*

When a dowel fits tight in a hole, it usually scrapes off the glue as it's driven home — unless the end of the dowel (the tenon) is fluted. I made flutes for the bench's dowels using an ordinary set of pliers (see drawing).

a.

When using my router table, I like to keep my fingers away from the bit. So for routing small pieces (like the rectangular leg brackets on the Shaker Bench), I made a safety shield that grabs the workpiece and protects my fingers from the bit (see photo at right).

The shield is made from a piece of ¼"-thick acrylic plastic with a pair of 1"-dia. dowel handles (see drawing above right).

A smaller piece of acrylic plastic

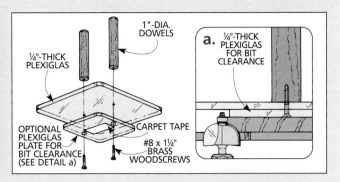

attached to the first is optional — it provides clearance for the nut or screw that holds the bearing on the bit when routing thin workpieces, or when

taking a deep cut (see detail 'a').

I use double-sided carpet tape to hold the workpiece firmly on the bottom of the shield.

Next, scribe around the bottom of each leg to indicate where they should be trimmed *(Fig. 25)*. Then remove the legs and trim off the ends. (I labeled the legs so they wouldn't get mixed up).

ASSEMBLE LEGS AND STRETCHER. Before the legs can be attached to the seat, a mortise must be drilled in each leg to accept the stretcher (see the Shop Tip below).

After the mortises are drilled, the stretchers can be glued into the legs, and the legs glued into the seat *(Fig. 26)*.

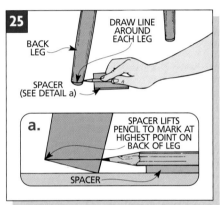

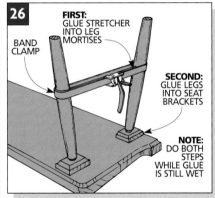

SHOP TIP ...... Drilling Into Angled Legs

To drill matching mortises in opposite legs, cut runners to fit across the legs, but short of the mortise height (6") *(Fig. 1)*. Then clamp the runners to the legs.

Cut a guide block to ride between the runners on "wings" *(Fig. 2)*, and drill a hole through it to match the tenon on the stretcher. Mark the bit at the desired mortise depth *(Fig. 3)*.

To drill the mortises, insert the bit through the block's hole and fit the block between the runners *(Fig. 4)*.

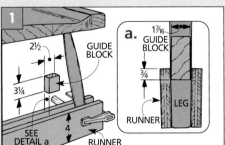

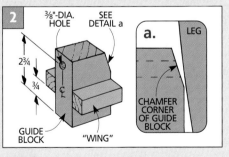

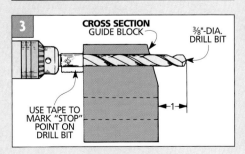

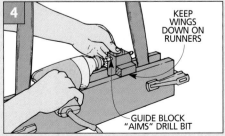

BACK REST

After the legs and stretchers are attached to the seat, I started on the back of the bench (a back rest connected with tapered spindles). The back rest secures the tops of the spindles.

CUT BACK REST. First, cut the back rest (E) to width and length from ³/₄" stock *(Fig. 27)*.

Then, to "blend" the back rest with the seat, trim angles off the ends *(Fig. 27a)*.

Next, sand a radius on each corner. (I used a drum sander in the drill press.)

MORTISES. Now lay out a series of mortises on the back rest to accept the spindles. To do this, I used the same template I had used earlier to lay out the holes along the back of the seat. First, align the centerline on the template with a centerline drawn on the back rest *(Fig. 27)*.

Then transfer the marks for the locations of the mortises from the template to the bottom edge of the workpiece.

Now the mortises can be bored in the back rest, centered on the thickness of the workpiece *(Fig. 28)*.

Note: A guide fence attached to the drill press holds the workpiece upright.

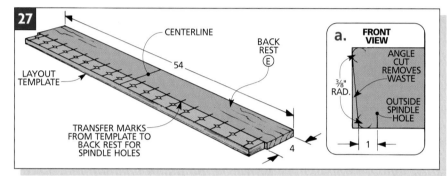

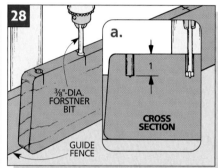

SPINDLES & FINAL ASSEMBLY

The back spindles on the bench actually start out as extra-long pieces of ⁵/₈"-dia. dowel rod. For a more graceful look, the dowels are then tapered from the bottom (thick) end to a thinner top (³/₈"-dia.) end *(Fig. 29)*. (See the Technique article beginning on page 122 for more information on this.)

After the dowels have been tapered, cut the spindles (F) to finished length by cutting off both ends *(Fig. 29)*.

Note: It makes it a lot easier to insert the spindles into the seat (A) if the bottom (thick) ends are lightly chamfered *(Fig. 29a)*.

RE-USE TEMPLATE. There's one last use for the layout template. First, enlarge each hole in the template to ⁵/₈"-dia. Then rip the template in half *(Fig. 30)*. Now the template can help align the spindles *(Fig. 32)*.

INSTALL SPINDLES. To install the spindles, first glue them into the holes in the back rest *(Fig. 31)*. Then, glue them into the holes in the seat.

Note: Because the spindles aren't tapered at the bottom ends, they can be "bottomed out" in the holes.

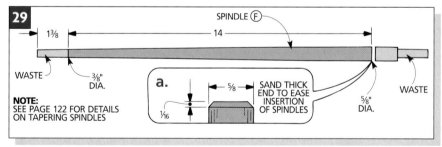

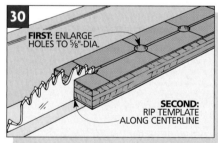

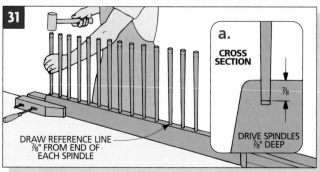

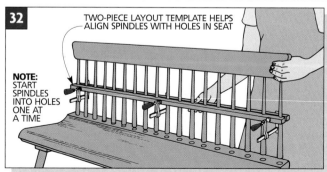

DESIGNER'S NOTEBOOK

If you don't have room for a long bench, you can still try your hand at making a Shaker-style seat. Just shorten the Shaker Bench, and you'll end up with a chair that's a little out of the ordinary.

CONSTRUCTION NOTES:

■ Turning the bench into a chair may be a fairly simple process, but the resulting piece of furniture will be anything but ordinary. Certain to be a conversation starter in whatever room it's displayed, this chair combines the style of the Shaker Bench with the size and convenience of a small seat.

■ To turn the bench into a chair, it's a simple matter of changing either the size or the number of a few key parts (see the Materials List below for specifics). All of the construction techniques are the same, so you can follow all of the original directions (and use the jigs shown on pages 122-125) to make the chair. You only need to make the following modifications.

■ The seat (A) is cut so its back edge has a *finished* length of 20" (instead of 53", as on the bench). The thickness and width (depth) of the seat remain the same (see drawing below).

■ The back rest (E) is also the same thickness and width as before, but is cut to a length of 21" for the chair (see drawing below).

■ The back spindles (F) are the same size as on the bench, but you only need seven (7) of them for the chair, instead of the eighteen (18) that were required for the bench (see drawing).

Note: Again, remember to have a few extra dowels on hand for test cuts and/or replacements.

■ There is one other significant difference between the bench and the chair. The seat brackets (B) that hold the legs wouldn't look right (or provide the proper balance and stability) on a chair if positioned the same as on the bench. So I positioned each of them with its inside edge 6½" from the center of the middle spindle (see drawing).

CHAIR

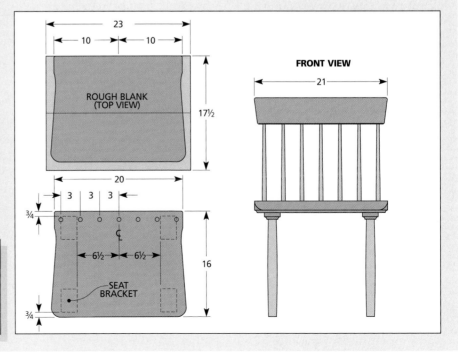

MATERIALS LIST	
CHANGED PARTS	
A Seat (1)	1¾ x 16 - 21
E Back Rest (1)	¾ x 4 - 21
F Back Spindles (7)	⅝ dowel x 18 rgh.

TECHNIQUE .... *Routing Spindles*

Turning a perfectly tapered spindle on a lathe takes time. And turning identical spindles takes even more time. I figure it would take me a full day to turn the eighteen identical spindles needed for the Shaker Bench on page 112.

Instead, I built a jig that uses an electric hand drill and a router (with a core box bit) to turn duplicate spindles — in a very short time. It took me about seven minutes to "turn" a ⅝"-dia. dowel into a spindle shaped like a tapered candle stick (with a very small amount of sanding required).

DUPLICATING JIG. The basic idea is that the jig acts as a cradle that holds the dowel. The drill, then, is the motor that turns the dowel. And the router bit does the cutting.

The router rides along a pair of tapered runners. As the router moves down the runners, the router bit shapes the tapered spindle.

LEG JIG. After building the spindle jig, I applied the same idea to a jig for duplicating the legs for the Bench. This jig works just like the spindle jig. The main difference is the shape of the runners — they're humped.

One more thing. For safety, find someone else to operate the drill for you. This way you can keep both hands safely on the router.

SPINDLE JIG

Sometimes projects (like jigs) just evolve. The first version of this spindle jig was built for use with a block plane.

The block plane slid across the top of the jig to "turn" the shape of the round spindle. But that was too slow — the plane had to remove too much waste. So I modified the jig for use with a router.

RUNNERS AND GUIDES. The router rides this jig much like a train rides a pair of tracks. The router (train) rides on two tapered runners (rails). The runners are supported by a base (track bed). And two guide blocks keep the router running straight. (I cut the parts from ¾" pine.)

Since I wanted a ⅛" taper along the length of each spindle, the router has to go "downhill" along the length of the jig. To do this, cut ⅛" tapers on the runners (A) *(Fig. 1)*. Then the guide blocks (B) are screwed to the runners.

Now the runner and guide block assemblies are ready to be screwed to the base (C) *(Fig. 1)*. The trick here is to screw the assemblies down so the base of the router just fits between the guide blocks.

Note: To determine how far apart the guide blocks should be, measure the diameter of your router's base plate and add ⅟₁₆". Also, when screwing the assemblies down, leave an overhanging lip at the front of the base. This is used to clamp the jig to the workbench.

TAILSTOCK AND HEADSTOCK. The ends of the jig are enclosed by two

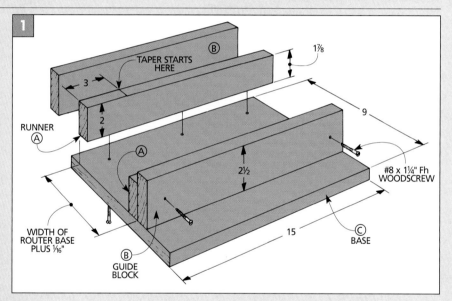

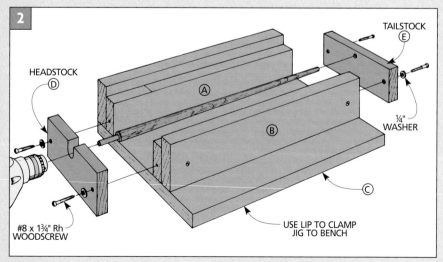

blocks. The headstock (D) is at the drill end of the jig *(Figs. 2 and 3)*. This piece has a short slot for the dowel to rest in.

The tailstock (E) at the other end of the jig has a shallow hole drilled in it for holding the free end of the dowel. (Due to the friction created by the spinning dowel, I used $^3/_4$" hard maple for the headstock and tailstock.)

Note: The dimensions shown on these pieces are specific to the diameter of the spindles for the Shaker Bench. But you could easily modify both of these blocks for other diameter dowels.

To allow for slight adjustments when setting up the jig for turning spindles, I drilled oversized screw holes in the ends of the headstock and tailstock (refer to *Figs. 2 and 3*). Use screws and washers to keep them in place.

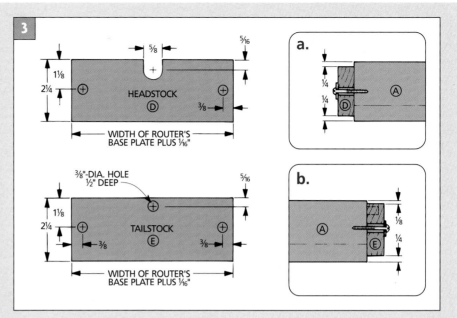

PREPARING DOWELS

The Shaker Bench requires eighteen spindles that are 14" long. But the dowels for the spindles must start a little longer (18") to allow room to "chuck" one end of the dowel in the drill and insert the other end into the jig.

BLANKS. To prepare spindle blanks, first cut a $^5/_8$"-dia. dowel rod to a rough length of 18" (see drawing at right).

Note: Use the straightest dowels you can find. And, when mass-producing parts like this, I'll usually cut a few extras. One is used to set up the jig. The others can be used for practicing the "turning" technique or replacing rejected spindles after they're made.

Now cut round, centered tenons ($1^3/_8$" long) on the ends of each dowel (see steps below). One of the tenons will be chucked in the drill. (I chose a drill with a $^3/_8$" capacity chuck.)

Note: If you're going to be using a $^1/_4$" drill, you'll have to cut one of the tenons smaller so it will fit the smaller-capacity chuck.

The other tenon will rotate in the

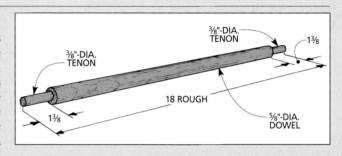

shallow hole drilled in the tailstock (refer to *Fig. 3* above).

After the tenons are cut, the dowels are ready to be "turned" into spindles. Adjusting the jig and turning the spindles are explained on the next page.

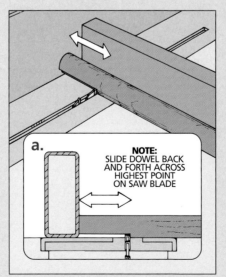

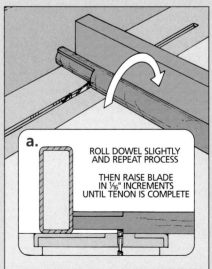

1 To cut a $^3/_8$"-dia. tenon, start by raising the saw blade $^1/_{16}$" above the table. Then position the rip fence to establish the shoulder of the tenon.

2 Now slide the dowel back and forth across the top of the blade. What you're doing is removing the waste with the sides of the teeth.

3 To continue cutting the tenon, rotate the dowel slightly and slide it back across the blade. Repeat this until the end has been reduced to a tenon.

USING THE SPINDLE JIG

The jig (as shown) is designed to taper a $5/8$" dowel to a diameter of $3/8$" at one end. But to get the correct taper, you have to make some adjustments to the jig.

Note: Test the taper on an extra dowel before tapering the actual spindles.

ADJUSTING THE JIG. To begin the adjustment, insert a spindle blank in the jig (see drawing below).

ADJUSTING HEADSTOCK. Now mount a core box bit in the router and lower it $1/4$" below the base of the router (Detail 'a'):

Then to check the alignment, place the router on the runners where the taper is to begin. For the spindles on the bench, the taper starts $4^1/8$" from the shoulder of the tenon (Detail 'a').

Now check the distance between the bottom of the bit and the dowel. If it's set up right, the blank should just touch the bit, and the router should rest flat on the runners. If any adjustments are needed, raise or lower the headstock.

ADJUSTING TAILSTOCK. Now move the router to the other end of the runners and check the tail end of the blank (Detail 'b'). The bit should just touch the tenon. If necessary, adjust the tailstock just as you did for the headstock.

With the jig adjusted properly, you can cut a test spindle.

CHUCK INTO DRILL. To do this, first chuck the end of the blank in the drill.

Note: A variable speed drill, turning clockwise, works best.

BLANK INTO JIG. With one end of the blank chucked in the drill, lubricate the other end that goes into the tailstock. (I used paraffin wax.) This reduces friction so the spindle blank can spin freely.

TURNING. The nice thing about using this spindle jig is it's a simple (but noisy) operation. It's probably best to find a friend to help. One person can operate the drill (it's just a matter of holding the drill and turning it on). But the person operating the router (you) will require a little more skill.

The idea is for the drill to turn the blank. Then the person operating the router sets the router on the runners (next to the drill), and moves the router slowly to the other end of the spindle. One pass, one smoothly tapered spindle.

Note: For the smoothest taper (that requires minimal sanding), the drill should turn the workpiece at a constant speed — about medium on most drills. And the router should be advanced very slowly (about $1/16$" per second). Otherwise, the result will look more like a "threaded" dowel than a tapered spindle (see "Troubleshooting" below).

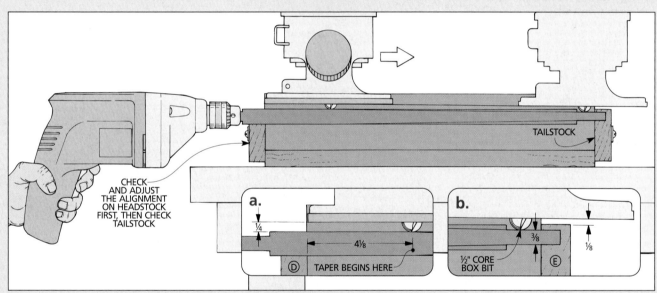

CHECK AND ADJUST THE ALIGNMENT ON HEADSTOCK FIRST, THEN CHECK TAILSTOCK

TAILSTOCK

a. $1/4$ — $4^1/8$ — (D) TAPER BEGINS HERE

b. $3/8$ — $1/8$ — $1/2$" CORE BOX BIT — (E)

1 To adjust the jig, first set the depth of the router bit $1/4$" below the base plate of the router. Then place the router on the runners at the drill end of the jig.

2 Next, check that the router bit is just touching the dowel where the taper begins. If adjustment is necessary, move the headstock up or down.

3 Now slide the router down the runners to the other end of the jig. Then check that the bit is just touching the tenon. Adjust the tailstock if necessary.

TROUBLESHOOTING

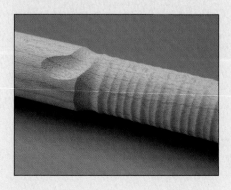

◀ If your dowel ends up looking like a threaded screw, you're moving the router too fast. Move the router very slowly — but fast enough so it's not standing still (about $1/16$" per second).

▶ If the dowel "chatters" as it spins, lower the drill's speed. If this doesn't help, tape a $1/4$"-thick block to the base plate, behind the bit with carpet tape. This keeps the dowel from whipping.

LEG JIG

The legs for the Shaker Bench could be turned on the lathe — but to make things easier, you could use a jig similar to the one for turning spindles. The only differences between the legs and the spindles are their length and shape. (The legs are longer and fatter in the middle like a cigar.)

The leg jig works like the spindle jig. A drill spins the workpiece while a core box bit in the router cuts the shape.

JIG DIFFERENCES. I started the leg jig just as I did with the spindle jig. First, the runners and the guide blocks are cut to size, then screwed together. Then they're screwed to a base *(Fig. 1)*. (For these, I also used 3/4"-thick pine.)

All the parts are longer to accommodate longer (24") dowels for the legs. And the runners have a small 1/8" "hump" (arc) in the center to produce the cigar-shaped leg.

Note: The headstock and tailstock pieces are also different *(Fig. 2)*. They have larger holes for supporting the larger diameter leg dowel. (And just like the spindle jig, I used 3/4" hard maple for the headstock and tailstock.)

After the jig is built, the next step is to prepare the dowels for the legs.

PREPARING DOWELS. Each leg starts out as a 24"-long, 1 1/2"-dia. dowel.

To prepare the dowels for the leg jig, tenons are cut on the ends *(Fig. 3)*. The smaller tenon will be trimmed off once the leg is cut to length. And the larger tenon will be used to mount the leg.

Also, to avoid plunging the bit into the dowel at the start of routing the cigar shape, I cut a relief notch near the smaller tenon *(Fig. 3)*.

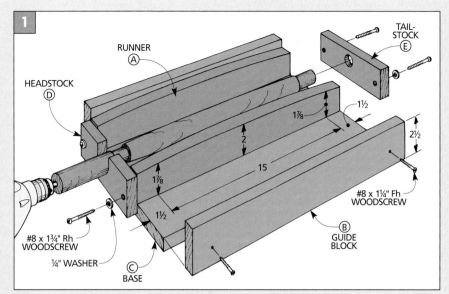

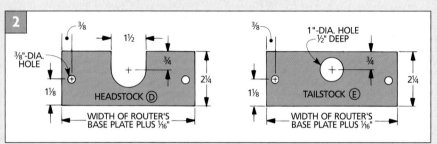

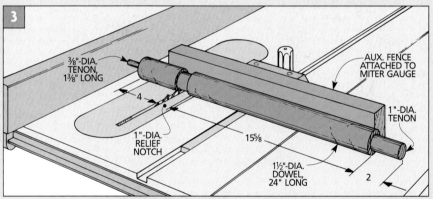

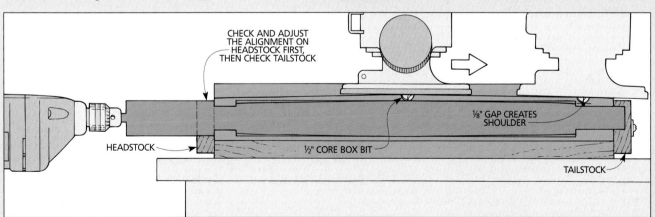

1 Before turning the legs, adjust the jig. To do this, first set the bit 1/4" below the base plate of the router. Then place the router in the middle of the runner.

2 Check that the bit is just touching the dowel, and the router base is on the runners. If necessary, move the headstock up or down until the bit just touches.

3 Next, slide the router over the larger tenon near the tailstock. If necessary, adjust the tailstock so there's a 1/8" gap between the bit and the tenon.

One thing we take into consideration when designing projects is whether the hardware is commonly available. Most of the supplies for the projects in this book can be found at local hardware stores or home centers, but sometimes you may have to order hardware through the mail. If so, we've tried to find reputable sources with toll-free phone numbers (see right).

Woodsmith Project Supplies also offers hardware for some projects (see below).

WOODSMITH PROJECT SUPPLIES

At the time this book was printed, the following project supply kits and hardware were available from *Woodsmith Project Supplies*. The kits include hardware, but you must supply any lumber, plywood, or finish. For current prices and availability, call toll free:

1-800-444-7527

Queen Anne End Table
(pages 26-37)
Full-size patterns for cabriole leg, transition block, and apron
.... No. 8005015

Computer Desk
(pages 48-61)
Hardware kit*............No. 7109100
Extension wing hardware kit
.................................No. 7109200

Oak Desk
(pages 62-75)
Hardware kit**.............No. 779100
Vanity panel hardware kit
.................................No. 779150
24" full-extension slides
(extra set) ....No. 1006120

Ladder-Back Chair
(pages 92-102)
Full-size patterns for leg, horizontal and vertical back slats
....No. 764300

*Doesn't include keyboard hardware (see sources at right).

**Includes one set of full-extension slides, but doesn't include vanity panel hardware.

KEY: TL07

MAIL ORDER SOURCES

Some of the most important "tools" you can have in your shop are mail order catalogs. The ones listed below are filled with special hardware, tools, finishes, lumber, and supplies that can't be found at a local hardware store or home center. You should be able to find many of the supplies for the projects in this book in one or more of these catalogs.

It's amazing what you can learn about woodworking by looking through these catalogs. If they're not currently in your shop, you may want to have them sent to you.

Note: The information below was current when this book was printed. August Home Publishing does not guarantee these products will be available nor endorse any specific mail order company, catalog, or product.

THE WOODSMITH STORE

2625 Beaver Avenue
Des Moines, IA 50310
800–835–5084
Our own retail store with tools, jigs, hardware, books, and finishing supplies. We don't have a catalog, but we do send out items mail order.

ROCKLER WOODWORKING & HARDWARE

4365 Willow Drive
Medina, MN 55340
800–279–4441
www.rockler.com
A catalog of hardware, tools, and accessories, including inlays, laminate trimming bits, keyboard tray hardware, full-extension drawer slides, and drawer pulls.

ADAMS WOOD PRODUCTS

974 Forest Drive
Morristown, TN 37814
423–587–2942
www.adamswoodproducts.com
A source for pre-made legs, including cabriole legs and other styles, in a variety of woods. Also turning squares in a variety of sizes.

LEE VALLEY TOOLS LTD.

12 East River Street
P.O. Box 1780
Ogdensburg, NY 13669-6780
800–871–8158
www.leevalley.com
Several catalogs offering keyboard tray hardware, knock-down hardware, full-extension drawer slides, drawer pulls and more.

GARRETT WADE

161 Avenue of the Americas
New York, NY 10013
800–221–2942
www.garrettwade.com
The "Bible" for hand tools, also a source for finishing supplies and accessories including drawer handles.

TREND-LINES

135 American Legion Highway
Revere, MA 02151
800–767–9999
www.trend-lines.com
Another complete source for hardware including full-extension drawer slides and threaded inserts, plus power tools and accessories.

WOODCRAFT

560 Airport Industrial Park
P.O. Box 1686
Parkersburg, WV 26102-1686
800–225–1153
www.woodcraft.com
This catalog has all kinds of hardware, including knock-down hardware, full-extension drawer slides, threaded inserts, pre-made cabriole legs and more.

WOODWORKER'S SUPPLY

1108 North Glenn Road
Casper, WY 82601
800–645–9292
You'll find a good selection of power tools, hand tools, and accessories, including reverse-cut jig saw blades, hardware for keyboard trays, threaded inserts, leg levelers, and full-extension drawer slides.

INDEX

AUGUST HOME
PUBLISHING COMPANY

President & Publisher: Donald B. Peschke
Executive Editor: Douglas L. Hicks
Creative Director: Ted Kralicek
Senior Graphic Designer: Chris Glowacki
Associate Editor: Craig L. Ruegsegger
Assistant Editors: Joseph E. Irwin, Joel Hess
Graphic Designers: Vu Nguyen, April Walker Janning, Stacey L. Krull
Design Interns: Heather Boots, Katie VanDalsem

Designer's Notebook Illustrator: Mike Mittermeier
Photographer: Crayola England
Electronic Production: Douglas M. Lidster
Production: Troy Clark, Minniette Johnson
Project Designers: Ken Munkel, Kent Welsh
Project Builders: Steve Curtis, Steve Johnson
Magazine Editors: Terry Strohman, Tim Robertson
Contributing Editors: Vincent S. Ancona, Jon Garbison, Bryan Nelson
Magazine Art Directors: Todd Lambirth, Cary Christensen
Contributing Illustrators: Mark Higdon, David Kreyling, Roger Reiland,
Kurt Schultz, Cinda Shambaugh, Dirk Ver Steeg

Controller: Robin Hutchinson
Production Director: George Chmielarz
Project Supplies: Bob Baker
New Media Manager: Gordon Gaippe

For subscription information about
Woodsmith and *ShopNotes* magazines, please write:
August Home Publishing Co.
2200 Grand Ave.
Des Moines, IA 50312
800-333-5075
www.augusthome.com/customwoodworking

Woodsmith® and *ShopNotes*® are registered trademarks of August Home
Publishing Co.

Oxmoor House®

Oxmoor House, Inc.
Book Division of Southern Progress Corporation
P.O. Box 2463, Birmingham, Alabama 35201

ISBN: 0-8487-2681-2
Printed in the United States of America

To order additional publications, call 1-800-765-6400.
For more books to enrich your life, visit **oxmoorhouse.com**